D1608209

Forensic Fictions

LAURA,
MERRY CHRISTMAS!
ENJOY!
LOVE,
THE MOM & THE DAD
12/25/99

FORENSIC
FICTIONS

The Lawyer Figure in Faulkner

· ·

JAY WATSON

THE UNIVERSITY OF GEORGIA PRESS
ATHENS AND LONDON

© 1993 by the University of Georgia Press
Athens, Georgia 30602
All rights reserved
Designed by Louise OFarrell
Set in 10/13 Linotype Walbaum by Tseng Information Systems, Inc.
Printed and bound by Thomson-Shore, Inc.
The paper in this book meets the guidelines for permanence and
durability of the Committee on Production Guidelines for Book
Longevity of the Council on Library Resources.

Printed in the United States of America

97 96 95 94 93   C   5 4 3 2 1

Library of Congress Cataloging in Publication Data
Watson, Jay.
Forensic fictions : the lawyer figure in Faulkner / Jay Watson.
p.   cm.
Includes bibliographical references and index.
ISBN 0-8203-1516-8 (alk. paper)
1. Faulkner, William, 1897–1962—Characters—Lawyers.
2. Lawyers in literature.   I. Title.
PS3511.A86Z98536   1993
813'.52—dc20   92–28216
                                      CIP

British Library Cataloging in Publication Data available

Excerpt from *The Town* by William Faulkner, copyright 1957 by William Faulkner,
copyright 1957 by the Curtis Publishing Co. Reprinted by permission of Random
House, Inc.

CONTENTS

. . . .

ACKNOWLEDGMENTS

Warner Berthoff and Elizabeth McKinsey helped me turn a rough pastiche of half-formulated ideas, half-sensed connections, and half-assimilated quotations into a doctoral dissertation and first draft of this book. For that invaluable service, along with their even-tempered advice and generosity of spirit, I owe them a world of thanks. Milner S. Ball also read the entire first draft, and his comments helped me recognize how much of its potential lay still unrealized. At a time when I was unsure whether to pursue publication, I found badly needed encouragement in his criticisms as well as his praise.

Joel Porte, Patricia Yaeger, Robert Kiely, Joseph Boone, John Norman, Amy Boesky, Michael Landon, Donald Kartiganer, Richard King, David Galef, and Bob Brinkmeyer have all read or heard portions of this book. These fertile minds have helped shape many of the ideas here, while confirming many others. Presenting drafts of my work before the Harvard University doctoral conferences on American literature and on narrative also led to fruitful, exciting discussions that influenced the shape and scope of this study. To my colleagues in both groups, and to the many others, too numerous to be listed here, who no doubt recognize their ideas and suggestions in these pages, I am indebted. I would also like to thank the Mrs. Giles Whiting Foundation for the Fellowship in the Humanities under whose auspices I was able to complete the first draft of this project.

Portions of this work have been previously published, albeit in altered form. Part of chapter one appeared as "The Failure of Forensic Storytelling in *Sanctuary*," *Faulkner Journal* 6 (Fall 1990/Spring 1991); part of chapter two was published as " 'Hair,' 'Smoke,' and the Development of the Faulknerian Lawyer Character," *Mississippi Quarterly* 43, no. 3 (1990): 349–66. I thank the editors of these journals for supporting this study.

To the anonymous readers who reviewed the manuscript for the University of Georgia Press, I can only say: I wish I could thank you by name, and in person. You were more than generous, more than tactful, and more than demanding with your suggestions and queries, all to my immeasurable benefit. Some of these suggestions I have no doubt failed to heed, but the flaws that appear here as a result are, of course, all my own. My editors at the Press I can most gladly thank by name. Karen Orchard, Madelaine Cooke, Matt Brook, Debbie Winter, and Malcolm Call guided this book through its many stages with deft and steady hands.

I also want to thank James Boyd White, whom I have never met but whose brilliant, eloquent, humane work awakened me to the myriad ways in which literature and law can, do, and *must* speak to each other.

I cannot begin to express my gratitude to my family, all of whom have been tireless sources of emotional (and material!) support during the many trying years over which this book has taken shape—and not just those years. I continue to draw sustenance from all of you. But this book is above all for Susan, without whose limitless patience, cheerful good humor, countless personal sacrifices (high among them the willingness to play second fiddle to Faulkner—or worse, to a laptop computer— at all sorts of unlikely and inopportune times), gentle encouragement, and nurturing companionship none of this would have been possible. I thank you for our beautiful Katherine, and for that even more precious gift, yourself. And that is only the beginning.

ABBREVIATIONS

. . . .

AA	Faulkner, *Absalom, Absalom!*
CS	Faulkner, *Collected Stories*
FAB	Blotner, *Faulkner: A Biography*
FD	Faulkner, *Flags in the Dust*
FU	Gwynn and Blotner, eds., *Faulkner in the University*
GDM	Faulkner, *Go Down, Moses*
H	Faulkner, *The Hamlet*
ID	Faulkner, *Intruder in the Dust*
KG	Faulkner, *Knight's Gambit*
LIA	Faulkner, *Light in August*
M	Faulkner, *The Mansion*
R	Faulkner, *The Reivers*
RFN	Faulkner, *Requiem for a Nun*
S	Faulkner, *Sanctuary*
SF	Faulkner, *The Sound and the Fury*
SL	Blotner, ed., *Selected Letters of William Faulkner*
SOT	Polk, ed., *Sanctuary: The Original Text*
T	Faulkner, *The Town*
UNV	Faulkner, *The Unvanquished*
WP	Faulkner, *The Wild Palms*

Forensic Fictions

The Faulknerian
Forensic Figure

As it is in our everyday experience, the law in Faulkner is a vast and multidimensional affair: at once a deeply normative cultural system, a vehicle of ideology (in its constructive and destructive manifestations), a force of social stability and control, an entrenched and often blindly self-interested institution, and not least of all a human vocation, a form of practice that in some instances achieves the status of a calling. While each of these overlapping aspects is more than worthy of detailed scholarly commentary, and while careful consideration of all of them informs the discussions that follow, this book finds its central subject and its most persistent concern in the last one: Faulkner's depiction, in what I call his *forensic fictions*, of the legal vocation and the practice of law, a practice that extends from the official space of the courtroom and the professional space of the law office to the farthest reaches of the community. Or perhaps I should simply say that this book is about the law in Faulkner as a way of life, a subject that continues to be neglected by students of Faulkner and his work even as current movements in Faulkner scholarship toward the analysis of ideology and other forms of discursive practice lead them (or lead them back) to the law as a field of inquiry (see for example Duvall, Moreland, and Morris).

Isn't Faulkner's fiction, after all, staggeringly rich in attorneys and other characters who have chosen the law as a way of life? Think of them for a moment: the roster would reach beyond Gavin Stevens and Horace Benbow, the most important lawyers in Faulkner and the principal figures of this study, to include Horace's father, Will Benbow (*Flags in the Dust*), Gavin's father, Judge Stevens (*The Town, The Reivers*), General Compson and his son Jason III (*The Sound and the Fury, Absalom, Absalom!*), Eustace Graham, Judge Drake, and the "Memphis jew lawyer" (*Sanctuary*), Justice of the Peace Jim Hamblett and Eulalia Bon's lawyer (*Absalom*), Judge Dukinfield ("Smoke"), Sam Galloway (from Faulkner's MGM screenplay *Country Lawyer*), Gail Hightower's grandfather (*Light in August*), Labove (*The Hamlet*), the unnamed advocates of "Wild Palms" and *A Fable*, the inexperienced public defenders who represent Mink Snopes (*The Hamlet, The Mansion*) and Monk Odlethrop ("Monk"), the young district attorney who prosecutes Homer Bookwright ("Tomorrow"), the anonymous judges who preside over the trial scenes of "Wild Palms," *Sanctuary*, and "Fire and the Hearth," the perplexed justices of the peace in "Barn Burning," *The Hamlet*, and the Quentin section of *The Sound and the Fury*, and finally law students such as Bayard Sartoris ("An Odor of Verbena"), Charles Bon, and Henry Sutpen (*Absalom*). Surely there are others as well. Their sheer number indicates that Faulkner's interest in them and their vocation was a profound and abiding one, as does the remarkable longevity of a character such as Gavin Stevens, who makes his first appearance in print in 1931 and his last in 1959.

As a rule, Faulkner resisted the temptation to define the forensic figure in narrow social or psychological terms. Unlike Charles Dickens's fictional lawyers, for instance, so often mere caricatures or humour characters, Faulkner's lawyers and judges frequently exhibit unusual versatility, subtlety, and vitality of character. His major forensic figures are among his most complex and broadly representative creations. Indeed, I can think of no other character type in Faulkner that encompasses such a variety of (often conflicting) cultural roles: raconteur and rhetor; polemicist and demagogue; narrator, historian, genealogist, and detective; actor and director; teacher, mentor, and student; advocate of the voiceless, adversary of the voiceless, and socratic midwife to the voiceless; champion of resistance to the symbolic order, public representative and principal defender of the symbolic order, and mediator between the individual and the symbolic order; reclusive Prufrock and gregarious Cincinnatus; alienated neurotic and nonalienated man of the world;· ambivalent son or brother, imperious father, and nurturing uncle; frustrated suitor and secure paterfamilias; hopeless romantic and resourceful pragmatist; lethargic voyeur and triumphant *écouteur;* meticulous professional and dedicated amateur; deluded abstractionist and disciplined empiricist—and, in the final analysis, *exponent* of culture and society, much as Faulkner, in his own multiple and contrary ways, was also. This is to suggest that in the figure of the lawyer Faulkner found his most habitual, and in many ways his most rewarding, authorial surrogate, a fictional alter ego on whom he could project, and through whom explore, numerous and often contradictory aspects of his personal experience, his family background, and his cultural heritage.

What is more, Faulkner discovered in the poetics, and ethics, of forensic practice an abundantly suggestive set of resources for cross-examining his own vocation. The example of the lawyer, for instance, offered Faulkner an insight that many of his critics have still failed to grasp: that, far from being some sort of ineffectual substitute for (or excuse for, or consolation in the absence of) action, language is itself a form of action, perhaps the most pervasive and powerful means by which we involve ourselves in our own and each other's lives. Lawyers, and especially litigators, do not choose between language and action, as some have suggested Faulkner's characters are obliged to do (see Watkins, for instance). They choose language *and* action, language as action. They know how to do things with words (though there is of course no guarantee that what they do will not be harmful or wrong), and I am convinced that the deeply performative nature of their craft contributed to, or at the very least confirmed, Faulkner's sense of his own. Furthermore, Faulkner, whose intuitive feel for the ins and outs of forensic procedure more than compensated for his lack of formal legal training, repeatedly demonstrates his understanding that courtroom law is at the most fundamental level a matter of rhetorical persuasion and narrative reconstruction. As such it is entirely commensurable with storytelling as he thought of it. From these insights it is but a short step farther to envision the lawyer as a kind of raconteur, and to measure forensic competence in terms of storytelling ability. As I argue in the chapters ahead, this logic informs a number of Faulkner's most important forensic fictions, and it also helps to illuminate the special and problematical relationship between his two most fully realized fictional lawyers.

Faulkner's interest in the forensic figure was in the most emphatic sense overdetermined, and in the remaining pages of this introduc-

tory chapter, I trace its roots in a number of different directions—bio-
graphical, psychological, rhetorical, regional, cultural, political. Faulkner spent his formative years and much of his adult life in the shadow
of what must have seemed an unending series of forensic Falkners,
forensic rivals, and forensic friends. The influence of these men upon
Faulkner could be inspiring or (more often) intimidating, but it was
almost never negligible. Faulkner's Oxford was a thriving small-town
legal community, seat of the Lafayette County court system and the
Northern Mississippi Federal District court, home of the state's leading
law school, and an important center for railroad law and litigation as
well. Further, as I have already begun to suggest, Faulkner had a keen
sense of the underlying rhetorical affinities between law and literature.
He recognized that the professional life of a lawyer or judge includes
a great deal of intrinsically literary activity. (As such he anticipates a
number of the guiding concerns behind the law and humanities movement of the past two decades, a movement now turning to his work
with increasing frequency as a source of inspiration and support.) It
should also be noted that Faulkner came of age in a regional society
that exalted the legal vocation for some of the same reasons he would
find it so intriguing. And he was remarkably sensitive to the role played
by the law in the articulation of that society's norms, codes, and boundaries. Finally, the idea of the forensic figure as lawyer-citizen, animated
by an ethic of service and typically aligned, for better or worse, with
communal values, exerted a powerful pull on Faulkner's imagination
throughout his career. This sense of the lawyer as *homo politicus,* and
of political life in Yoknapatawpha County as inherently and primarily
verbal, discursive, colloquial, must be reckoned with by anyone seeking to understand the origins and development of fictional attorneys
such as Gavin Stevens and his ilk.

FORENSIC FRIENDS, FORENSIC FOREFATHERS,
AND FORENSIC RIVALS

The lawyer is a conspicuous and complicated presence in Faulkner's
personal history: at once a figure to admire and to emulate, a figure to
avoid and to resent, a figure to compete with, and above all a figure to
cope with. When one considers the sheer number of Faulkner's friends,
relatives, and other, more troubling acquaintances who practiced law

or received legal training, and when one inquires further into the specific nature and tone of Faulkner's relationships with these figures, it becomes difficult not to maintain that they played a crucial role in inspiring, or provoking, Faulkner to write forensic fictions, and to write about the forensic figure in the particular ways he did.

Faulkner's circle of local friends and acquaintances would seem to substantiate a recent critic's picture of Oxford as a town "almost overrun with lawyers" (Snell, "Phil Stone and William Faulkner" 171). Dean R. J. Farley of the law school and his son Robert, Governor Lee M. Russell (who practiced with Faulkner's grandfather and uncle before his political career took off), General James Stone and his sons Phil and Jack, agent and fellow novelist Ben Wasson, hunting buddy Jim Kyle Hudson, and Lucy Somerville Howorth (a fellow founding member of the Marionettes): all were, at one time or another, practicing attorneys and all were, at one time or another, close friends of the Faulkner family.[1] Yet a far more imposing and immediately problematical collection of forensic figures confronted the artist closer to home.

Faulkner was born into a family with a history of achievement and training in the law. His great-great-great-uncle, John Wesley Thompson, was a district attorney and circuit judge in Ripley, Mississippi. His great-grandfather, and Thompson's nephew and ward, William Clark Falkner ("the Old Colonel"), passed the Mississippi bar in 1847, and went on to a distinguished and multifaceted career as a lawyer, planter, military leader, best-selling author, and railroad tycoon. His grandfather, John Wesley Thompson Falkner ("the Young Colonel"), practiced privately in Oxford before serving as deputy United States district attorney for Mississippi's northern district and later as Lafayette County Attorney. His "Uncle John," J. W. T. Falkner, Jr., also practiced privately (where, Falkner family lore has it, he earned the nickname "The Lion of the Courtroom" and "never lost a killing case" [J. Faulkner 66]) and later served as judge of the state's third judicial district, a position to which he was appointed twice but never elected. And two members of the novelist's own generation became lawyers: his cousin J. W. T. Falkner IV, and his younger brother Murry C. ("Jack") Falkner, who practiced briefly in J.W.T. Jr.'s firm before embarking upon a long career with the Treasury Department and the FBI.[2]

As a male member of a family in which the legal vocation ran five generations deep, William Faulkner must have experienced the au-

thority and even the identity of his Falkner forefathers as importantly
and perhaps inseparably linked to that vocation. Lawyers who bore
the mantle of authority and mastery that Jacques Lacan attributes to
the symbolic role of the Name-of-the-Father, the Falkners were, no
less significantly, fathers who bore the Name-of-the-Lawyer, the badge
of legal training, professional accomplishment, and cultural valida-
tion.[3] No doubt the peculiar aura of veneration and legend that arose
in the Falkner family around powerful paternal figures such as the
Old Colonel and the Young Colonel derived at least in part from their
vocation, though the reasoning here could just as easily be reversed
and the authority of the Falkners as forceful fathers cited in order to
derive and confirm their authority as lawyers. Either way, the experiences these men collectively represented—apprenticeship to working
lawyers, formal legal education, admission to the Mississippi bar—sig-
naled and guaranteed, in institutionally sanctioned form, their initiation into the Lacanian symbolic order, the order of law and culture that
according to Lacanian theory plays a primary role in articulating every
human subject, and to which every healthy subject learns to accede.

Yet the Falkner forefathers achieved these goals largely as a result
of their own force of will and personal ambition: their own fathers did
not figure prominently in their rise to success. The Old Colonel, for
example, ran away from his father in Missouri after a violent family
quarrel, and he was admitted to his foster father's legal practice in
Mississippi only after he had educated and proven himself in the law.
Likewise, J. W. T. Falkner, Jr., in a clear declaration of filial independence, chose for his first law partner an attorney who had recently
broken away from the Young Colonel's law firm. This kind of Oedipal tension—sons admiring, emulating, and yet resisting their fathers,
fathers loving their sons but also capable of impeding their progress
in the family vocation—would also afflict William Faulkner, a Falkner
man and an eldest son, taking the form of a typically Falknerian ambivalence toward the profession of choice among so many of his forensic
forefathers.

William's own father, however, seems to have prefigured this ambivalence, throughout his life drifting indifferently through a series of
jobs, none of which was even remotely connected with the vocation
that had claimed his grandfather, father, and brother. Murry Falkner
was also himself a weak father, a much less authoritative family pres-

ence than his wife, Maud. Unwilling or unable to align himself with the Name-of-the-Lawyer, that is, Murry found himself divested as well of the Name-of-the-Father and the legitimacy ordinarily conferred by that symbolic mantle. If Murry's mixed feelings about his patrimony, then, prefigured his son's, there is also the matter of that son's ambivalence toward him. This ambivalence ultimately led William Faulkner to declare his independence from father and forefathers alike. He became a writer, a move guaranteed and perhaps engineered to puzzle and provoke his father, but what is more he became a writer who returned habitually to forensic issues, subjecting the lawyer figure to his own authorial control in novel after novel—in every Yoknapatawpha novel, in fact, except *As I Lay Dying*. He resisted the calling of law yet created a host of forensic alter egos. If Faulkner projected his own mixed feelings toward the forensic Falkners into his fiction, perhaps this is why he made his greatest lawyer character, Gavin Stevens, a decidedly avuncular figure, wielder of a gentler, less problematical brand of authority.

It is also certainly significant that the three men who most strenuously attempted to thwart the relationship between Faulkner and Estelle Oldham were forensic figures. Estelle's father, Judge Lemuel E. Oldham, repeatedly expressed his disapproval of the match, fearing (not unreasonably at the time) that Faulkner would never amount to anything. Oldham, however, approved of Cornell Franklin, a law student at the University of Mississippi, and he encouraged the young man as a suitor for Estelle. To make matters worse, Phil Stone also disapproved of Faulkner's relationship with Estelle, but for a different reason than Judge Oldham. Stone, Faulkner's mentor and best friend at the time, feared that the star-crossed romance with Estelle would prove a negative influence on his protégé, a budding poet, and he told Faulkner as much. Unable to convince Faulkner to elope, Estelle eventually married Franklin in 1918, and the two moved to Hawaii, where Franklin first practiced law and then became a federal judge. Through avatars like Franklin and Guy Lyman, a New Orleans attorney to whom Faulkner lost another of his early loves, Helen Baird, we see a new side of the lawyer figure emerging: the forensic rival, in competition with the artist not only for public laurels but also for romantic laurels as well.[4] Is it merely a coincidence, then, or is it a deliberate authorial response, that Faulkner's most important lawyer characters, Horace Benbow and

Gavin Stevens, suffer troubled love lives and are pointedly depicted as second husbands and stepfathers, rather than husbands and fathers? The irony could not have escaped Faulkner, however, that these roles were also his own, that the way he vented his spleen against the forensic figure in his fiction was only to make this figure more like himself.

As every reader of Susan Snell's illuminating Stone biography well knows, Phil Stone's influence on Faulkner extended well beyond affairs of the heart. If the mature Faulkner was to proclaim himself "Sole Owner and Proprietor" of Yoknapatawpha County, Stone sought to establish a virtual literary proprietorship over his young friend, in ways Faulkner was to find both liberating and constraining. In Stone's eyes, his own role would be to flood an untutored genius with the raw materials of poetry and story and so preside (whether as midwife or as proud father) at the birth of a literary giant. He served as Faulkner's patron, mentor, and first literary agent. He discussed literature endlessly with Faulkner, criticized his work, corrected his spelling, supplied him with countless ideas, anecdotes, and character types, even gave the lonely poet a place to stay in New Haven, when the Oldham-Franklin wedding sent Faulkner running northward in 1918. He even chaperoned the shy Faulkner on dates (see Blotner, "Author-at-Law" 10; see also 12, 19). All in all, Stone was the most important force behind Faulkner's early progress as a writer, and he helped the young artist through some difficult personal times as well.

The price of these contributions, as we might expect, was control. Sensitive and impressionistic, delighted to find anyone who shared his love of literature, Faulkner deferred at first to Stone's superior knowledge and experience and formed easily beneath his elder's ready hands. For a while, at least, Faulkner was as happy to listen and write as Stone was to talk and read. Stone reacted to such adulation possessively. "This poet is my personal property," he wrote to the *Yale Alumni Weekly* in November 1924, in a notice for Faulkner's first volume of poetry, *The Marble Faun*. "I urge all my friend and class-mates to buy his book" (quoted in FAB 373). Such confident mastery would be only temporary, however, and when Faulkner finally rebelled against Stone's influence,[5] Stone became convinced of Faulkner's ingratitude and spoke more and more unkindly of the writer and his work. Certainly Stone's financial insolvency and his gradually deteriorating mental health contributed to the growing element of tension in the relationship. Even so, however, the cool distance that emerged between the two men never fully degenerated into hostility.[6]

It is no overstatement to say that Phil Stone incarnated the many dimensions of the forensic figure in a more ambivalent way than anyone Faulkner had ever known before. This is no doubt one reason why so many of Faulkner's lawyer characters seem modeled, in one way or another, after him. Clearly the paternalistic impulse in Stone ran strong. Full of outrageous opinions about Estelle, he also sought to control Faulkner's relationship with an even more intimate partner: his muse. Further, as a reputable lawyer in a small southern town, Stone enjoyed a standing in the community that Faulkner himself was not to earn until he won the Nobel Prize (if indeed then). In 1921, for instance, at the precocious age of twenty-eight, Stone was appointed assistant United States district attorney for the Northern District of Mississippi. That title was longer than any of Faulkner's book titles or any royalty statement he was to receive for a long time. Stone thus emerges as something of a forensic rival himself, though a rival for public recognition rather than female affection. "The Honorable Phil Stone," as Snell puts it, "had an identity the provincial southern community would certify," no matter how little he might have actually accomplished to deserve it ("Phil Stone and William Faulkner" 170). Faulkner, on the other hand, was a black sheep and a ne'er-do-well, still emphatically uncertified. Was Stone's local reputation as a literary lawyer a slap in the face of the apprentice poet, or did it light a fire under him? One thing that seems clear is that Stone, who more than any other single figure introduced Faulkner to modern literature and the writerly vocation, served notice that the lawyer is of necessity a figure of language, particularly spoken language. Litigation is, after all, a fundamentally verbal activity that occurs when real, existential disputes are rechanneled into narrative disputes. All the more reason, then, for Faulkner to make the forensic competence of his fictional lawyers a direct function of their linguistic competence, their storytelling skill.

What composite image of the lawyer emerges from this collection of ancestors and coevals? A compelling but also disturbing figure, part mentor, part competitor. A kindred soul to the writer as fellow humanist and rhetor, yet also an authority figure, possessed of the power and status that Faulkner no doubt coveted for himself but resisted in others. Precisely the kind of figure, that is, who, in more than one incarnation, confronts young Bayard Sartoris in "An Odor of Verbena," one of the subtlest and most suggestive of Faulkner's forensic fictions.

"An Odor of Verbena" opens at an important milestone in the life of its narrator, Bayard Sartoris. At twenty-four, beginning his final year of legal study at Oxford, Mississippi (UNV 258), Bayard is clearly poised on the brink of manhood, and as he prepares to be initiated into a vocation that signifies maturity and status, to accede to the Name-of-the-Father in tacit exchange for something of its authority, he suddenly learns that his father, Colonel John Sartoris, has been murdered by Ben Redmond, a former business partner who is also, not insignificantly, a lawyer. (The fact that the circumstances of Colonel Sartoris's death roughly parallel those of William Clark Falkner's only makes this material more fascinating.) As Bayard returns home for the funeral, he is confronted by a moral dilemma whose specifically Oedipal overtones John T. Irwin noted long ago. Should Bayard fulfill the community's expectations and kill Redmond? This dilemma is compounded by Bayard's deep, unconscious ambivalence toward Redmond—a lawyer, and thus a figure to be emulated and respected by the young law student (a kind of father, even, to the young apprentice-at-law), but also a murderer, a figure to be despised and punished by the aggrieved son, as well as a figure to be brought to justice by any aspiring lawyer worth his salt. Furthermore, Bayard cannot but be aware at some level that, by orphaning him, Redmond has also liberated him from the potentially oppressive authority of John Sartoris, a demanding, larger-than-life paternal figure who, if not actually a practicing attorney, is specifically described on one occasion in the text as "forensic" (UNV 265).

Bayard, however, is not about to submit to the authority of his liberator. In a climactic showdown, he faces Redmond unarmed, repudiating the code duello and, by implication, the whole set of obsolescent cavalier values represented by his father and his father's killer alike. Vanquished—indeed, completely humiliated—by Bayard's abjuration of violence, Redmond flees Jefferson, leaving Bayard free to create a space of authority for himself in the Jefferson law community and in the Sartoris clan. By besting the man who bested his father, Bayard avenges the murder in his own way, and he also overcomes the troubling shadow of John Sartoris by emerging as his own man. He thus acknowledges and repudiates both of the forensic fathers who have imposed their wills upon his existence.[7]

I repeat: acknowledges *and* repudiates. For "An Odor of Verbena" seems uneasily to advocate both submission and resistance to the order of law and culture. The denouement would seem to imply that Bayard has acceded to the symbolic order. In accordance with cultural expectations, he has defended Sartoris honor and assumed a prominent role in the public life of his community. He has, moreover, literally received the Name-of-the-Father, in accepting the mantle of "The Sartoris," the honorific that traditionally designates the clan leader (UNV 247). He might thus seem to be fully vested in symbolic power. But has there not also been a degree of willful resistance involved in each of these acts? That is, doesn't Bayard assume the role of paterfamilias on his own terms rather than terms dictated to him from the outside, through the symbolic order and its agents? Doesn't he challenge, and ultimately surmount, the authority of both of his forensic fathers? And doesn't the story's climax involve an outright subversion of the symbolic order, as Bayard singlehandedly dismantles the southern ethic of honor and violence endorsed by his father's entire generation? He refuses, after all, to carry a pistol, phallic weapon of choice in the deep South, with him to Redmond's office. And on the way there he rejects an offer from George Wyatt, a former soldier under Colonel Sartoris, to kill Redmond for him. His words, in fact, seem to anticipate the pathologically individualistic credo of Flannery O'Connor's Misfit, a sworn enemy of the order of law and culture if ever there was one: "I'm tending to this. You stay out of it. I dont need any help" (UNV 284). These are hardly the words of a man who has made his peace with the symbolic covenant. Interpreted this way, Bayard becomes the most happily misunderstood of rebels in Yoknapatawpha, and "An Odor of Verbena" emerges as a kind of narcissistic fantasy, a dream of morally begetting oneself, of leapfrogging the symbolic covenant and coming into possession of phallic authority without first bowing to that authority. Of doing all right by yourself, the Misfit might say. All things considered—especially the analogies between Colonel Sartoris and the Old Colonel—it is difficult not to read the story's mixed responses to the lawyer/father/Other as a projection of the author's own.

If the image of the lawyer thus remains locked in a frustrating but also productive ambivalence, perhaps we should ask what it meant for Faulkner to write, again and again, about the lawyer. Was it a gesture of mastery, a way to subject the forensic authority figure to the novelist's

authority—and thus a form of resistance to the symbolic order and its
paternal(istic) representatives and imperatives? "In literature," a recent
Faulkner critic has reminded us, "one defeats the authority and priority
of one's fathers—both literal and literary—by becoming an author, by
creating a progeny to which one is prior" (Grimwood, *Heart in Conflict*
53). Or could writing about lawyers have been, on the contrary, a form
of submission, a way for Faulkner to ease himself toward the symbolic
order through the mediating agency of the forensic alter ego? I like to
think that forensic fiction offered Faulkner a third alternative, a means
of exploring his orientation toward the symbolic order, a strategy that
in itself foreclosed neither the possibility of authorial mastery and resistance, nor the possibility of authorial humility and submission. By
this I mean, in the most fundamental sense, that Faulkner's forensic
fiction raises the issue of the symbolic order, and the individual's stance
toward it, toward culture and power, through images of lawyerly resistance and lawyerly submission. We read Faulkner's forensic fictions
most expansively and profitably, I think, when we leave the tension
between resistance and submission suspended, rather than attempt to
resolve it in one way or another. If this seems a simple enough interpretive stance to map out and occupy, it is on the contrary a very difficult
one to maintain, since there are so many seductive competing stances
from which one might push the dynamic toward some sort of puta-
tively final resolution.[8] If, however, I am right to recommend that we
leave the dialogue between the subject and the symbolic open, unresolved, and thus a means of asking questions rather than answering
them, then we can see yet another reason why Faulkner so often made
storytelling ability the litmus test of legal skill. By judging his lawyer characters according to novelistic standards of creativity, rhetorical
accomplishment, and narrative power, he made these characters even
more effective vehicles for authorial self-discovery, self-examination,
even self-creation.

This raises the distinct possibility that the discovery of the forensic
character and its fictional possibilities played an important part in the
process by which Faulkner became "Faulkner," the mature "genius"
who has been reified and all but deified by an entire scholarly industry.
It was, let us remind ourselves, in the same novel, *Flags in the Dust*,
that Faulkner unveiled his first extensively delineated lawyer character, Horace Benbow, and first began to mine the well-nigh inexhaust-

ible resources of his apocryphal county. Note the conjunction of these breakthroughs. On the one hand, Faulkner discovers perhaps his most characteristic fictional alter ego, in the lawyer figure. On the other hand, and in the same bold move, he finds, in the cultural complexity of Yoknapatawpha, his own peculiar objective correlative for the order of law and culture—against which he will test his principal forensic figures (and indeed all his principal characters) in novel after novel. This is the moment, I would suggest, that marks the arrival of the mature Faulkner. If *Flags* is the first novel of his major phase, as many agree, it is perhaps due to more than the emergence of Yoknapatawpha alone.

The scenario of authorial ontogenesis I sketch here is strikingly evocative of the Lacanian mirror stage, the scene of a fundamental shift in the infant subject's sense of itself, from a *corps morcelé*, or "fragmented body-image," to a *corps propre*, a totalized, insular ego— a transformation catalyzed by the discovery and "jubilant assumption" of the imago or specular image (*Écrits* 2–4; see also Gallop 79–80). What if, however, we replace the *corps* with a *corpus*, taking our cue from Faulkner himself and adding the letter "u" to the word, substituting for the idea of the infantile body in Lacan's scheme the idea of a body *of work*? Can we postulate a *writerly* mirror stage, in which William Faulkner, the writing subject, produces "Faulkner," jubilantly assuming an authorial (and authoritative) self, as a result of discovering and confronting, in imaginary form, his great theme, the individual's struggle with the symbolic? And isn't *Flags in the Dust* precisely the site of this transition? Consider the pre-*Flags* corpus: isn't it indeed a *corpus morcelé*, a mélange of largely unrelated stories, plays, poems, essays, reviews, drawings, handmade books, apprentice novels, and unfinished manuscripts? The importance of this material, after all, has emerged in retrospect, after the fictions of the late twenties, the thirties, and the forties put "Faulkner" on the literary map. On the other hand, isn't the work after *Flags* something much more like a *corpus propre*, dominated as it is by the Yoknapatawpha material, material with clear integrity and focus? (Think of the many who have approached this material as a single unified "saga.") If so, then I want to suggest that the discovery of the lawyer character, in all its richness, ambivalence, and specular potential, played a principal role in catalyzing the transition from *corpus morcelé* to *corpus propre*, and from William Faulkner, writing subject, to "Faulkner," canonical institution; and that it is thus high

time to put an end to the condescension and outright neglect that have
for decades characterized scholarly work on Horace Benbow. Clearly,
Benbow is no mere working sketch for later, more fully delineated characters such as Quentin Compson, Gail Hightower, and Henry Sutpen.
The logic of the writerly mirror stage reveals Horace as a truly seminal
figure, who makes not only his later Prufrockian avatars, but also in a
very real sense his author, "Faulkner," possible.

FORENSIC POETICS

> One day in Sicily, in the fifth century B.C., a dispute between two parties
> ended in violence, with damages. The next day they appeared before the
> authorities empowered to decide which of the two was guilty. But how to
> reach such a decision? The dispute did not occur before the eyes of the
> judges, who were unable to observe and ascertain the truth. When the
> senses are powerless, only one means remains—to hear the narratives of
> the litigants themselves, whose position is thereby altered, for their prob-
> lem is no longer to establish a truth (which is impossible) but to approach
> it, to produce an impression of it. And this impression will be stronger in
> direct proportion to the skill of the narrative. To win the trial, it is more
> important to speak well than to have behaved well. (Todorov 80)

The moral of Todorov's forensic fable is one Faulkner knew well and
demonstrated repeatedly in his fiction: the moment an act of litigation begins, we leave the illusion of unmediated knowledge behind and
enter a realm of representation. Before witnesses, litigants, attorneys,
judges, jurors, and gallery members alike lies the collaborative task
of resolving a dispute between two parties, a dispute to which no one
any longer enjoys direct access. The arbiter's only recourse is thus the
conflicting versions of "the facts" (re)presented by the claimants and/
or their advocates. In this way, the "real," historical dispute yields to a
narrative dispute, a contest of stories.[9]

As Todorov argues, there is a direct historical connection in Western culture between the emergence of the law court and the birth of
rhetoric as a discipline emphasizing the persuasive value of language.
In fifth-century Greece, for instance, the rise of the *rhetores* (professors
of oratory) paved the way for revolutionary changes in the practice of
law and for the emergence of a professional class of lawyers (Casson

123–26), and 2,500 years later the lawyer's professional day still consists largely of spoken and written conversations intended to persuade (White, *Heracles' Bow* 4). This is even more true of the litigator. When verbal accounts of an event clash in the courtroom, language itself becomes the star witness, "an autonomous entity governed by its own laws and susceptible of being judged for itself. The importance of words exceeds that of the things they were supposed to reflect" (Todorov 80). Thus verisimilitude, rather than referential accuracy, emerges as the goal of every courtroom speaker. If rhetoric fetishizes public opinion, in essence subordinating reality to it, then litigation does the same thing by embodying public opinion directly in courtroom listeners such as judges and jurors, the principal targets of forensic discourse.

If litigation is thus an essentially rhetorical act, it is also an inescapably narrative one. Clients typically articulate their needs to lawyers in story form. Witnesses offer narrative versions of events by testifying in court or by giving depositions, and lawyers are constantly beseeching them to "tell the Court what happened." Lawyers of course advocate by narrating, by telling their clients' stories in the language of the law. Even written documents such as criminal indictments tend to exhibit a strong narrative component: individual actors are named, dates are given, events are placed in sequence, and causality is assigned. Further, the lawyer works these individual stories selectively into a composite narrative sequence—the case—that holds meaning and suasive power.[10] Prosecutors and defense attorneys typically put the same narrative raw material to very different uses in the construction of their cases, and they frequently endorse very different interpretations of a story offered as evidence.

Had Faulkner explicitly sought confirmation of the links between advocacy and narration, he could have turned to the story of his great-grandfather's first brush with fame, which, as it happens, occurred at the very point of convergence between law and literature. In 1845, soon after he began reading law, W. C. Falkner was recruited into a posse that tracked down a murder suspect named Andrew McCannon. Family legend has it that Falkner

almost saw a lynching when an angry crowd demanded the prisoner
on [the posse's] return. In a brilliant and desperate stroke, McCannon
promised that if they would give him the time, he would reveal the story

of his life, including the actual details of the . . . murders. McCannon
was illiterate, and for amanuensis he chose William Clark Falkner, who
would do his best both for the subject and for himself. Suddenly time
became crucial once more. When McCannon was tried and sentenced to
hang, Falkner set off on the seventy-mile ride to Memphis, waited there
while the printer worked at top speed, and then rode through the night
to carry the pamphlets back to Ripley. He arrived just in time to hawk
them at the actual moment of their subject's execution. Apparently, he
pocketed a tidy profit. . . . (FAB 14–15)

Here, a full two years before he passes the bar, the Old Colonel's career
as advocate really begins, in an act of storytelling, at the same moment that his writing career launches itself in a lucrative act of advocacy, and the result is the McCannon pamphlet: part affidavit, part
potboiler, part Scheherazade-like narrative reprieve—and an early and
suggestive glimpse of the interrelations between the two vocations that
intrigued William Faulkner as no others would.

The orality and aurality of courtroom litigation are also among its
most important features. The passage from Todorov reemphasizes the
relative unimportance of the eye in juridical proceedings (hearings)
and the preeminence of the voice and the ear. The old proverb that
"Justice is blind," and the blindfolded icon, bearing aloft her scales,
which illustrates the adage on the walls of courtrooms throughout
America, are further reminders of the logocentric bias of courtroom
law. Even tangible or "material" artifacts such as weapons, damaged
goods, personal belongings, and written documents, are irrelevant unless incorporated into larger oral narratives. Nor does the belated and
supplementary stenographic transcript record the entire story of a legal
proceeding. First of all, it fails to attend to paralinguistic features of
courtroom discourse such as nuances of tone, hesitations, pauses and
other changes of tempo, laughter and stammering, variations in volume and pitch—all of which can be highly charged with meaning
(see P. Brown 22–23). Moreover, the written transcript can be edited,
whereas the actual discourse of litigation is recorded in memory in
a fuller context, relatively free from editing or erasure.[11] Any lawyer
worth his rhetorical salt knows how to exploit these crucial differences
between what is spoken and what is transcribed: leading, inappropriate, or even scabrous comments may be stricken from the record, but

no juror instructed to disregard such comments can ever do so with the total and ideal amnesia of the stenographer. Thus courtroom utterance can secure a rhetorical effect even in its "official" graphological absence.

Many of these observations are supported by the etymology of common legal terms. The origins of the word "forensic," for instance, stretch back to the great public gatherings of the Roman forum, where law and rhetoric converged frequently and intimately. "Verdict," defined as "a jury finding," stems from the Latin *verus* + *dictum:* "a true-saying." Yet, in a lexical evolution that parallels exactly the declension of truth value into verisimilitude, the term acquires a secondary sense of "opinion" or "judgment." "Conviction," legally "a guilty finding," is also in a more quotidian sense "belief," as if to underscore the fact that trials issue not in truth or knowledge but rather in persuasion, someone's being convinced. (The accused is convicted when the jury is convinced.)[12] Likewise, a "sentence," legally a specification of punishment, derives from the Latin root *sententia,* meaning "feeling" or "opinion." To "pronounce" a sentence seems to promise the unbiased objectivity of "reporting forth" (*pro* + *nuntiare*), but the more subjective legal sense of sentencing as "passing judgment upon" reveals once more the inseparability of the speaker and the arbiter.[13]

In the rhetorically charged environment of the courtroom, then, the success of the lawyer depends utterly upon his or her effectiveness as a speaker. Litigators must be penetrating inquisitors, receptive to the give and take of courtroom dialogue and debate. They must also be convincing raconteurs capable of editing their remarks on the fly, as the situation around them changes. And they must constantly adapt their performances to the needs, moods, and tastes of an audience of jurors whom they have had a hand in selecting. This latter skill, which a contemporary theorist of conversational storytelling calls "recipient design" (Polanyi 46), demands an unusual sensitivity to nuances of idiom. "[T]he lawyer," James Boyd White emphasizes, "must always start by speaking the language of his or her audience, whatever it may be" (*Heracles' Bow* 33).

When forensic discourse downplays its own rhetoricity, however, and passes itself off as transparent, referential, or all-comprehensive, the interests of justice are threatened if not subverted outright. Roland Barthes has argued that all speech inherently gravitates toward an au-

thority which involves the capacity to punish, a fundamentally conservative force, appearing "not in what is said but in the very fact of
speaking," which he associates with the law ("Writers, Intellectuals,
Teachers" 192). The voice of the law, whose punitive side is apparent
not only in the phenomenon of sentencing but also in the root meaning
of the verb "convict" ("to vanquish together"), wants to hear itself talk,
typically at the expense of others, and in the courtroom its victims are
often those who do not or cannot speak themselves: the silent and the
inarticulate.[14]

As Barthes's ideological analyses of two sensational murder trials in
France vividly demonstrate, the primacy of rhetoric in the law court
pushes justice in the direction of literature and creates an insatiable demand for stories (see *Mythologies* 43–46, and *The Eiffel Tower* 67–69).
Theoretically, this demand is balanced by legal guarantees for the silent
(the Fifth Amendment, for instance), but if the right to remain silent is
not respected, the judicial process may be disrupted. Legal procedure
is at its most pathological when one side controls the discourse, and this
is precisely what happened at the Dominici and Dupriez trials. From
their example, Barthes concludes grimly that in every courtroom situation there lies the possibility of being "deprived of language, or worse,
rigged out in that of our accusers, humiliated and condemned by" an
objectifying, intrusive, and alienating discourse. Nor should Americans
think that their adversary system is free from the dark side of forensic
rhetoric or always exemplary in its attentiveness to the voiceless and
the marginal. The farcical trial of Quentin Compson for kidnapping in
The Sound and the Fury—a model of polyglot chaos that would not be
out of place in a Kafka story—offers plenty of evidence to the contrary,
as do the great courtroom scenes of *Sanctuary*.

Or consider the Mink Snopes trial in *The Hamlet*. After his arrest
for the murder of Jack Houston, a bruised throat sustained during an
unsuccessful suicide (or perhaps escape) attempt leaves Mink practically dumb at his trial, capable only of "a dry, croaking sound" (H 258).
From the start, therefore, the verbal deck is stacked against this voiceless litigant. Yet as he cranes his injured neck to look for his cousin
Flem Snopes, whom he believes will save him, Mink is not even listening to the stories that will determine his fate, and when he does
finally summon the wherewithal to speak, it is only to curse the cousin

who abandoned him to the prattle of his inexperienced lawyer and the conviction of the jury.[15]

The threat of tyrannical or terroristic forensic discourse places the lawyer under a special obligation to listen to and for those often critically different voices guaranteed a hearing in the courtroom (see Soifer). The lawyer-as-listener must be willing to allow a place for silences and hesitations in the aural spaces of testimony and cross-examination, to maintain a healthy skepticism about referential claims for courtroom rhetoric, and to recognize the appeal to linguistic transparency as a "mythological," ideological strategy to usurp the language of the accused or suppress it altogether. Nor does the advocate's obligation to listen end with the act of litigation. Along with his client, the lawyer is the major source and vehicle of courtroom narrative, and what empowers him to speak is the fact that, well before judge and juror, he has already heard everything. In his interviews with clients and witnesses, he collects raw story material and arranges that material within the larger narrative structure of the case he will present to other listeners in court. "The lawyer," argues Peter Brooks, "is the arch-narratee," "he who listens to, and enters into, all the secret, buried stories of a society" (233). As both principal narratee and original narratee, the lawyer illustrates both senses of Brooks's term.

If the litigator's job is to put together a rhetorically effective narrative account of contested events, it is important to note that this account is rarely, if ever, a completely seamless affair. On the contrary, as Brooks implies, the lawyer is a collector of buried stories, pieces of stories, partial remains of older stories that are exhumed and incorporated into new designs. Nor are these patchwork efforts doomed to incoherence or indeterminacy. The fragmentary nature of the lawyer's narrative and evidentiary materials only reinforces the fact that in the courtroom, storytelling is most often an act of recuperation and reconstruction. As bits and pieces of information, often insignificant in their own right, begin to accumulate and be given narrative form, uncertainty can be transformed into plausibility. This habit of building up workable artifacts out of diverse and fragmentary parts links the lawyer with the *bricoleur,* the resourceful jack-of-all-trades described by Claude Lévi-Strauss in *The Savage Mind* (16–36).[16]

Bricolage serves Lévi-Strauss as a metaphor for the general "sci-

ence of the concrete" by which preliterate cultures give meaning and
structure to the physical universe. As opposed to the engineer, hero
of modern culture, who favors the abstract and conceptual over the
concrete, the *bricoleur* is characterized by resourcefulness, improvisa-
tion, a habit of imaginative reconstruction, and a limited repertoire of
available moves and materials. The *bricoleur*'s credo, in other words, is

> always to make do with "whatever is at hand," that is to say with a set of
> tools and materials which is always finite and is also heterogeneous be-
> cause what it contains bears no relation to the current project, or indeed
> to any particular project, but is the contingent result of all the occasions
> there have been to renew or enrich the stock or to maintain it with the
> remains of previous constructions or destructions. The set of the "brico-
> leur's" means . . . is to be defined only by its potential use or, putting this
> another way and in the language of the "bricoleur" himself, because the
> elements are collected or retained on the principle that "they may always
> come in handy." (Lévi-Strauss 17–18)

In much the same way, the litigator can only work with the resources at
hand, the stories and physical artifacts provided by clients, witnesses,
investigators, and the like. The litigator does not invent these materials
but inherits them—or, if particularly industrious, the lawyer gathers
them as the case progresses, against the moment when they will become useful. Since any story "may always come in handy" later, the
good lawyer, like the *bricoleur*, forgets nothing, throws nothing away.

The litigator will draw upon the same skills when it becomes necessary to research a point of law, since, as Joseph Vining has observed,
legal research is at bottom "a search for the right quotation," in which
the lawyer raids a rich repertoire of "digests, indexes, commentaries,
and glosses" for statements and opinions that will "come in handy," if
you will, by lending authority to the lawyer's construction of the law.
(Note how appropriate the concept of "construction" becomes in this
context. As the etymologies suggest, to construe the law is inevitably
to construct it.) And these statements and opinions are in turn "inter-
laced with quotations and references, often to the point where the page
looks like a collage" (Vining 189). Thus the Lévi-Straussian "savage
mind" persists into the heyday of literate culture, where it can still be
found haunting many a law library and legal archive.

Since the *bricoleur* must sift through the debris of culture in order to renew, enrich, or maintain his stock, these "odds and ends" are never completely fresh, never free from the imprint of history. On the contrary, as Lévi-Strauss explains, "they are not raw materials but wrought products," and as such, they cannot be put to just any use or given just any meaning. They already signify. "[T]hey have *had a use*," as parts of some earlier configuration, and, after this configuration is dismantled by time or human effort, "*they can be used again*," reappropriated in new contexts. Even then, however, they still carry the fossilized traces of earlier meanings and uses. For this reason the possibilities of combination will "always remain limited by the particular history of each piece and by those of its features which are already determined by the use for which it was originally intended or the modifications it has undergone for other purposes" (22, 35–36, 19; Lévi-Strauss's emphasis). The analogy with courtroom storytelling is readily apparent here. The stories that make up the greater part of the lawyer's raw materials are also wrought products, given shape and meaning by their original tellers in their original contexts, and while they too can be used again, reappropriated in a new structure (the case at hand), they can never be wrenched entirely free of their earlier history. As an inevitable constraint on meaning, this history must be honored and fully accounted for, lest the litigator risk having his stories discredited by opposing counsel. James Boyd White writes of statutory and especially constitutional law in much the same way, as disciplines that require of lawyer and judge alike the ability "to put together the prior texts that are the material of law in new compositions, which, while respecting the nature of each item, so order them as to create a new arrangement with a meaning of its own" (*Justice as Translation* 214). For these reasons, the legal imagination must be not only narrative but also deeply historical, even "archeological" (White, *The Legal Imagination* 209).

The task of assessing what role(s) a given tool or technique can be made to play in the labor of reconstruction and repair is a crucial element of *bricolage*. The *bricoleur* accomplishes this task by making a mental inventory of the entire repertoire, going through it piece by piece and assigning to each item a set of potential values.

> His first practical step is retrospective. He has to turn back to an already existent set made up of tools and materials, to consider or reconsider what it contains and, finally and above all, to engage in a sort of dia-

logue with it and, before choosing between them, to index the possible
answers which the whole set can offer to his problem. He interrogates all
the heterogeneous objects of which his treasury is composed to discover
what each of them could "signify" and so contribute to the definition
of a set which has yet to materialize but which will ultimately differ
from the instrumental set only in the internal disposition of its parts.
(Lévi-Strauss 18)

In the emergence of this "internal disposition" or structure lies the
essence of *bricolage*. A working whole is (re)constructed out of disparate
parts. Order is created out of disorder.

The litigator subjects her own repertoire of stories to the same sort
of interrogation in order to combine them in the most effective way for
courtroom presentation. What is a judge or juror likely to think about
this piece of evidence, coming at this particular moment in my case?
What will it signify? What is its potential? Which story in my repertoire most persuasively establishes this particular point? When should
this witness take the stand? Early in the case, or later? Am I arranging
my material in a way that develops an argument, that allows an overarching story, an "internal disposition," to emerge? Like the primitive
fix-it-man, the forensic *bricoleur* must "cross-examine his resources"
before proceeding with his work (Lévi-Strauss 19).

There is also a morality to *bricolage*, an ethic of reconstruction, that
deserves comment. Confronted with the degeneration of culture into
ruin or of meaning into indeterminacy, the *bricoleur* wastes little time
bemoaning the situation (as a modernist might) or celebrating it (as
a postmodernist might), but instead sets about changing it, fixing it
on the spot, as it were, using whatever means are available. For the
bricoleur, the analytical impulse to tear things apart and to hoard the
shards of culture is always tempered by the synthetic impulse to put
them back together again—though not necessarily in the same configuration as before (Genette 3). To keep culture going—this is the goal
of *bricolage*, and it is also one of the primary goals of the court of law.
Litigation, after all, evolved in order to keep culture going, to provide
a forum for individual disagreement without endangering social stability, and thereby to bring "a rhetorical coherence to public life by
compelling those who disagree about one thing to speak a language
which expresses their actual or pretended agreement about everything

else." Courts legally remake conflict as "an idealized conversation," rendering it "both intelligible and amenable to resolution" (White, *Justice as Translation* 179). In this sense, the ethic of reconstruction, as practiced by attorney and *bricoleur* alike, is a conservative one, but its conservatism is ultimately constructive rather than delimiting.

In his own remarks upon his craft, Faulkner often describes an activity that suggests *bricolage*. He liked to speak of himself as a kind of literary fix-it man, reaching into the lumber room of his imagination for the materials and techniques he needed to meet the aesthetic requirements of the particular job at hand—or as he put it at the University of Virginia, "hunting around in the carpenter's shop to find a tool that will make a better chicken-house" (FU 68). A number of Faulkner's critics have noted his *bricolage*-like "habit of building up his works from fragments" (Pikoulis 153). Donald Kartiganer, for example, finds "[t]he fragmentary structure to be the basic building block of Faulkner's narrative imagination" (*The Fragile Thread* xiii). Faulkner's fiction, argues Kartiganer, "splinters a commonly, conventionally known world into the vital reality of its separate pieces, and then makes its own recovery, its struggle for a comprehensive design, the central drama" (xv). The restless experimentation of the Faulkner novel thus offers the reader an "internal disposition" that is not quite the same as that of the world of which it is built. Nor is it this world only, or the knowledge of it, that is "splintered" in the Faulkner text. A master of the twice-told tale, Faulkner habitually raided his previous fictions for situations, characters, anecdotes, and other material to be revised or otherwise recycled into new narrative configurations, especially in the later years of his career (see Moreland on Faulkner's aesthetic of "revisionary repetition," and Creighton on his "craft of revision"). He also made the rediscovery, reconstruction, and recounting of old stories a principal theme in much of his greatest fiction (Minter, "Notes" 251). One critic has argued, in fact, that we should interpret Faulkner's career itself as a constantly evolving, *bricolage*-like process driven by "the perpetual reconstitution of new designs out of old ones" (Stonum 30). One important result of these fictional strategies is to make a kind of *bricoleur* out of the Faulkner reader, who is confronted in text after text with "the problem of fitting pieces together" (Slatoff 1) and must answer that challenge with an openness to interpretive strategies that are reconstructive, improvisatory, even performative.[17]

The narrative and rhetorical dimensions of law are not confined to individual acts of litigation alone. Even in the largest institutional or anthropological sense, the law is a product of story and discourse. As what Clifford Geertz calls a cultural system, a network of symbolic forms by means of which human beings, both individually and collectively, order and also actively *shape* the experience of the real, every legal system encompasses more than simply a *corpus juris*. It also invokes a distinctive language and rests upon a set of narratives that provide it with significance and authority as a *nomos*, or normative universe (Cover 9). Similarly, the creation of new legal meaning, a phenomenon legal scholar Robert Cover calls jurisgenesis, is always a culturally mediated process grounded heavily in narrative (11). "Once understood in the context of the narratives that give it meaning," Cover writes, "law becomes not merely a system of rules to be observed, but a world in which we live," a world that articulates itself, anchors itself, perpetuates itself, and constantly remakes itself by means of stories (4–5). The law thus emerges as a central mode, and the courtroom as a central site, of cultural performance.[18]

Faulkner frequently emphasizes this aspect of courtroom procedure by exploring the inherent theatricality of forensic activity, and by calling attention to the larger and more representative drama that the law court itself stages for society. "Courtroom drama" has become such a tired cliché that we may too easily discount its accuracy. For elements of the drama are built into the structure of every act of litigation, causing one legal scholar to wonder "whether a court that lacks a properly theatrical aspect is really a court at all" (Ball 44).[19]

The geometry and architecture of the courtroom immediately suggest the theater. From a public gallery in the rear of an enclosed room, we witness a performance before us (a balcony often provides additional seating). Behind us stands a kind of usher, the bailiff, guarding against unnecessary disturbances and other interruptions. The principal actors are separated from the audience by a bar that demarcates the space of performance, much as the proscenium stage indicates the boundaries of dramatic illusion. It is by crossing this bar (with its occasional Tennysonian implication) that the individual is initiated into the inner circle of speaking performers, the *dramatis personae* of the trial.

Appropriately enough, this point of crossing is a point of speech: the spectator rises, proceeds to the stand, takes an oath, and enters the courtroom drama officially, to become a part of the written record. With this act, of course, the nature of one's "witnessing" changes.

The lines of sight and sound in the courtroom typically converge on two central points, the Bench and the witness box; at any given moment the principal speaker and the principal listener sit side by side—and often elevated—in the visual and aural center of attention. The theater of the courtroom, moreover, is a self-conscious one, providing us with an onstage audience, the jury, comprised of citizens like ourselves. These onstage listeners are ideally courteous. Silent and attentive, they rarely advertise their presence. Yet we notice them, for their reactions in some sense mirror, anticipate, or corroborate our own, as if to remind us of the pragmatic orientation of all forensic discourse.

There are further similarities. The witnesses, for instance, are akin to actors. They speak severally, and their roles are often familiar, conventional ones (the friend of the family, the psychiatric expert, the nosy neighbor, the jealous spouse, the arresting officer, and so on). Each of these actors, like the performer on the stage, assumes a fictive personality that is not to be confused with his or her existential identity. In fact, as Ball points out, everyone involved in the courtroom production speaks through masks, or *personae juris*, which function as much to protect and amplify individual voices as to inhibit or repress them (86–88). Furthermore, as in the theater, there are no objective criteria that allow us to privilege one speaker over another, to distinguish the honest individual from the liar. So, like Shakespeare's audience, we do well to allow a degree of truth to each speaker and thus to accede to a certain indeterminacy that is not without aesthetic pleasure. The way we respond to the stories before us, however, will affect real persons, palpably and often dramatically changing their lives.[20] The tangibility of interpretive consequences in the courtroom is no doubt the most important reason why the legal system typically places such a premium on resolving issues that literature and literary criticism are content to leave ambiguous (though there are other pragmatic constraints on legal indeterminacy as well; see Graff 405–13). It may also make us yearn for an overarching evaluative presence to help us narrow the range of our own interpretive options.

This presence is embodied in the lawyer, in the capacity of a director who participates in the performance itself—as opposed to the theatrical director, who typically remains offstage, behind the scenes.[21] From an onstage vantage point, the lawyer makes interpretive decisions at every moment of a trial, by choreographing action, prompting gesture, and influencing the pacing of the production (moving for a recess, perhaps). In addition, the lawyer makes decisions about costume and strategizes with the performers about the most effective means of delivering individual lines and speeches. If the audience is unable or unwilling to judge the production on its own merits, the lawyer may seek another, more impartial audience by requesting a change of venue. It should be noted, however, that the lawyer's authority as a director is challenged from the start by the efforts of the opposing counsel to stage a more persuasive drama. In this context it is left to the jury to decide which performance will carry the day, much as playgoing citizens in ancient Greece were called upon to judge contests of theater.

To the performances-in-miniature directed and produced by the opposing advocates must be added a second type of "judicial theater," the overarching spectacle of the trial as a whole. If the former is intended for an audience of judge and jurors, the latter is performed for the general public. As such it bestows order upon society, confers legitimacy upon the legal system, and "is importantly an end in itself." As Ball puts it, "the judicial branch does not merely utter decisions, disembodied words. It is the exemplar of the law. In its ceremony, its costuming, its performance, and its treatment of participants, it embodies the legitimate exercise of power within a given sphere" (62).[22]

The criminal justice system in the antebellum South offers us a revealing look at judicial theater in action. This system secured social order in a number of ways—not only by immobilizing and punishing interlopers, but by promoting interaction between the classes in a stratified social climate, supplying the region with sorely needed intellectual leadership, and serving as "a setting in which the community could celebrate in high drama the momentary triumph of good, the temporary eradication of evil" (Wyatt-Brown 370). This cultural spectacle, in which aristocrat and professional, yeoman and poor-white alike played significant roles, balanced "a rigid rank-conscious placement of individuals" with a more egalitarian, "communal sense that provided for wide participation in rendering the final verdict" (390). Furthermore, the systematic exclusion of slaves and free blacks from these roles is itself culturally significant and constitutive. The judicial theater of the Old South, then, reveals a world view not unlike the one E. M. W. Tillyard assigned to the Elizabethans: a great chain of being—in which, regretfully, some beings found themselves in chains.

Judicial theater may even be broken down into distinct subgenres, many of which could be characterized as pathological: the saturnalia, for instance, in which passion predominates over procedure and the lines between participants and spectators are hopelessly blurred; or the morality play, in which the human participants are allowed only allegorical significance, as opposed to the richer symbolic significance of the *persona juris;* or the theater of the absurd, in which certain participants deliberately abandon or subvert courtroom protocol, most often as a form of protest against inequities in the legal system (Ball 54–57). For better or worse, that is, in sickness and in health, judicial theater gives the community an image of itself in action.

The Dionysian trial scene of "Wild Palms," for instance, reveals a community blind to, and blinded by, its own provincial assumptions about sexuality and gender. When the adulterous affair between Charlotte Rittenmeyer and Harry Wilbourne culminates in Charlotte's death from a botched abortion, Harry, who performed the operation, is charged with manslaughter. If his trial initially furnishes the languid coastal town with the occasion for a "communal morality play," as one critic has suggested (Duvall 51), it goes on to evoke other categories of judicial theater as well. Ultimately, in fact, a morality play is precisely what this trial is not, what it refuses to become.

That the community *intends* to stage a morality play is clear enough from the start, when the "businesslike" jury selection indicates a disposition, on the part of the defense as well as the prosecution, to move along briskly with a trial whose outcome is, by implication, a foregone conclusion (WP 316). The leading roles, preassigned by consensus, are conventional and allegorical. Wilbourne, doubly outrageous as adulterer and murderer, is expected to deny all responsibility for the crime, thus requiring the explicit instruction in morality and guilt that it is the office of the court to provide. Francis Rittenmeyer, doubly bereft as cuckold and widower, elicits sympathy in the role of victim, but he is also expected, by virtue of the same talionic ethic that confronts Bayard Sartoris in "An Odor of Verbena," to avenge Charlotte's death upon her killer—and thus to underwrite reigning communal narratives of honor, violence, and gender. The judge, who looks like "a Methodist Sunday School superintendent" (317), appears just as ready to pronounce upon sanctity as upon legality. And the community, of course, awards itself the role of ordinary, god-fearing citizens only too eager to impose a moral upon the story: adulterers, like all sinners, come to a bad end.[23]

The morality play, however, is subverted from the outset. Wilbourne, for instance, won't play his assigned role. He admits his guilt freely and forthrightly to the court. Nor does he offer his plea in hope of receiving a lenient sentence. He is prepared to face the consequences of his actions, and as such, he undermines, and humanizes, the community's image of him. Moreover, Rittenmeyer enters the courtroom bent on mercy rather than vengeance. Not only is he unarmed (as Bayard Sartoris was), missing a crucial prop—the judge is shocked and the gallery scandalized to learn this—he has actually come on behalf of his would-be victim. He wishes to make a plea, he says, but what does he mean by this? What role does he have in mind? That of a character witness, pleading for a lenient sentence on Wilbourne's behalf? That of an advocate, entering his client's plea? Or perhaps most subversively, that of a fellow conspirator, entering his own plea alongside Wilbourne's guilty one and thus acknowledging his complicity, however remote or attenuated, in what has transpired? Whatever the answer, the effect of Rittenmeyer's appearance at the trial is to render Wilbourne even more human and thus to expose the community's allegorizing practices as implausible and strained.

On other occasions forensic procedure itself is subverted at Wilbourne's trial, edging the courtroom drama toward theater of the absurd. The district attorney wants to arraign Harry on a murder charge, though the indictment against him is only for manslaughter. Entering his guilty plea, Wilbourne addresses the court directly rather than through his advocate, and the judge's testy response ("Dont speak from there!") barely disguises his anxiety about the prospect of such unorthodox and unmediated contact (318). Rittenmeyer asks to speak on Harry's behalf well after the latter's guilty plea has technically closed the case to further testimony. And the jury is ready to return a verdict against Wilbourne without ever having retired! These self-conscious distortions of courtroom protocol reveal the law court as a space of representation in which reality is always constructed, controlled, and politically inflected, rather than simply presented in "objective" form.

In this respect they are not unlike the alienation-effects of Brechtian epic theater.

As the allegory continues to unravel, there is a corresponding break-down of social order in the courtroom, and the trial turns saturnalian. Deprived of its tidy moral categories, the gallery grows incapable of channeling its indignation or even making sense of the trial. It vents its fury indiscriminately against Rittenmeyer as well as Wilbourne. There are cries of "Lock them up together!" and "Hang them both!" (321), collapsing the distinction between victim and villain. Soon all social distinctions collapse, and the gallery becomes a mob. As its "droning murmur" (317) yields first to a "long in-sucking" of "amazement and incredulity" and then to an outright roar of screaming voices and trampling feet (320), the crowd increasingly resembles the lynching parties of *Sanctuary* and *Intruder in the Dust*, and even as the judge frantically attempts to restore order, the sound of outrage and chaos beats on outside the courtroom, like the sound of the wind in the palms.

THE FORENSIC CITIZEN

As Garry Wills has brilliantly demonstrated, American concepts of citizenship originated in Enlightenment ideals of civic duty and political virtue finding their most perfect embodiment in the legendary figure of Cincinnatus, the Roman citizen who, called from the plow to lead his people against an invading army, responded by routing the enemy, restoring public order, and, after only sixteen days in office, surrendering the dictatorship to retire to his farm. As a private citizen with a resoundingly public conscience, and as a man who answered the call to duty and power without abusing it, Cincinnatus exemplified classical values (self-sacrifice and disinterestedness) especially prized in a neo-classical age. Americans of this age found their Cincinnatus, as we all know, in George Washington, the soldier-citizen who "perfected the art of power by giving it away" (Wills 3).[24] But though Washington was the most visible individual representative of the Cincinnatus-ideal in the young nation, and though other examples of the soldier-citizen were to be found in the Society of the Cincinnati, it could be argued that the role of Cincinnatus in revolutionary and republican America was more characteristically, and perhaps even more dutifully, performed by lawyer-citizens. For throughout the years of rebellion and early nationhood, lawyers, more than soldiers, ministers, doctors, or the members of any other vocation, were the leading figures in American intellectual, political, and even literary life. Thirteen of the first sixteen presidents, for instance, were trained in the law (Ferguson 11). So were twenty-five of the fifty-six signers of the Declaration of Independence, thirty-one of the fifty-five representatives at the Constitutional Convention in Philadelphia, and twenty-seven members of the First Congress (Boorstin 205). Moreover, a number of the most important literary figures of the early national period (and a substantial number of their readers) were lawyers.

The swiftness with which lawyers rose to cultural preeminence in America is astonishing. As late as the early federal period, many Americans saw the lawyer as the very antithesis of the good citizen. To some, "the mystery of the law was a gigantic conspiracy of the learned" against the "helpless integrity" of the common folk. Others persisted in "the old Puritan hostility to lawyers as being men sworn to advocate any case regardless of its merits" (Miller 102, 104). By the 1770s and 1780s, however, Americans found themselves faced with the almost unfathomable intellectual task of creating a political framework, a national rhetoric, and, not least of all, a legal system for a fledgling republic woefully short on established national traditions. And where their ancestors might have turned to minister-citizens for guidance, they turned to lawyers, who developed a revolutionary rhetoric with a decidedly legalistic character. What is more, Revolutionary lawyers turned this legalistic discourse against their main rivals for cultural authority, the minister-citizen and the soldier-citizen, driving them "away from civic podiums and the positions of communal control" with vitriolic protests against "religious intolerance and standing armies." They thus insured their own hegemony as spokesmen for American ideals and interests (Ferguson 12, 17).

It is also important to note that these lawyer-citizens believed their effectiveness as statesmen and as practicing attorneys to derive in large part from their training in letters. They were individuals of liberal learning and wide vision, self-conscious generalists whose "enlarged and comprehensive intellectual power" helped them meet the enormous demands of nation-building (Miller 135). Throughout the republic, young lawyers were urged to study history, philosophy, government, grammar, oratory, rhetoric, mathematics, the natural sciences, and most of all belles lettres and the classics (R. B. Davis 355; Ferguson

28–30). This curriculum reflected the basically Ciceronian attitude that humanistic wisdom was the very bedrock of freedom, "the surest guarantee of a precarious liberty" (Ferguson 5). Furthermore, as "the only educated Americans who regularly met and spent time together as a matter of course," circuit-riding lawyers "constituted a rare intellectual forum" in republican America, in which ideas of a political or belletristic nature could be debated and disseminated. The lawyer-citizen thus emerged as "a gentleman of letters defending cultural ideals" (Ferguson 69–70).

This image, and the configuration of law and letters that supported it, dominated the intellectual and political scene in America into the Jacksonian period. By the time of the Civil War, however, the lawyer as learned generalist and litterateur was rapidly becoming an anachronism. There were many reasons for this decline. Nineteenth-century courts and legislatures redirected the emphasis of American law from the protection of individual rights and the articulation of communitarian values to the aggressive promotion of economic development, thus creating new areas of legal practice and new niches for legal specialists. Other new branches of law emerged in the aftermath of the War of 1812 (Miller 127). American case law proliferated dramatically in the decades leading up to the Civil War, virtually insuring specialization. And in the 1830s, charges of elitism leveled against the bar by Jacksonian Democrats gradually forced lawyers to base their claims for legitimacy less upon broad learning than upon the specialized services they, and they alone, could offer their clients.[25]

After the Civil War, the growing industrialization and urbanization of American society created an even greater demand for trained experts in specialized legal fields. The rapid settlement and development of the American West also contributed to the new flush times for lawyers, as did the emergence of large law firms and the growth of professional schools of law. In the latter, the case method of instruction approached law as a system of rules that could be determined by inductive, quasi-scientific procedures, rather than as a subject of humanistic or political inquiry. All of these factors contributed to the demise of the lawyer-citizen and the rise of the lawyer-businessman and the lawyer-technician (Hall 211–21).

Modernization, urbanization, and industrialization came later to the predominantly rural, agrarian South, however, and the ideal of the classically trained lawyer-citizen held its ground against the encroach-

ment of specialization and narrow professionalization a good deal
longer there than in other parts of the nation. Legal historian Maxwell Bloomfield has described the antebellum southern lawyer in terms
that evoke the Cincinnatus image in rather pure form: as a man in
whom agricultural and political interests coincided (50–51). Opting for
more self-consciously mythical terms, Allen Tate christened this figure
"Cicero Cincinnatus," a title that bespeaks literary- as well as civic-
mindedness (587–88).

On the wane elsewhere in the nation, the old ideal actually strength-
ened its grip on the southern mind during the turbulent 1850s and
1860s, when sectional antagonism boiled over and the South, declaring itself a separate nation, faced the necessity of rediscovering, re-
appropriating, and reenacting the gestures with which an earlier group
of lawyer-citizens, the Founders, had called a nation into being in
1776. The search for these gestures secured the continuing cultural and
political relevance of southern lawyer-citizens throughout the crisis
years. And when the Confederate experiment failed, postbellum lawyers emerged as the leading advocates for a defeated southern society,
preaching a rhetoric of regional apology abroad and arguing the ex-
pediency of reconciliation before the unreconstructed back at home
(Ferguson 290–93).

Furthermore, the courthouse persisted as a visible center of community life in the thinly populated, predominantly rural South of the
nineteenth and early twentieth centuries. For the southern country
folk, scattered among isolated homesteads and small farms, the courthouse served as a meeting place where news, gossip, and stories could
change hands, as the following description of court week in turn-of-
the-century North Carolina will attest:

> There were no hard-surfaced roads or automobiles to facilitate inter-
> course among the people of the country, and so court week, by custom,
> became the most important event in their lives. They could meet each
> other, take a look at the new judge, hear his charge to the jury, exchange
> views, swap lies and horses, drink good liquor (which was plentiful),
> and occasionally raise a little hell on the side. . . . During its sessions the
> courtroom was packed with interested spectators who enjoyed the tilts
> between the lawyers and the occasional embarrassment of witnesses by
> vigorous cross-examinations. (A. Brooks 21–22)

For many of these people, shackled to the soil and starved for any kind of diversion, courtroom trials served as an important form of entertainment, a poor-man's playhouse, as it were (see Braden 30–31; Bloomfield 52; and Mueller 6). Their interest in litigation helped insure the continuing visibility of southern lawyers as citizens active in the life of their community.

The image of the lawyer as learned humanist and concerned citizen, then, survived relatively intact in the South into the early decades of the twentieth century—the time of William Faulkner's youth. Throughout the novelist's formative years, law remained the vocation of choice among civic-minded young southerners, and legal study continued to be perceived as the logical extension of a liberal education for those who considered themselves gentlemen. To Faulkner's brother Jack, for instance, the study of law simply "seemed the thing for one of our generation and of my family to do" (M. Falkner 118). Ben Wasson spoke of his legal career in much the same terms. Faulkner himself may have resisted the call of this tradition, but it clearly influenced his sense of the literary possibilities of the lawyer character. In figures like General Compson, Judge Stevens, and Sam Galloway, socially prominent attorneys and jurists who are also guardians of the commonweal, Faulkner explored the image of the lawyer-citizen with a characteristic blend of sympathy and irony. In the figure of Gavin Stevens, however, he created his most detailed version of the lawyer as Cincinnatus—making the comparison explicit in *Requiem for a Nun* (RFN 43, 184). What is more, in Stevens's hermitic, and hermetic, project of translating the Old Testament back into classic Greek, Faulkner found a rough equivalent of the fabled plow of Cincinnatus: a synecdoche for the entire private realm the good citizen willingly forsakes in order to answer the call to duty. In "Go Down, Moses," "Knight's Gambit," *The Town*, and *The Mansion*, Gavin's willingness—or unwillingness—to refrain from immersing himself in the translation functions as a barometer of his commitment to an ethic of public service and self-sacrifice.

It is also interesting to note that in the late forties and early fifties, the very time Gavin Stevens came to dominate the Yoknapatawpha fiction, Faulkner began to take increasingly public stances on regional, national, and even international issues; as he deepened and complicated his depictions of the lawyer-citizen, the novelist was also refining his own sense of civic responsibility. Faulkner appropriated the Cincinnatus role, however, in a way that more nearly resembled George Washington than Gavin Stevens. The uneasy conjunction of Faulkner's aggressive emergence as a public figure and his "retirement" into the persona of a gentleman-farmer who jealously guarded his privacy and pronounced himself unqualified to offer literary opinions (often before crowds gathered specifically in honor of his prodigious literary achievements), should not be dismissed by Faulkner scholars as simply a matter of the novelist's fabled contrariness or his fondness for gratuitous role-playing. The roles of citizen and farmer coexisted much more intimately than that. For Faulkner discovered, just as Washington had, that he could legitimate and even strengthen his authority as a leading citizen and public spokesman precisely by appearing to renounce that authority. By retiring to his farming duties, his ostensible first love, he sought to whet as much as to escape public interest in his political views.

Finally, it should be apparent that the integrity of the lawyer-citizen is a direct function of the integrity of the community on whose behalf he speaks and acts. If its values are basically sound, he emerges as worthy of respect and emulation, but if they are narrow or intolerant, he is often all the more so. The lawyer as aspiring Cincinnatus may be tempted to align himself uncritically with destructive or intolerant communal practices and views. He must be prepared to resist this temptation. Indeed, a provincial community is often best served by the citizen who challenges its values—even, perhaps, its laws. In Faulkner, the moral authority of the symbolic order is often open to question in this way. The lawyer must remain sensitive to the needs of individuals as well as the community and must treat the legal code not as an end in itself but as a means to the greater ethical ends of individual freedom and social stability. He must also know when and how to bend the code or to circumvent it, on those occasions where the law is irrelevant, inequitable, or inapplicable. "There's somewhere you stops," Ned McCaslin of *The Reivers* says to a local constable whose authority verges on tyranny. "There's somewhere the Law stops and just people starts" (R 243). It is worth noting that Ned's words have a salutary effect on the angry deputy, as though he, too, is capable of acknowledging the validity of resistance to the order of law and culture. The same novel, however, stresses the necessity of observing the dictates of the symbolic order and protecting the public good, at the comical trial of Boon Hogganbeck and Ludus, a driver for the Priest family (15–17). For emptying his pistol at Ludus and grazing an innocent bystander in the process, Boon must replace the injured girl's ruined dress and buy

her a bag of candy. Ludus is also implicated in the offense, since his insults initially provoked Boon's rage. Because the two offenders have for
the most part disturbed only each other and the peace, however, Maury
Priest and Judge Stevens come up with a punishment appropriate to
the crime:

> "I want both of them [Priest says], Boon and this boy, put under bond to
> keep the peace: say, a hundred dollars each: I will make the bond. Only,
> I want two mutual double-action bonds. I want two bonds, both of which
> will be abrogated, fall due, at the same moment that either one of them
> does anything that—that I—"
>
> "That dont suit you," Judge Stevens said.
>
> "Much obliged," [Priest] said. "—the same second that either one of
> them breaks the peace. I dont know if that is legal or not."
>
> "I dont either," Judge Stevens said. "We can try. If such a bond is not
> legal, it ought to be." (R 16)

Behind the humor here lurks an important ethical point. The double-
action bond restricts Boon and Ludus no more than socially responsible
behavior, behavior under the sign of the symbolic, restricts anyone. The
sentence placed on the two men is thus ultimately less one of bondage than of bonding, of acknowledging their mutual participation in
the social order and their mutual obligations to that order. Civilization
itself, as Freud, for one, knew well, is a kind of double-action bond, at
once alienating and enabling, and in acknowledging this truth, Priest
and Stevens manage to preserve the dignity of individual Yoknapatawphans as well as the integrity of Yoknapatawpha itself. As such, they
honor what White calls "the burden of acknowledged responsibility for
what you do with the law" (*Heracles' Bow* 58).

Absalom, Absalom! also supplies powerful positive and negative
images of the lawyer-citizen and his ethical responsibility to individual
and community. General Compson, for example, intervenes on behalf
of Valery Bon at an indictment hearing that promises only disaster for
the young man, who refuses to speak in his own defense. Compson
acts with sympathy, beneficence, and an awareness that the law must
sometimes be subordinated to human dignity and kindness. Realizing that as long as the youth remains in Jefferson, he risks exposure
as a mulatto (though unaware that Bon is also a Sutpen), the general
offers Bon a chance to escape this oppressive community and establish
himself somewhere else, where he can be exempt from the sins of his

fathers and the prejudices of his peers (AA 255–56). Compson's offer, however, though incontestably generous, reveals something of these very prejudices. For this lawyer-citizen, recognizing the threat that Bon, as a living third term, poses to the strictly binary ideology of race upon which the social and economic stability of Yoknapatawpha (and indeed "the southern way of life" in general) depends, would rather simply coax the problem into leaving than attempt to solve it. That is, he attempts to address an individual injustice while acquiescing to the systematic injustice that made it possible.

If General Compson thus fulfills the role of Cincinnatus-at-law only equivocally, Eulalia Bon's lawyer categorically rejects it. In his brief career, he directly or indirectly brings about the complete ruin of everyone around him in his lust for power and wealth. Unlike the lawyer-citizen, this attorney exists in a purely private realm, never emerging from the confines of his fortresslike office, where he reigns with absolute authority. (Beware of the cloistered attorney in Faulkner.) Nor is he a storyteller in the many senses discussed earlier in this chapter. He speaks on only two occasions in the narrative: once in getting Charles Bon safely off to the University of Mississippi (388–89), and once in order to determine whether Bon has actually fallen in love with Judith Sutpen (422–23). Since these are the moments that will make or break his plan to destroy the Sutpen dynasty, the implication is that the lawyer doesn't risk talking under any but the most urgent circumstances. For talking is a rather risky proposition for him, just as it typically is for Thomas Sutpen.[26] The lawyer, in fact, almost gets himself killed for insulting the name of Judith Sutpen in front of the chivalrous Bon. Small wonder, then, that the lawyer is almost wholly a figure of writing. His every move is literally scripted, his entire world built upon a foundation of concealment and cryptic inscription. The "secret paper" on which he plots against the house of Sutpen, for instance, "maybe a chart with colored pins stuck into it like generals have in campaigns, and all the notations in code" (375), is, though utterly inimical to the Sutpen design, itself the dark reflection of that (also dark) design, its written equivalent: a document of pure power, an utterly private communication answering to no morality other than blind self-interest. And while the lawyer waits for the Sutpens to reach maximum value and probes for a weak spot in the Sutpen empire, he keeps Eulalia Bon in ignorance of her former husband's whereabouts with a series of counterfeit communiqués that throw her off the scent (380). These written exercises are merely preliminary, however, to the lawyer's most masterful composition of all, the letter introducing Charles Bon to Henry Sutpen at Ole Miss (392–94). Obsequious, overwritten, all but anonymous in the way it so insistently defers identifying its author, this letter proclaims everywhere its own humility, disinterestedness, and good intentions, but it is actually the most malignant act of communication in the entire novel, a model of writerly duplicity that essentially seals the doom of the Sutpens. Safe among the impersonal spaces of his letter, the lawyer escapes indictment as the author of Sutpen ruin, but the reader attributes his evil, at least in part, to his repudiation of the role and ethic of lawyer-citizen.

The chapters that follow test the working model of the Faulknerian forensic figure outlined in this introduction against Faulkner's two most extensive portraits of the attorney-at-law. Horace Benbow, the first lawyer of any consequence in Faulkner's fiction, appears in two novels, *Flags in the Dust* and *Sanctuary*, where his forensic skill and professional conduct are part of a thoroughgoing inquiry into the possibilities of human contact and communion in a world on the cusp of modernity. Gavin Stevens, who appears in seven novels and a number of short stories, emerges in Faulkner's late fiction as a Yoknapatawpha genius loci, presiding over Jefferson and its environs as historian, genealogist, moral conscience, knight-errant, custodian of local apocrypha, and even, in one critic's evocative phrase, "uncle-creator" (Samway, "Gavin Stevens"). Furthermore, Benbow and Stevens are linked in an intricate characterological evolution that leaves them unable to coexist within the boundaries of a single Faulkner text. As I hope to demonstrate, it is no mere coincidence that the former's unceremonious exit from the Faulkner oeuvre yields almost immediately to the latter's more effectual entrance there.

These two characters have attracted much scholarly attention, yet few have really examined them as lawyers. Benbow, for instance, has been described as an innocent man forced to confront his own complicity in evil (C. Brooks, *The Yoknapatawpha Country* 116–38), and a "pathetic, hedonistic esthete," an ironic veteran of the Great War whose ennui is not so much *après guerre* as fin de siècle (Pilkington 30; see also Bleikasten, "For/Against" 37). He has been criticized for self-conscious Keatsian mannerisms but also compared to Endymion (Hodgin, McDaniel). He has been identified as a Pierrot or Prufrock figure, a character type which recurs often in Faulkner's early fiction (Sensibar xvii–xviii). His incestuous fixation upon his sister, his desire for his stepdaughter, and his habit of voyeurism have been painstakingly analyzed (Hurd; Matthews 247–55; Wittenberg 71–72, 97–99; Mortimer 105–6; Irwin 169; Parker 71–73). He has been called a "Victorian" representative of an older, aristocratic order assaulted by modern forces of alienation and relativism (Singal 167–70). He has been accused of escapism, role-playing, and a damaging tendency to erect abstract concepts between himself and the actual world (Vickery, *The Novels of William Faulkner* 24; Broughton 50). He is also a lawyer, however, and his vocation substantially enriches our understanding of his character. The same goes for Gavin Stevens, who remains largely neglected as a forensic figure despite having received even more intense critical scrutiny than Benbow.

Since Benbow's abrupt departure from Yoknapatawpha clears the way for the advent of Gavin Stevens, it is tempting to conclude that the latter is merely a replacement for the former. Stevens does, after all, resemble his predecessor in a number of ways. Both are tall, thin, balding men who have been educated abroad. Both exude what Faulkner has called elsewhere an air of perpetual bachelorhood, though both eventually marry. Both play the roles of uncle, brother, and stepfather. Both are garrulous, waxing rhapsodic, aphoristic, or elegiac at a moment's notice. And on more than one occasion, Stevens is attributed lines that actually belonged to Benbow in earlier texts (compare FD 177 and KG 164, S 134 and RFN 112).[27]

When we consider Benbow and Stevens as lawyers, however, their very real differences begin to emerge. Benbow seems destined from the beginning to fail both inside and outside the courtroom, and this constant inadequacy necessitates his early retirement. Stevens, on the other hand, finds success as an attorney. He wins cases for both the prosecution and defense, exhibiting a versatility Benbow lacks. It seems inevitable that the Yoknapatawpha chronicle would eventually require a figure who could not only endure in the courtroom but prevail there, and Horace Benbow is not that figure. So he gives way to the county attorney, and the result is not a simple substitution but an evolution, with all the deepening and progression implicit in that concept.

Chapter 1 examines the depiction of Horace Benbow in *Flags in the Dust* (1927) and *Sanctuary* (1931), focusing in particular on his legal career. His inauspicious debut in the earlier novel, which reveals him as "a lawyer by default" (Bassett, "Faulkner, Sartoris, Benbow" 49), paves the way for his disastrous experiences as a litigator in the later novel. The transition from forensic failure to storytelling lawyer-citizen is the subject of chapter 2, which explores four of Gavin Stevens's earliest appearances on the Yoknapatawpha stage. In "Hair" (1931), "Smoke" (1932), *Light in August* (1932), and "Go Down, Moses" (1941), Stevens emerges as an accomplished raconteur, a victorious prosecuting attorney and protector of the polis—and a spokesman for the community in some of its less flattering moments.

Chapters 3, 4, and 5 trace Stevens's role in, respectively, *Intruder in the Dust* (1948), *Knight's Gambit* (1949), and *Requiem for a Nun* (1951)—novels that gain in value and interest when taken together as a forensic trilogy, an anatomy of the lawyer figure as *homo politicus* and, equally important, as *homo loquens*. It is also necessary in these chapters to address some of the more unreasonable critical charges levied against Stevens. Critics who have vilified the Stevens of *Intruder* for his gradualist politics and long-winded polemic, for instance, tend to overlook a subtle but significant strain of storytelling on his part that emerges as a profoundly affirmative act with important moral consequences, especially for his young nephew, Chick Mallison. In the *Knight's Gambit* tales the emphasis shifts from forensic telling to forensic listening, and readers who object to Gavin Stevens's basic exemption from "legwork" in these stories, and his preference for all-but-pervasive acts of conversation and conjecture, miss Faulkner's point that the art of detection, upon which the safety and stability of the agrarian community hinge time after time in this volume, is a fundamentally colloquial affair. This is why, in the oral economy of Yoknapatawpha, the lawyer makes such an appropriate, and effective, sleuth. In *Requiem for a Nun* the focus shifts once more, to the activity of teaching to speak. Here Stevens draws on all of his forensic skills in order to elicit, from a desperate young woman, a deeply repressed, traumatic story of guilt and complicity, a story that may, however, lead her toward wisdom and purgation.

Chapter 6 grapples with Faulkner's reappraisal of the forensic figure in *The Town* and *The Mansion*. Not only is Gavin Stevens largely ineffectual as an attorney in these novels, he is a fairly uninspiring character in general. His rhetorical ability, well-documented in earlier fictions, now abandons him at inopportune times. His achievement as lawyer-citizen is compromised by his interpretation of the Snopeses as irrevocably alien monsters, his stubborn refusal to acknowledge them as products of the same ideology that has created him. This provincialism he shares with the community he represents. In addition, Faulkner assigns the county attorney a secondary role in the Snopes trilogy that threatens to distract us from his primary role as lawyer, to the point of obscuring that role altogether at times. This secondary role—that of a rather absurd, ineffectual romantic hero—evolves out of the depiction of Labove in *The Hamlet* and is anticipated by the portrayal of Stevens himself in "Knight's Gambit."

One unavoidable consequence of focusing my discussion so closely on the Benbow and Stevens material is that a number of other forensic novels and stories by Faulkner must be relegated to a subordinate position in this book. The admittedly suggestive forensic characters, scenes, and other motifs in *The Sound and the Fury*, *Absalom, Absalom!*, "An Odor of Verbena," "Wild Palms," *The Hamlet*, and *The Reivers* could undoubtedly sustain more exhaustive analyses than I offer here. But my research on storytelling and on one of our greatest twentieth-century creators of narrative has convinced me that my own scholarly work must exhibit a strong, and selective, narrative thrust, must itself pursue a central story line; and the story I am telling in this book centers above all on Benbow and Stevens. My intent has been to draw on Faulkner's other forensic fictions to amplify, clarify, and contextualize this primary story line. The role played here by these other texts is by design a strictly supplementary one, limited largely to this introductory chapter and its working descriptions of forensic fiction and of the lawyer figure in Faulkner's work. I have opted for this approach in confidence that *Absalom, Absalom!*, *The Hamlet*, and the other texts named above will figure more and more prominently in the work of future scholars of the law in Faulkner, myself included.

In his depictions of the forensic figure, Faulkner hit upon a way to interrogate and at the same time to legitimate his own calling. An important subtext of his forensic fictions is the conviction that the values and concerns of the storyteller can and must carry over from a limited, private, aesthetic realm into a public world outside, where verbal creations can reinforce, challenge, or otherwise inform social norms. This is a final important reason why the Faulknerian forensic figure typically stands or falls on the basis of his narrative ability and his fidelity to the ideal of the lawyer-citizen, as we will discover in the pages ahead.

CHAPTER ONE

. . . .

The Failure of the Forensic Storyteller:
Horace Benbow

Nothing is more emblematic of the character and tone of Horace Benbow's tenure in Yoknapatawpha County than the fact that he enters the
published fiction already under erasure. "His strange destiny in Faulkner's fiction," observes André Bleikasten, "was to be twice sacrificed"
to editorial concerns (*The Ink of Melancholy* 217). The Benbow of *Sartoris* (1929), Faulkner's third published novel, is only a shadow of the
more complex figure of the 1927 typescript, *Flags in the Dust*. To meet
the demands of Harcourt, Brace and Company, Faulkner was forced to
trim the typescript by almost one-third, and, as textual scholars have
noted, much of the excised material focused on Benbow (Dennis 188;
Millgate, *The Achievement* 82–85). Similarly, while Horace is certainly
among the most important characters in *Sanctuary*, he was an even
more forceful, and focal, presence in the original version of the novel
(published in 1981 as *Sanctuary: The Original Text*), though this time
the decision to emend his role came from the author himself. In the
context of these early disappearing acts, Horace's premature departure
from Yoknapatawpha is not quite the bolt out of the blue that it may
initially seem. Indeed, Faulkner carefully prepares us for this departure by tracing, over the course of both novels, Benbow's inadequacy
as a practicing attorney and as a functioning member of his community. The novelist's first forensic figure thus sets a standard of forensic
failure that few, if any, of his Yoknapatawpha colleagues can surpass.

. . . .

Flags in the Dust is the story of a group of young veterans who return
from a Europe ravaged by World War I to Jefferson, where their efforts

to reintegrate themselves into family and community traditions that have survived relatively intact at home are more or less fruitless. Foremost among these veterans is Bayard Sartoris, who has lost his brother Johnny in the war and who is himself doomed to perish under the pressures of family legends detailing reckless bravery, romantic heroism, and glamorous death, legends that have claimed the lives of at least three generations of Sartoris men before him. Next to Bayard is Horace Benbow, whose own personal mythology seems as decadently romantic as Bayard's. Horace is a minor character in *Flags in the Dust*, perhaps not even the most important minor character. He argues no cases here, though we are introduced to his practice. But he does serve a constant function of counterpoint, standing outside both the Jefferson old order and the postwar generation, who lack the hypocrisies and also the characteristic virtues of their precursors. The ambivalence between romantic nostalgia and modern skepticism not only characterizes Horace but also pervades the novel itself on a number of levels, including the meaning of the past, the function of myth and history, the stability of society and psyche, the possibilities of love, the transmission of order, value, and responsibility, and, most crucially, the function of language and the prospects of human communication.[1] *Flags in the Dust* abounds with venerable raconteurs and their inarticulate posterity. Where the ancestors exchange stories, their descendants merely swap silences and halting, tentative fragments of discourse, and neither group entirely escapes indictment.

As a veteran, an aesthete, a southern aristocrat, and an attorney, however, Horace represents the potential for a rare point of contact between old ways and new, antique certainties and contemporary indeterminacies. Horace's thorough grounding in the tenets and postures of modernity insures his skepticism and self-consciousness, yet his vocation demands commitment and selflessness. Horace should be the happiest of hybrids in *Flags in the Dust*: a modern man who, thanks to the rhetorical and ethical imperatives of his calling, manages to avoid the threat of solipsism. Yet he never fulfills these utopian expectations.

Flags in the Dust repeatedly demonstrates that the art of storytelling persists among members of the older generation. In the novel's opening scene, for instance, old man Will Falls and old Bayard Sartoris overcome the obstacles of old age, faulty hearing, and fading memory, as they share the story of Colonel John Sartoris's daring escape from Yankee troops, a narrative that evokes themes of family, community, and shared suffering (FD 3–5).[2] Falls's energetic roaring is matched by old Bayard's active collaboration as listener, and familiar literary kinds contribute additionally to shared meaning. The traditional oral genres of family anecdote, Civil War history (the veteran's reminiscence), and tall tale combine in an entertaining story with a powerful regional grounding and a moral and didactic value for its hearer—whose own youthful heroism, incidentally, is celebrated in the tale. Furthermore, Falls's presentation of the dead Colonel's pipe to old Bayard emphasizes an element of barter always present in their intercourse. In a culture that still recognizes its roots in folk customs, a story, presented lovingly, is a gift that equals or even exceeds the value of any material object that may be exchanged for it. This intimacy accounts in large part for the incantatory power of Falls's narrative, its ability to re-present its subject even after sixty years. The text salutes this power, simultaneously the raconteur's highest aim and his richest reward: "As usual, old man Falls had brought John Sartoris into the room with him. Freed as he was of time, he was a far more definite presence in the room than the two of them cemented by deafness to a dead time and drawn thin by the slow attenuation of days. He seemed to stand above them, all around them, with his bearded, hawklike face and the bold glamour of his dream" (5). The tale transcends the teller and his audience; the absent becomes more present than the living participants in the scene. Falls speaks, then yields, with the intuitive grace of the born taleteller, to his own verbal creations, in a moment of pure invocation.

These formulas recur and deepen in subsequent encounters between the two men. The boisterous prose ballad of John Sartoris and Zeb Fothergill (244–52), by turns mythical contest narrative, unreconstructed rebel yarn, and Sartoris family legend, reemphasizes the prominent place of storytelling in Jefferson's folk economy, and this time old Bayard matches Falls's gift with one of his own, a parcel of tobacco and peppermint candy. Significantly, Falls unwinds the Fothergill anecdote as he dabs a homemade ointment onto a cyst on Bayard's face, and the conjunction of remedy and tale suggests a therapeutic dimension of storytelling. Stories, we find, serve not only as valuable gifts but also as salves, treatments, with healing properties all their own, and this conviction only grows firmer when the prescription proves successful and Bayard's wen, as it were, "Falls" (268).

In his third and final performance in the novel, the economical fable of Colonel Sartoris and the Burden carpetbaggers (262–64), Falls effaces himself and actually becomes his Confederate hero. "He crossed his arms on his breast, his hands in sight, and for a moment old Bayard saw, as through a cloudy glass, that arrogant and familiar shape which the old man in shabby overalls had contrived in some way to immolate and preserve in the vacuum of his own abnegated self" (263). As his corpselike attitude suggests, Falls momentarily dies out of life in order to make John Sartoris live again, as if to illustrate that storytelling is not without its own attendant dangers and sacrifices. If the raconteur is not quite an unqualified success—the resurrected Colonel's image is "cloudy," mediated—his ability to bring Bayard almost face-to-face with his long-departed father is a tribute to the power of story in a culture rapidly growing indifferent to it.

Old Bayard's aging aunt Jenny Du Pre also exemplifies the penchant for storytelling among the Yoknapatawpha ancien régime. Like Will Falls before her, she unravels her tales of Sartoris glory in situations that encourage intimacy and active collaboration between speaker and listener. In the friendly environment of a family gathering, Jenny is capable of a verbal magic that binds Sartorises and outlanders alike in a web of shared meaning, as she does in recounting the death of her brother, the "Carolina Bayard," at second Manassas.

> [A]s she grew older the tale itself grew richer and richer, taking on a mellow splendor like wine; until what had been a hair-brained prank of two heedless and reckless boys wild with their own youth, was become a gallant and finely tragical focal-point to which the history of the race had been raised from out the old miasmic swamps of spiritual sloth by the two angels valiantly and glamorously fallen and strayed, altering the course of human events and urging the souls of men. (14)

There is undeniably an element of irony at work in this passage. The old woman is, after all, sentimentalizing behavior that is at best childish and at worst blatantly self-destructive. But Jenny's performance also demonstrates how, related in warm and personal circumstances, stories can become both invested with meaning and redolent of meaning, can create and perpetuate complex responses that involve emotions and values as well as documented historical facts.[3]

Jenny's powers of invocation approach those of Will Falls. She too summons a ghostly "presence" to re-present itself before her and her audience at the moment of narration: "The flames leaped and popped on the hearth and sparks soared in wild swirling plumes up the chimney, and Bayard Sartoris' brief career swept like a shooting star across the dark plain of their mutual remembering and suffering, lighting it with a transient glare like a soundless thunder-clap, leaving a sort of radiance when it died" (22). And her story is also a loving gift— a Christmas gift, we learn—to the Mississippi Sartorises. Later in the novel, at the great Thanksgiving dinner scene over which Jenny presides (324–30), family efforts to create and share meaning through story also incorporate outsiders, who represent the potential for new narratives and fresh perspectives.

The novel's younger generation finds its major representatives in young Bayard Sartoris, Horace Benbow, and Horace's sister, Narcissa. Imprisoned in self, frustrated and psychically wounded by the war and its aftermath, these characters are left estranged and uncommunicative, in stark contrast to their loquacious forebears. Holding themselves aloof from love, language, and social contexts that foster dialogue and conserve meaning, these isolated figures offer little to brighten the bleak prospects of human communion in the twentieth-century South.

Young Bayard, for instance, is unable to articulate the trauma of his war experience, in particular the death of his brother. The Sartoris family understands his visceral need to give meaning to Johnny's death, to find a story for it, but everything he tells them bristles with self-hatred and self-recrimination. When he does try to describe Johnny's death to Narcissa—his only attempt in the entire novel to reach out to another person through language—the effort quickly sours, and Bayard resorts to force in order to hold his listener literally captive.

> It was a brutal tale, without beginning, and crassly and uselessly violent and at times profane and gross, though its very wildness robbed it of offensiveness just as its grossness kept it from obscenity. . . . "Please," she whispered. "Please!" He ceased and looked at her and his fingers shifted, and just as she thought she was free they clamped again, and now both of her wrists were prisoners. She struggled, staring at him dreadfully, but he grinned his white cruel teeth at her and pressed her crossed arms down upon the bed beside him. (280–81)

Though the context of this passage is therapeutic (with Narcissa's help, Bayard is recovering from an auto accident), the tale itself is not. It is merely another way for Bayard to abuse living and dead, himself and others.

Narcissa's own response to others is to retreat into silence and to insulate herself from the world behind a barrier of books. She seems to believe that reading absolves her of the responsibilities and the rewards of communication. She would rather read to Bayard than converse with him, "as though she were crouching behind the screen of words her voice raised between them" (272), and on at least one occasion, her reading actually silences Bayard's attempts to talk to her (243). When misunderstandings arise between Narcissa and her brother, she once again hides behind a book (283).[4] Throughout the novel, her silence and serenity are her most salient and conspicuous characteristics. They seem, for instance, to be the traits with which her brother is obsessed.

Into this rich context of raconteurs and reticents steps brother Horace, whose communicative skills, however, are ironized before he even sets foot in Jefferson. He enters the novel doubly circumscribed by language: in a half-bemused, half-exasperated conversation with Jenny Du Pre, Narcissa describes a perplexing message she has received from New York concerning her brother's imminent return:

> "Speaking of children [Jenny quips]: What's the news from Horace?"
>
> "Oh, hadn't I told you?" the other said quickly. "I had a wire yesterday. He landed in New York Wednesday. It was such a mixed-up message, I never could understand what he was trying to tell me, except that he would have to stay in New York for a few days. It was over fifty words long. . . . It was such an incoherent message . . . Horace never could say anything clearly from a distance." (32)

Right away, the telegram exposes Horace as prodigal of language as well as money. Its hyperbole communicates little or nothing, since Narcissa knows no more of his plans after reading it than before. What is more, his homecoming is of a piece with his telegram. In "clean, wretchedly fitting khaki," Horace steps off an afternoon train "like a somnambulist" (170), and his reunion with Narcissa is merely an occasion for his own monologic babbling (172). It does not take long for Benbow to establish his inane logorrhea as the novel's most infuriating voice, as the following encomium on his Venetian-glass urns demonstrates:

> "And the things themselves! Sheerly and tragically beautiful. Like preserved flowers, you know. Macabre and inviolate; purged and purified as bronze, yet fragile as soap bubbles. Sound of pipes crystallized. Flutes and oboes, but mostly reeds. Oaten reeds. Dammit, they bloom

like flowers right before your eyes. Midsummer night's dream to a sala-
mander." His voice became unintelligible, soaring into phrases which
she did not herself recognise, but from the pitch of his voice she knew
were Milton's archangels in their sonorous plunging ruin.

Presently he emerged, in a white shirt and serge trousers but still
borne aloft on his flaming verbal wings, and while his voice chanted in
measured syllables she fetched a pair of shoes from the closet, and while
she stood holding the shoes, he ceased and touched her face again with
his hands after that fashion of a child. (180)

The fact that such Demosthenian flights of rhetoric can issue from a
man incapable of picking out his own shoes makes it difficult to take
Horace seriously as an adult, let alone a raconteur or citizen.

We expect communicative skill from Horace because he is a lawyer,
but *Flags in the Dust* gradually reveals how ill-suited he is for this most
demanding of rhetorical careers. Horace thinks he is only being coy
when he describes the law as "the final resort of the lame, the halt,
the imbecile and the blind" (199), but his insincere bon mot all too
accurately describes his own incompetence. In fact, Horace's bohemian
avocation probably reveals more about him than his vocation does.
Horace is a glassblower, and the transparent, ephemeral bubbles into
which he breathes life are striking emblems of all his creative efforts,
each "a small chaste shape" not only "fragile" but "incomplete" (179).
His "war-orphans," as Narcissa misnames them, are more appropriately Keatsian brides of quietness, foster children of an ideal silence—
much as Narcissa herself is in her brother's eyes. He apostrophizes
glasswork and sister alike in gushing "moments of rhapsody over the
realization of the meaning of peace and the unblemished attainment
of it" (190–91).

If the elusive peace Horace seeks is the private product of a purely
personal utterance, it may seem odd that this would-be artist is called
to the intersubjective career of law. What calls him there, as it happens,
is literally the Name-of-the-Father. Benbow enters the legal profession,
the narrator explains, "principally through a sense of duty to the family
tradition," even though "he had no particular affinity to it other than a
love for printed words, for the dwelling-places of books" (183–84). His
is literally, and in the worst way, a private practice: the urge to retire
to the hermetic nooks and crannies of his forensic father's musty law
office contradicts the civic obligations of the attorney. His simplistic

association of the law with the static printed word points forward ironically to *Sanctuary*, where he enters the public domain of the courtroom with insufficient respect for the fundamental orality and dynamism of litigation. Further, the "family tradition" to which Horace defers seems but a thinly veiled reference to his father, the tellingly named Will Benbow. Predictably, this element of paternal control only increases after the elder Benbow's death, as the "will" of the father is progressively reified into the Name-of-the-Father. For Will Benbow no sooner dies than he reaches from beyond the grave to direct his son into the family practice and away from a very different ambition:

> [O]n the homeward boat [from Oxford] he framed the words with which he should tell his father that he was going to be an Episcopal minister. But when he reached New York the wire waited him saying that Will Benbow was ill, and all thoughts of his future fled his mind during the journey home and during the two subsequent days that his father lived. Then Will Benbow was buried beside his wife, and . . . next day but one Horace opened his father's law office again. (193–94)

If we may be tempted to thank Will Benbow for posthumously saving Horace from a vocation potentially even more disastrous than the one he pursues, the real point of this passage lies in those words of self-assertion that Horace is never allowed to express before his father. As happens so often during his short career, there is a gap between what Horace plans to say and what he actually does say, a gap that always works to his disadvantage.

Thus Horace settles speechlessly into his father's practice, safe from excitement or challenge. Ensconced in the dusty recesses of his office, Horace performs an inconsequential dance of communication with his clients, locking lawyer and client alike the more securely in their solipsistic worlds: "His practice, what there was of it, consisted of polite interminable litigations that progressed decorously and pleasantly from conference to conference, the greater part of which were given to discussions of the world's mutations as exemplified by men or by printed words." Words like "polite" and "pleasant" serve only to anesthetize these already dull exchanges, which wend "their endless courses without threat of consummation or of advantage or detriment to anyone involved" (194). The man at law here panders himself to the meanest kind of social elbow-rubbing.

The more closely we scrutinize Horace's practice and clientele, the more unpromising his situation appears. Nowhere in the novel, for instance, do we see Benbow actively solicit a case, enter a courtroom, or offer his services to a client. Rather, Horace seems content to receive passively the roster of clients bequeathed to him by his father. Nor does the elder Benbow's crippling influence end here. The most arresting feature of Horace's monastic cell of an office is also a direct legacy from his father, a "fire-proof cabinet" that works an ironic twist on Horace's beloved Grecian urn. Impervious to time, change, or catastrophe, this indestructible cabinet contains not funerary ashes but the next best thing,

> a number of wills which Horace had inherited and never read, the
> testators of which accomplished their lives in black silk and lace caps
> and an atmosphere of formal and timeless desuetude in stately, high-
> ceiled rooms screened from the ceaseless world by flowering shrubs
> and old creeping vines; existences circumscribed by church affairs and
> so-called literary clubs and a conscientious, slightly contemptuous pre-
> occupation with the welfare of remote and obtusely ungrateful heathen
> peoples. (194)

To his unwilling son, Will Benbow thus wills only more wills, dooming Horace to a legal life among the dead and dying.

Behind the "black silk and lace caps" of Horace's unvanquished spinsters we may catch a glimpse of Jenny Du Pre, a glimpse that complicates things. For there is more to Jenny and others like her than the "formal and timeless desuetude" that Horace is so quick to notice. The resources of community are all around Horace, were he only to turn from the dead documents of his elders to their living stories, to enter the immense, rich dialogue that is social life in Yoknapatawpha. The fire-proof cabinet, however, continues to exert its powerful inertia.

Like his professional skills, Benbow's social savvy leaves much to be desired. He seems absolutely unable, for example, to talk to women without making a fool of himself. His foredoomed flirtation with a young girl named Frankie (197–204) descends all too quickly into a lascivious interior monologue worthy of Joyce's Leopold Bloom. When talking to the girl, Horace makes no attempt to edit his wholly private discourse, and his inappropriate remarks scare her away:

> "You ought to run in a cheese-cloth shimmy on hills under a new
> moon," Horace told her. "With chained ankles, of course. But a slack

chain. No, not the moon: but in a dawn like pipes. Green and gold, and
maybe a little pink. Would you risk a little pink?" She watched him
with grave curious eyes as he stood before her lean in his flannels and
with his sick brilliant face and his wild hair. "No," he corrected himself again. "On sand. Blanched sand, with dead ripples. Ghosts of dead
motion waved into the sand. Do you know how cold the sea can be just
before dawn, with a falling tide? Like lying in a dead world, upon the
dead respirations of the earth. She's too big to die all at once. Like elephants . . . How old are you?" Now all at once her eyes became secretive,
and she looked away. "Now what?" he demanded. "What did you start to
say then?"

"There's Mr Mitchell," she said. (203–4; Faulkner's ellipsis)

How expedient is it to mention "chained ankles" to a woman you are
trying to seduce? A man who had indulged in less poetry and more
sincere social exchange would not fall prey to such indiscretion.

Benbow's last onstage appearance in the novel, which takes place
after he leaves Jefferson with Belle Mitchell, his partner first in adul-
tery and later in marriage, is marked by further Bloomian reveries, but
even more striking are his halting attempts to misrepresent himself in
a letter to his sister that he well knows is thoroughly incomprehensible.
"Horace's pen ceased and he gazed at the sheet scrawled over with his
practically illegible script, while the words he had just written echoed
yet in his mind with a little gallant and whimsical sadness, and for the
time being . . . that wild and delicate futility of his roamed unchal-
lenged through the lonely region into which it had at last concentrated
its conflicting parts" (397). Estranged from family and community,
Horace embraces a silent and lonely existence that directly contradicts
the social role we expect of the lawyer. His new hometown of Kinston
holds no real future for him (he has little in common with his "kin"
there, his new wife and stepdaughter), and we hear nothing of his practice there. His final quoted words (406), wrenched free of any but an
inaccessible interior context, address only himself.

In the wake of Horace's abdication, it is Narcissa Benbow Sartoris
who presides over the closing pages of *Flags in the Dust*. These pages
witness the final encroachment of alienation upon the Sartorises. Bayard has abandoned his pregnant wife and his family, and his final days
are characterized by futile attempts to elude the possibility of com-

munication in an alcoholic stupor (411–16)—or, preferably, to outrun communication, to attain a kind of escape velocity beyond which the world of shared contexts and values falls away and only the individual, in solipsistic glory, remains. His postcards, already outdated by the time they reach Jefferson, only emphasize the distance (metaphysical as well as physical) that separates him from family and community (407). And when Bayard does resurface, it is only to die, to achieve his exalted speed in a disintegrating test aircraft whose final screaming power dive silences him for good.

Horace, by contrast, survives, though in typically attenuated fashion, leaving the novel much as he entered it. His correspondence from Kinston makes no more sense to Narcissa than the fifty-word telegram that introduced him to us. "Each week she got a whimsical, gallantly humorous letter from Horace: these she read . . . with serene detachment—what she could decipher, that is. She had always found Horace's writing difficult, and parts she could decipher meant nothing. But she knew that he expected that" (410–11). Even Jenny Du Pre is relatively muted as the novel moves toward its conclusion.

The uncomfortable impression of discursive opportunities missed haunts the final tableau of *Flags in the Dust*, a parodic reenactment of the scenes between Will Falls and old Bayard. With characteristic tenacity and common sense, Jenny continues to interrogate the Sartoris tradition at novel's end, but Narcissa simply stares past the old woman and out the window, not listening. Her piano playing, like her earlier reading efforts, serves as a screen behind which her "rapt inattention" voids any possibility of contact or communion (433). Her indifference settles like a judgment over the Sartoris homestead and, by extension, Jefferson, signaling the final triumph of a numbing isolation. The victory seems irreversible, and among the self-enclosed monads of this disheartening closing scene, Horace's voice is significant only in its absence.

. . . .

While Horace Benbow plays a relatively minor role in *Flags*, and while that novel offers us only a few preliminary glimpses of his vocation, *Sanctuary*, from its very beginnings, directly interrogates his competence as a lawyer. The novel traces the efforts of defense attorney Benbow to enlist the aid of a rape victim, Temple Drake, in the acquittal of his innocent client, Lee Goodwin. "The problem of determining the meaning of the work" thus rests heavily on "the problem of understanding Horace's characterization" (Hurd 428), but scholarly discussion of these problems has been dominated by psychoanalytic perspectives ever since the 1930s, with the result that Benbow's forensic performances in the novel have failed to elicit the critical attention they are due.[5] Faulkner revised the *Sanctuary* galleys away from what had been a Jamesian immersion in Benbow's consciousness, and toward a tougher, leaner, hard-boiled prose, after the style of Hemingway and Hammett.[6] This objective style frees the reader to a degree from Horace's often cloying personality and allows us to observe the lawyer from the outside, in a wider social context, where he assumes his place among the host of characters implicated in the novel's central "metaphor of trial" (Kinney 191).

As we have seen in the introductory chapter to this book, forensic narrative has the power to forge consensus in the courtroom and to create (at least in part) the legal reality of which it speaks. As preeminently a spoken thing, it is capable of immediate, reciprocal interaction with other voices both inside and outside the official spaces of law. If it is also in important ways a broken thing, a patchwork of other, prior stories and story fragments, its motley nature often seems to enhance its flexibility, credibility, and fidelity to human experience. And if it is ultimately intended to move listeners, to convince (and convict), this does not necessarily prevent it from informing and illuminating as well. All of these characteristics, of course, are morally neutral, capable of being put to devastating as well as liberating uses. But at its best—as we will find it, for instance, in parts of chapters 3, 4, and 5 of this study—forensic telling drives toward the reconciliation, at least for brief moments, of rhetoric and reality, verisimilitude and justice.

At its worst, however, forensic telling in Faulkner collapses into forensic lying, untruth in service of further untruths; or, perhaps even more unforgivably, it is forfeited altogether, yielding to silence or to blatant ineptitude. Both scenarios emerge in *Sanctuary*, a novel in which forensic telling is never presented favorably—in which, indeed, all telling is corrupt, impotent, or simply absent, and precious little of it interactive. *Sanctuary* is an extended meditation—Faulkner's earliest and most terrifying—upon the dark side of forensic storytelling, not only in the embarrassing stammers and silences of Horace Benbow, but also in the false rhetoric and malevolent courtroom theatrics of Temple Drake and Eustace Graham. Perhaps *Sanctuary*'s unflinching attention to this dark side proved cathartic for Faulkner, paving the way for later, sunnier versions of forensic telling. In any case he seems to have been unwilling or unable to assign an affirmative role to this narrative mode before he had fully sounded the depths of its failure in his bleak 1931 novel.

These failures are already evident in *Sanctuary*'s well-known opening scene, an unsettling encounter between Horace and the Memphis gangster Popeye that doubles as a prophetic litmus test of legal ability. The scene is ingeniously staged as a cross-examination:

> From his hip pocket Popeye took a soiled handkerchief and spread it upon his heels. Then he squatted, facing the man across the spring. That was about four oclock on an afternoon in May. They squatted so, facing one another across the spring, for two hours. Now and then a bird sang back in the swamp, as though it were worked by a clock; twice more invisible automobiles passed along the highway and died away. Again the bird sang. (S 5)

Confronted over the Narcissus-spring by this ominous secret sharer, a mechanical man armed and by all signs dangerous, Horace would do well to start talking, to probe through speech the stranger's motives, the full extent of his threat, and gradually to uncover his story—in short, to do the very things the litigator does at work in court.

Yet here, as almost everywhere else in *Sanctuary*, Horace's speech fails him, yielding to Popeye's watching, as the two silently survey each other over the spring. We shall find this surveillance associated with Popeye and his world everywhere throughout the novel, taking over as a technique of domination and control when narrative is no longer effective. While the promise of speech and telling is to unite individuals, to invite them together and by means of its immanence to provide a medium for interaction, *Sanctuary* makes it clear that watching holds them apart, establishes the space of their separation, reaffirms their impenetrable privacies, their inscrutable purposes. The many cross-examinations of the novel tend to be displaced out of the realm of speech and into the realm of silent (super)vision. Horace, however, never masters this visual mode. He is unable to bridge the ocular gap that separates him from Popeye, so the scene at the spring merely stale-

mates. In his two-hour cross-examination of Popeye, Benbow learns
nothing from his tight-lipped interlocutor, as the latter's reticence and
stasis dominate the proceedings. Popeye's silent stare, thoroughly in
keeping with his name, infects Horace, implicates him in a voyeurism that extends to the outermost reaches of the hermeneutic circle.
Horace's few attempts to initiate conversation are intercepted and subverted by Popeye, who in a series of odd reflections turns Benbow's
spoken peace offerings immediately into further confrontations that
lead only to further impasses:

> The drinking man knelt beside the spring. "You've got a pistol in that
> pocket, I suppose," he said.
> Across the spring Popeye appeared to contemplate him with two knobs
> of soft black rubber. "I'm asking you," Popeye said. "What's that in your
> pocket?"
> The other man's coat was still across his arm. He lifted his other hand
> toward the coat, out of one pocket of which protruded a crushed felt hat,
> from the other a book. "Which pocket?" he said.
> "Don't show me," Popeye said. "Tell me."
> The other man stopped his hand. "It's a book."
> "What book?" Popeye said.
> "Just a book. The kind people read. Some people do."
> "Do you read books?" Popeye said. (4)

> "I want to reach Jefferson before dark," Benbow said. "You cant keep
> me here like this."
> Without removing his cigarette Popeye spat past it into the spring.
> "You cant stop me like this," Benbow said. "Suppose I break and run."
> Popeye put his eyes on Benbow, like rubber. "Do you want to run?"
> "No," Benbow said.
> Popeye removed his eyes. "Well, dont, then." (6)

In these representative exchanges, Popeye and not Horace is clearly
doing the cross-examining. If he says little, it is by design. His silence
is a consciously adopted strategy that makes visual mastery possible,
rather than, as in Benbow's case, a failure or breakdown of speech.
Popeye's rubbery eyes do his talking for him: to be seen by him—by
them—is to be made subject to his power, quite literally "put upon."
The repeated attention to those eyes also emphasizes the fact that Popeye absorbs more information than he reveals. Benbow, on the other

hand, has more faith in his ears than in his eyes, so he asks questions, which are turned back against him.[7] Thus unable to move or to speak effectively, he can only wait, in a stillness punctuated intermittently by invisible sources: the song of the hidden bird and the indifferent rumblings of automobiles from the road above. These ambiguous sounds merely add to the tension that pervades the scene at the spring, a tension that leaves Horace incapable of performing even the simplest of linguistic acts (he cannot name the mysterious bird).

On his way to the old Frenchman place, where the uncommunicative Popeye will ironically introduce him to community, or at least to a simulacrum of it, Benbow edges his way back toward language, but the precedent has already been set for all his future cross-examinations and all the legal maneuvers he will perform in *Sanctuary*. The four terse pages of this opening scene offer us the novel in miniature, as the silences and the implied violences of Popeye's nihilistic world challenge the efficacy of speech, justice, authority, and human interaction, principles that ostensibly find their champion in the man at law.

Horace's ordeal at the spring, and his subsequent encounter with Popeye's accomplice Lee Goodwin and his stern but hospitable gang of bootleggers at the Frenchman place—an encounter in which there is again little meaningful interaction—take their place against a pervasive background of epistemological uncertainty. Indeed, all human contact in *Sanctuary* is arguably reduced to a single appalling synecdoche, Popeye's brutal parody of intercourse with Temple Drake. There is nothing here to compare with the hearty fables of Sartoris heroics recounted by Will Falls or Jenny Du Pre in *Flags*, or with the Shegog sermon in *The Sound and the Fury* (SF 339–43)—no one to help *Sanctuary*'s dislocated cast of characters shore the fragmentary remains of southern culture against their ruin. Aunt Jenny does live on in *Sanctuary*, but her chances of breaking through the autism of the young moderns around her seem even slimmer here than in the bleak conclusion of *Flags*. The jabbering Ole Miss students whom Horace encounters on an Oxford-bound train vividly illustrate the vacuousness of modern discourse in this "desperately perverse and noisy world" (Ross 48). Their parodic, private language consists almost entirely of indecipherable slang and innuendo:

> [One student] began to whistle between his teeth, a broken dance
> rhythm, unmusical.

"Do you eat at Gordon hall?" the other said.

"No. I have natural halitosis." The conductor went on. The whistle reached crescendo, clapped off by his hands on his knees, ejaculating duh-duh-duh. Then he just squalled, meaningless, vertiginous; to Horace it was like sitting before a series of printed pages turned in furious snatches, leaving a series of cryptic headlines and tailless evocations on the mind.

"She's travelled a thousand miles without a ticket."

"Marge too."

"Beth too."

"Duh-duh-duh."

"Marge too."

"I'm going to punch mine Friday night."

"Eeeeyow."

"Do you like liver."

"I cant reach that far."

"Eeeeyow."

They whistled, clapping their heels on the floor to furious crescendo, saying duh-duh-duh. The first jolted the seat back against Horace's head. (178–79)

Such is the verbal white noise over which the novel's minority of earnest communicators must struggle to be heard. In such a world, speech ceases to be a medium of human interaction and instead only confirms the isolation of individuals, and the traditional links among the spoken word, the law, justice, and authority become irrevocably blurred. Thus it is fitting that the symbolic genius loci of the old Frenchman place is a figure incapable of speech and utterly without authority, the mute, sightless, grotesque scarecrow Pap, a kind of caricature of blind justice who reveals himself to be aptly named when he greets Benbow at the Goodwin dinnertable with a nauseating pabulum: "Benbow watched him take a filthy rag from his pocket and regurgitate into the rag an almost colorless wad of what had once been chewing tobacco, and fold the rag up and put it into his pocket" (13). And this failed icon of legal equity is not only blind but deaf, as powerless to hear stories as he is to tell them or to watch them unfold.[8]

Though Pap, in sober contradiction of another sense of his name, seems to have fathered no one in this novel, Temple attempts to assign him a paternal role, adopting him as a surrogate for her own absent father, who, as Temple is wont to tell us in moments of crisis, is a judge (55, 57, 59). Judge Drake is one of Faulkner's typical forensic fathers, in whom paternal and legal authority coincide, but he can offer little help to his hapless duckling in Frenchman's Bend. During her ordeal there, Temple thinks more than once of the judge, sitting at home on his porch in Jackson (54, 57)—reveries most likely triggered by her first unsettling sight of Pap (who, like the judge, walks with the aid of a stick) on the porch of the Frenchman place (44–45). This rudimentary associationism lies behind Temple's wild invocations, as if to suggest that she will turn to any judge in her plight; and the ironies resonate even further when the girl brings the deity himself into her dense tangle of judges and fathers.[9] Terrified by the bootleggers, however, Temple cannot recall "a single designation for the heavenly father" as she tries to pray, so she substitutes instead only mantralike repetitions of the phrase, "My father's a judge," which, we now realize, is hardly the non sequitur it seems at first.

Pap, Judge Drake, God the Father: these parodic, actual, and eternal judges reappear to be judged themselves during the rape scene. As Popeye silently stalks Temple in the corncrib (in what is surely the most macabre nursery scene in modern literature, complete with depraved "Daddy," incestuously abused adoptive daughter, a "crib" that cruelly metamorphoses into a torture chamber, and a corncob that is not a simple plaything but a weapon), she turns desperately to Pap, in an effort she already knows to be vain:

> She could hear silence in a thick rustling as [Popeye] moved toward her through it, thrusting it aside, and she began to say Something is going to happen to me. She was saying it to the old man with the yellow clots for eyes. "Something is happening to me!" she screamed at him, sitting in his chair in the sunlight, his hands crossed on the top of the stick. "I told you it was!" she screamed, voiding the words like hot silent bubbles into the bright silence about them until he turned his head and the two phlegm clots above her where she lay tossing and thrashing on the rough, sunny boards. "I told you! I told you all the time!" (107)

Here impotent telling falls on deaf ears. From his porchside seat of judgment, Pap merely looks away. His awful silence seems but an extension of Popeye's, implicating the old man in the most culpable kind of consent—consent that, moreover, by virtue of the connections among judges and fathers that Temple herself has pursued, implicates both Judge Drake and an even higher authority as well.[10]

The silent world, of course, is Popeye's world, through which he moves effortlessly. An orphan, he answers to no father, and his indifference to the spoken word makes him all but immune to it, subject neither to the integrating power nor to the restrictive, punitive dimension of speech that Roland Barthes, following Jacques Lacan, calls "the Law"—"all speech is on the side of the Law" ("Writers, Intellectuals, Teachers" 191). One hallmark of this imperviousness is the fact that Popeye's name is hardly mentioned at the Goodwin trial, a trial at which he should actually be the defendant, the principal subject of courtroom storytelling. In *Sanctuary* he seems to be above language rather than beneath it, and to be above language in this novel is literally to be above the law. In place of communication, of reciprocal give and take, Popeye erects an elaborate structure of surveillance, in which eyes are constantly bulging (or popping) to see behind doors, ears straining to hear around corners—a system that rests upon the same foundation of panoptical control described by Michel Foucault in *Discipline and Punish*, "in which the techniques that make it possible to see induce effects of power, and in which, conversely, the means of coercion make those on whom they are applied clearly visible" (170–71).[11] It is probably this aspect of the novel more than any other that inspired Michael Millgate's interesting comparison of *Sanctuary* and *Measure for Measure* (*The Achievement* 119–21), though the novel's silent overseer, as opposed to Shakespeare's, is clearly malignant.

In the absence of effective narrative interaction (or intervention), and with direct visual confrontations like the one at the spring dissolving into occasions of pure power and threat, almost all human interaction in *Sanctuary* short of outright violence becomes reducible to spying and eavesdropping. The moment Popeye and Horace arrive at the Frenchman place in chapter 1, the gangster and Tommy eye each other cautiously, "with a glance at once secret and alert," over a whiskey jug (S 10). Ruby Lamar conceals herself behind a door to listen in on Horace's almost incomprehensible autobiographical ramblings on the porch (13–17). At the moment Gowan Stevens's car plunges into a tree, Temple catches a glimpse of "two men [Popeye and Tommy] peering from the fringe of cane at the roadside" (40). Popeye's watchful eye first precipitates, then constantly monitors, Temple's interminable dashes through the house and around the grounds. Temple herself joins Ruby in the kitchen, where the two overhear "harsh, abrupt, meaningless masculine sounds from the house" (58). And when Temple shuts herself in the bedroom in order to retreat out of the sight and minds of the drunken bootleggers, there follows a surreal concatenation of scenes that constitute a hierarchy of watching. At the center of the concentric rings of surveillance, Temple watches herself, in her tiny compact (75). Outside, Tommy spies on her through the window (73–75). A short time later, inside the room, Tommy watches Goodwin watch Popeye and Van (78–79). Then Ruby watches Tommy watch Popeye (82). The escalating tensions of this spying upon spying culminate in a shifting, Chinese box pattern of narrative perspective, at the outermost level of which Ruby Lamar stands, watches, and listens:

> She stood just inside the door. She could tell all of them by the way they breathed. Then, without having heard, felt, the door open, she began to smell something: the brilliantine which Popeye used on his hair. She did not see Popeye at all when he entered and passed her; she did not know he had entered yet; she was waiting for him; until Tommy entered, following Popeye. Tommy crept into the room, also soundless; she would have been no more aware of his entrance than of Popeye's, if it hadn't been for his eyes. They glowed, breast high, with a profound interrogation, then they disappeared and the woman could then feel him, squatting beside her; she knew that he too was looking toward the bed over which Popeye stood in the darkness, upon which Temple and Gowan lay, with Gowan snoring and choking and snoring. The woman stood just inside the door. (84–85)

The formal symmetry of the paragraph, in which Ruby's perspective literally frames the sequential actions of Popeye and Tommy, is representative of this complex scene as a whole. At one point five individuals are joined in the chain of surveillance. The web of monitoring here is so subtle that even the slightest tactile sensations serve as feedback for the observer: "she felt Tommy move from beside her, without a sound, as though the steady evacuation of his position blew soft and cold on him in the black silence" (85). There is nothing inherently malevolent about all this surveillance, of course. In the case of Ruby, Tommy, and Goodwin, it is basically benign, directed toward protecting Temple. But

Popeye's spying culminates directly in the twin violences of murder and
rape. Indeed, it is not implausible to suggest that Popeye rapes Temple
with a corncob—by hand—in order to be able to *see* all the better what
he is doing to her, much as he kills Tommy—with a silenced pistol, no
less, whose report is "no louder than the striking of a match" (107)—
in order not to be seen doing it.[12]

The strategy of observation continues and even heightens in Memphis, where Popeye takes over as Temple's "Daddy" (249), setting her
up in Miss Reba's house of ill repute in order to control, protect, and
above all watch her. The earlier, more attenuated ministrations of Pap,
Judge Drake, and Gowan Stevens seem only distant memories. Among
the denizens of the Beale Street underworld, Popeye is the law, and the
general corruption over which he presides extends to precinct house
and courthouse alike. Popeye turns Miss Reba's brothel into a virtual
labyrinth of locked doors, prying eyes, and inquisitive ears, a textbook
example of what Foucault calls the Panopticon, at once a site and a
mode of institutionalized coercion and control based on the principle
of constant, ubiquitous, nonreciprocal surveillance.

According to Foucault, the Panopticon works by setting up, in some
centralized area, a gaze that extends the threat of punitive violence to
every inmate. Whether the threat will be carried out or not depends, of
course, on what is seen, but the real purpose of the panoptical gaze is
to render violence unnecessary,

> to induce in the inmate a state of conscious and permanent visibility that
> assures the automatic functioning of power. So to arrange things that
> the surveillance is permanent in its effects, even if it is discontinuous in
> its action; that the perfection of power should tend to render its actual
> exercise unnecessary. . . . To achieve this, it is at once too much and too
> little that the prisoner should be constantly observed by an inspector: too
> little, for what matters is that he knows himself to be observed; too much,
> because he has no need in fact of being so. (201)

It is the mere possibility, however remote, of being seen that creates
conformity. Popeye, of course, is just such an absentee inspector as
Foucault describes, and Temple just such an inmate—though she is
not the only one. For there are also the police chiefs and congressmen
lured by Miss Reba's girls to the brothel, where Popeye can keep an
eye on them, while he goes about his own business undetected, unseen,

elusive as ever. Popeye, in other words, takes legally sanctioned techniques of observation—perfected, it should be noted, on his own fellow misfits in prisons, hospitals, and asylums—and turns these techniques to his own advantage. Foucault's Panopticon is turned inside-out: the outlaw becomes its silent overseer, while the official representatives of law and the law-abiding are reduced to inmates, the inspected. Popeye has beaten the law at its own game.

So completely is the act of watching fetishized in the brothel that it takes precedence over sex itself.[13] Unwitting eavesdroppers like Virgil Snopes and Fonzo Winbush, who figure in the novel's most darkly humorous subplot (see 203–15), are complemented by witting ones such as Virgil's vulgar cousin Senator Clarence Snopes, Miss Reba's most parsimonious patron, who would rather peep through keyholes than indulge in other, more expensive transactions. If Clarence likes to watch, however, he can do so only at the risk of being watched himself, as he finds out when Minnie, Miss Reba's maid, catches him *in flagrante spectatione* and runs him out of the house. And Popeye, of course, is content to whinny blissfully from the foot of Temple's bed while his hired stud Alabama Red performs in his place with the girl (245, 269–73). Perhaps watching Temple and Red is the only alternative he has to raping her again.

We are now prepared to recognize the full significance of the novel's opening scene, in which Popeye, that figure of overwhelming visuality, faces Horace, the dubious disciple of forensic speech, and quickly reduces him to silence and a kind of diluted voyeurism of his own (ocularity triumphant over orality). These figures clash again behind what are quite literally the scenes of the Goodwin trial, where Horace tries to redeem his failure at the spring—to turn the lawyer's rhetorical training to Lee Goodwin's benefit and to bring Popeye to justice. In order to arrive at a cohesive re-presentation of the facts that will not so much inform as persuade a jury, Horace must construct, out of the stories and spoken depositions he hears, a narrative of Goodwin's innocence, negotiating his way among fragmentary and not altogether consistent accounts of the events at the Frenchman place. In order to fabricate a convincing legal fiction, he must be an attentive listener, a tactful editor, an earnest and eloquent speaker—that is, a consummate storyteller and a resourceful courtroom *bricoleur*, ready to assess the strengths and weaknesses of his audience and to tailor his performance accordingly.

His efforts, however, are frustrated almost from the moment he takes the case.

Horace is engaged in a struggle with his own clients for narrative control. He well knows that in the courtroom knowledge is power and that speech is at once the source and vehicle of that knowledge. As Horace explains to Goodwin, "the lawyer should know all the facts, everything. He is the one to decide what to tell and what not to tell" (138). Yet Goodwin won't talk. His fear of Popeye prompts his reticence, and the rhetorical ploys of the lawyer fail to elicit any further information.

> "Is he that good a shot?" Benbow said. "To hit a man through one of those windows?"
> Goodwin looked at him. "Who?"
> "Popeye," Benbow said.
> "Did Popeye do it?" Goodwin said.
> "Didn't he?" Benbow said.
> "I've told all I'm going to tell. I dont have to clear myself; it's up to them to hang it on me." (119)

This clipped dialogue so closely recalls the circular exchanges at the spring, where words redound with hostile force upon the speaker, as to rule out mere coincidence. As we approach the halfway point of the novel, Benbow is for all intents and purposes back at his starting place, getting nothing out of his interlocutors, still stymied by their silence.

The communicative short-circuit in this scene points ominously forward to the darker, grimmer scene at Miss Reba's Memphis brothel, where Horace interviews Temple (chapter 23). The story he extracts (or extorts) from her there at once facilitates and obstructs his efforts to (re)construct his forensic argument. Temple's narrative (225–31), if it can truly be called that, is a surreal, twisted tale that is called immediately into doubt by the problematic circumstances of its transmission and the pressures of Temple's own disturbed personality. She insists on turning out the light before she speaks, and even then she still wants to hide beneath the bedcovers in a room not her own (223), as if to remove the "view" from the interview. Certainly this instinctive shrinking from every possibility of intimacy is a corrective against the intrusive surveillance of the brothel world, but in making the circumstances of her telling as alien as possible, Temple jeopardizes its effectiveness as an act

of communication. Having made herself unseen, she remains frustratingly unclear about what she has seen. When she does speak to Horace,
she uses her story as a kind of weapon, a threat, then as a bargaining
chip. "Dont think I'm afraid to tell," she says. "I'll tell it anywhere.
Dont think I'm afraid. I want a drink" (225). But whiskey only slurs
the tongue, blurs the memory, and works directly against articulation.
Isolated in her room, estranged not only from human sympathy but
also from human dialogue, Temple does all in her power to negate the
discursive bond between speaker and listener, to corrupt her own telling. Victim of Popeye's horrific parody of intimacy, she offers none in
return, only a deposition that keeps Horace literally and figuratively in
the dark.

When Temple at last begins her narrative, she insists on telling it
in her own way, with her own distortions, lacunae, compressions, and
rarefactions, and her story proves just as notable for what it omits as for
what it actually says. Behind her odd transferences, her grotesque pene-
tration fantasies, her imaginary gender reversals and other improbable
psycho-physiological maneuvers, there is no mention at all of her rape
or Tommy's murder. Instead, she offers what Harold Bloom would call
a strong misreading, in which the traumatic Sunday morning at the
Frenchman place is simply transumed.

> Sitting up in the bed, the covers about her shoulders, Temple told
> [Horace] of the night she had spent in the ruined house, from the time
> she entered the room and tried to wedge the door with the chair, until
> the woman came to the bed and led her out. That was the only part of the
> whole experience which appeared to have left any impression on her at
> all: the night which she had spent in comparative inviolation. Now and
> then Horace would attempt to get her on ahead to the crime itself, but
> she would elude him and return to herself sitting on the bed, listening to
> the men on the porch, or lying in the dark, while they entered the room
> and came to the bed and stood there above her. . . . [S]uddenly Horace
> realised that she was recounting the experience with actual pride, a sort
> of naive and impersonal vanity, as though she were making it up, looking
> from him to Miss Reba with quick, darting glances like a dog driving
> two cattle along a lane. (225–26)

Whether or not it is "made up," this testimony promises little in the way
of favorable evidence for the defense, so Horace merely dismisses it.

He leaves Memphis still ignorant of Temple's rape and thus totally un-
prepared for Eustace Graham's brilliant, reprehensible tour de force at
the Goodwin trial.

District Attorney Graham excels in the very areas where Horace is
most deficient as a lawyer. Motivated solely by the persuasive effects
he seeks, Graham is an example of what the philosopher of rhetoric Richard Weaver calls the "base" rhetorician, one for whom self-
serving ends justify any persuasive means (11). Handicapped physically,
Graham knows the emotional value of his affliction; indeed, the rhetoric of his crippled body played a large part in getting him through college and law school (S 275–76). To be fair, however, Graham's club foot
is no mere substitute for legal ability, for he has real talent. His visual
perspicacity, for instance, expressed in "a certain alert rapacity about
the eyes" (275), links him with Popeye, in whose cause he ultimately
acts, but it also aids and abets his forensic skills. This last ability is
present early in Eustace's career, as evidenced by the anecdote, known
throughout the town, of his poker-playing exploits in law school.

> When, two years out of school, he got elected to the State legislature,
> they began to tell an anecdote of his school days.
>
> It was in the poker game in the livery stable office. The bet came to
> Graham. He looked across the table at the owner of the stable, who was
> his only remaining opponent.
>
> "How much have you got there, Mr Harris?" he said.
>
> "Forty-two dollars, Eustace," the proprietor said.
>
> Eustace shoved some chips into the pot. "How much is that?" the
> proprietor said.
>
> "Forty-two dollars, Mr Harris."
>
> "Hmmmm," the proprietor said. He examined his hand. "How many
> cards did you draw, Eustace?"
>
> "Three, Mr Harris."
>
> "Hmmmm. Who dealt the cards, Eustace?"
>
> "I did, Mr Harris."
>
> "I pass, Eustace." (276)

Another cross-examination successfully, and profitably, executed.
Graham's gambling skills—knowing your opponent, knowing the face
value of a bluff, trusting to the intimidating power of your reticence
and your gaze, knowing that the truth of your hand is nowhere near as

important as your opponent's impression of it—translate directly into legal skills, especially courtroom skills, where the players bluff with narratives rather than cards and the stakes are substantially higher than forty-two dollars.

The poker anecdote (in which, to add insult to Mr. Harris's injury, Eustace has dealt his own hand) reveals how aware Graham is at all times of his audience and the effects on it of his words and gestures. He brings an equal attentiveness to his courtroom audience. As district attorney, an elected official, Graham is by necessity in touch with a broad constituency of voters. Eustace well knows that "the first principle of law is, God alone knows what the jury will do" (277), but since the jury is selected from the voting public itself, the better the district attorney knows his constituency, the more he knows by implication about his courtroom narratees. In *Sanctuary*, it is Graham and not Benbow who plays the role of lawyer-citizen—though the role is terribly ironic, since the citizens he represents are so prone to intolerance, lewdness, and violence. Graham also lacks the ideal disinterestedness of the Cincinnatus-at-law, for he turns his public skills aggressively toward his own personal advantage in court. If, in so doing, he happens to serve the provincial interest of his constituency as well, all the better.

Benbow's failures as lawyer-citizen, on the other hand, prove especially costly to his client. The novel gives every indication that this former probate lawyer is unused to practicing law before a broad audience. True, he may have learned a thing or two from his father, but his observations on courtroom tactics seem arrived at intellectually rather than experientially. At one point he warns Lee Goodwin, "You're not being tried by common sense. . . . You're being tried by a jury" (138), but Horace doesn't fully heed his own words. He is a competent enough figure among the country folk and the Jefferson citizenry, "stopp[ing] now and then and talk[ing] with them in unhurried backwaters," but how well does he really know, or care to know, these men and women? What might Horace learn, for example, from a Saturday afternoon stroll among his fellow Yoknapatawphans around the town square?

> The sunny air was filled with competitive radios and phonographs in the doors of drug- and music-stores. Before these doors a throng stood all day, listening. The pieces which moved them were ballads simple in melody and theme, of bereavement and retribution and repentance

metallically sung, blurred, emphasised by static or needle—disembodied
voices blaring from imitation wood cabinets or pebble-grained horn-
mouths above the rapt faces, the gnarled slow hands long shaped to the
imperious earth, lugubrious, harsh, and sad. (116)

These ordinary, hardworking squaregoers are the very people who sit
on juries. The music they listen to, the tales they tell and hear, offer a
wealth of information about them and their tastes and biases, information that could and should guide a young lawyer in his efforts to as-
semble a forensic narrative with suasive power. A straightforward case
invoking familiar motives and urges is obviously the most effective way
to win the minds of such listeners; yet relying as he does on intuition,
assuming as he does that his jury is capable of subtle discriminations
and impervious to emotional appeals, forgetting as he does that what
is obvious to the lawyer may be befuddling to the layman, Horace fails
to tailor his case to his audience. Eustace Graham's pragmatically oriented narrative, and not Horace Benbow's semantically oriented one,
will give the jury what it wants to hear, what it will respond to: a story
of cold-blooded murder, fornication, and unnatural rape.

And so, on the first day of summer, the trial begins.[14] Horace's case
itself hinges on Ruby Lamar's testimony, which introduces Popeye and
Temple to the record and establishes their presence at the scene of
the murder. Over his client's self-defeating objections (Goodwin still
fears Popeye's retribution more than any sentence the jury can hand
down), Horace gets Ruby's story out, only to have it immediately under-
mined by a masterful rhetorical question from Eustace Graham in
cross-examination.

> The District Attorney now faced the woman.
> "Mrs Goodwin," he said, "what was the date of your marriage to Mr
> Goodwin?"
> "I object!" Horace said, on his feet.
> "Can the prosecution show how this question is relevant?" the Court
> said.
> "I waive, your Honor," the District Attorney said, glancing at the
> jury. (283)

Glancing at the jury. Eustace, who well knows the couple are unmar-
ried, also knows that his immaterial question may go unanswered or be

stricken from the record, but it is not likely to be erased from the minds of the jurors. The subtle hint of immorality now taints Ruby as a witness, and the keystone of Goodwin's defense is compromised. Graham's strategy is maddeningly economical; with the slightest rhetorical gesture or tone, he can call into doubt an elaborately constructed argument. Benbow later dismisses Graham's move: "Dont you see your case is won?" he asks Goodwin. "That they are reduced to trying to impugn the character of your witness?" (284). But in the original text Horace acknowledges the power of the prosecution's ploy. After Graham's telltale glance juryward, Benbow immediately assesses the situation and awards a symbolic victory to his opponent. "Damn! Horace thought. He took me then" (SOT 261). Only it is Goodwin's forty-two dollars that has been tossed into the pot.

As every reader of the novel knows, the whole timbre of the trial changes with the entrance of Temple Drake. Her appearance takes the fight out of Horace, who sees immediately that she has been enlisted in Graham's, and Popeye's, cause—a witness dealt from the bottom of the deck. What is more, Temple seems to inspire Eustace, who grows sharper than ever in the courtroom. At this textual turning point, Graham's tactics, and the narrative itself, acquire a dimension of theatricality that will pervade the remainder of the trial. His own acting, and his directorial management of Temple's performance, begin to move beyond bare narration into the supple dramatic rhetorics of pose and gesture gauged for maximum audience effect.

The hint of theater actually enters the Goodwin case before Temple does, with the entrance of the courtroom audience. Between the lines of Faulkner's succinct sketch of the gallery and the chamber itself, we glimpse an expectant dramatic audience milling about, climbing to the balconies, buzzing eagerly among themselves, settling into their seats in anticipation of the show to come.

> Above the seat-backs Horace could see their heads—bald heads, gray heads, shaggy heads and heads trimmed to recent feather-edge above sun-baked necks, oiled heads above urban collars and here and there a sunbonnet or a flowered hat. . . . The windows gave upon balconies close under the arched porticoes. The breeze drew through them, bearing the chirp and coo of sparrows and pigeons that nested in the eaves, and now and then the sound of a motor horn from the square below, rising out of

and sinking back into a hollow rumble of feet in the corridor below and on the stairs. (S 295–96)

This depiction is redolent with irony, largely at Benbow's expense. Among the suggestive gallery of heads Horace surveys are no doubt many of the same townspeople and country folk he has ignored on the town square in the passage quoted earlier. Again he fails to attend to them, to the "shaggy heads" and "sun-baked necks" listening not only from the balconies but also, we assume, from the jury box. How then could Horace be aware, as Graham is aware, of what engages these listeners, what moves them? Moreover, in the "chirp and coo" of resident songbirds and the noise of a car on the square, we hear echoes of the novel's opening scene, the silent confrontation between Horace and Popeye over the spring, with the minimal aural accompaniment provided by the "fishingbird" and the sounds of unseen automobiles. We know Horace failed as an inquisitor there, and, after this ominous detail, we cannot but be skeptical of what is to come.

Benbow basically folds his hand the moment he sees Temple. He commits a forensic cardinal sin: he simply stops listening. "After a while Horace realised that he was being spoken to, a little testily, by the Court" (297). Distracted by the pigeons in the eaves and the bailiff's monotonous intonations, he makes little or no effort to discredit Temple's testimony, to minimize his (and Goodwin's) losses—though it should be noted that Horace is caught in something of a double bind here: to challenge Temple's perjured account would probably be unwise, since maligning an apparently helpless, "innocent" young rape victim in front of the jury might damage his case more than help it. And if all this isn't enough, Eustace Graham becomes more outrageously theatrical, more rhetorical, more immaterial in his own questioning than ever before:

> "You have just heard the testimony of the chemist and the gynecologist—who is, as you gentlemen know, an authority on the most sacred affairs of the most sacred thing in life: womanhood—who says that this is no longer a matter for the hangman, but for a bonfire of gasoline—"
> "I object!" Horace said: "The prosecution is attempting to sway—"
> "Sustained," the Court said. "Strike out the phrase beginning 'who says that,' mister clerk. You may instruct the jury to disregard it, Mr Benbow. Keep to the matter at hand, Mr District Attorney."
> The District Attorney bowed. (298)

Horace catches Eustace this time, but his objection is already too late. Graham's inflated encomium on southern womanhood could come straight from a Ku Klux Klan rally, as could the lynching he so unprofessionally recommends. But to the jury, which we learn here is comprised entirely of men, Graham's remarks become an urgent, earnest appeal to the gyneolatry that, W. J. Cash has argued, has been part and parcel of the mind of the South from its earliest days forward (87–89).[15] As Graham knows, no amount of tampering with the record will erase the full affective value of his remarks from the minds of the jurors; the immediacy with which it is recorded in memory guarantees speech in the courtroom an imperishability that the mutable written transcript does not enjoy. Eustace punctuates his melodramatic oration with a timely bow, the mark of a self-acknowledged performer, and he soon puts his directorial skills to good use in his interrogation of Temple Drake:

> "What is your name?" [Graham] repeated, moving also, into the line of her vision again. Her mouth moved. "Louder," he said. "Speak out. No one will hurt you. Let these good men, these fathers and husbands, hear what you have to say and right your wrong for you."
>
> The Court glanced at Horace, his eyebrows raised. But Horace made no move. He sat with his head bent a little, his hands clutched in his lap. (S 299)

Graham here prompts his witness to deliver her lines on cue and to project to her audience. Like a good, though slightly mechanical, actress, Temple responds. Meanwhile, the stern countenance of the law settles on Horace, who yet again finds himself silently stared at.

Temple's own gaze, however, is curiously distracted, "fixed on something at the back of the room" (299). While critics have wondered at whom Temple might be staring (her brothers? Her father? Popeye? One of Popeye's cronies sent to insure her compliance?), it seems to me that to posit a definite object for her gaze is to miss Faulkner's point.[16] Rather, within the context of courtroom drama developed throughout the trial scene, Temple is simply playing to the back of the house, as actors are routinely instructed to do—looking at nothing and no one in particular as she lies, once again, about what she saw. A well-coached courtroom performer, Temple plays her role of violated debutante to the hilt, and what she seems to leave unsaid, Graham's leading, and again at times immaterial, questions eventually bring out. When

Horace finally summons the self-possession to object, the court's response indicts both attorneys: "I have been on the point of warning you for some time, Mr Attorney, but defendant would not take exception, for some reason" (301). As we might expect, Graham's own response is again to bow, with the false humility of a rhetor who has his listeners right where he wants them.

At this point the narrative shifts perspective slightly to consider the effect of the prosecution's little drama on its listeners. "The room sighed, its collective breath hissing in the musty silence. Some newcomers entered, but they stopped at the rear of the room in a clump and stood there" (301). The effect of both of these sentences is to collapse individual auditors together in a single "clump," a rapt audience whose behavior anticipates that of the mob. As we all too uncomfortably recognize, it is not a long way from Temple's cathartic story of her rape, offered here misleadingly, to the purgative gasoline fire of the lynch mob. That the audience acts and reacts this way is a tribute to the prosecution's compelling production and also a chilling foretaste of the speed and power with which the collective mentality of the rabble works to obliterate individual morality and accountability. This trial is well on the way to what Milner S. Ball describes as "saturnalian" judicial theater, in which the boundaries separating spectators from the official participants in the trial begin to break down (56–57).

The audience—"it"—listens on as Graham arrives at the climactic rape and murder (S 302–3), and it sighs hissingly again when the telltale stage prop is produced. The bloody corncob triggers a final concatenation of Graham's inflammatory rhetoric, Temple's anesthetized staring, the gallery's outrage, and Benbow's unprotesting silence, as a new judge—Temple's father—enters and stops the trial.

> [T]he heads turned as one and watched a man come stalking up the aisle toward the Bench. He walked steadily, paced and followed by a slow gaping of the small white faces, a slow hissing of collars. . . . He walked steadily up the aisle in a slow expulsion of silence like a prolonged sigh, looking to neither side. He passed the witness stand without a glance at the witness, who still gazed at something in the back of the room, walking right through her line of vision like a runner crossing a tape, and stopped before the bar above which the Court had half-risen, his arms on the desk.

"Your Honor," the old man said, "is the Court done with this witness?"

"Yes sir, Judge," the Court said; "yes, sir. Defendant, do you waive—"

The old man turned slowly, erect above the held breaths, the little white faces, and looked down at the six people at the counsel table.

Behind him the witness had not moved. (303–4)

Again, and more destructively than ever, Horace waives the opportunity to cross-examine. Or, more precisely, we never learn his response to the court's question; Judge Drake's withering glance cuts him off before he can answer, and Temple is gone. Again, watching silences telling, and Benbow makes no effort to expose the courtroom drama that has distracted everyone from the facts. Around him, no doubt as a kind of judgment on his ineptitude, the audience grows more and more agitated. "The room breathed: a buzzing sound like a wind getting up. It moved forward with a slow increasing rush, on above the long table where the prisoner and the woman with the child and Horace and the district attorney and the Memphis lawyer sat, and across the jury and against the Bench in a long sigh" (305). And from a smaller audience of twelve angry men, a verdict against Goodwin is not long in coming. "The jury was out eight minutes" (306). In brief, rave reviews for the command performances of Temple and Graham.

The guilty verdict, though no surprise to Horace, essentially crushes him into aphasia. As he realizes, it is just as much a verdict against him as against Goodwin. Though he talks with Narcissa after the trial, his words are basically meaningless.

"Do you want to go home?" Narcissa said.

"Yes," Horace said.

"I mean, to the house, or out home?"

"Yes," Horace said. (306)

The blatant non sequitur here reveals a distracted, utterly demoralized man. Further, Goodwin's lynching, which Horace witnesses, only reiterates the ascendancy of silence, the power of rhetorical deception, and the unconditional surrender of spoken language that mark the trial's, and novel's, end. Like Temple's rape, which opens the case that the vigilant, voyeuristic mob closes, the swirling bonfire infects the scene around it with a tangible, vorticular silence,[17] a roaring stillness in which Horace says and hears nothing, only helplessly and complicitously watches (310–11). That the victim of so much watching is here forced to watch the man his forensic storytelling could not save become a victim (and silent spectacle) is perhaps the novel's bitterest irony. No wonder Horace returns to Kinston defeated and stammering—less a Cincinnatus triumphantly retiring than a near-scapegoat ignominiously fleeing.

His swan song there is no mere afterthought on Faulkner's part but a powerful coda to the communicative inadequacies that have plagued the hapless attorney throughout the novel. He makes a telephone call to his stepdaughter, Little Belle, in a last-ditch attempt at contact that is also, ironically, an attempt at surveillance: having just witnessed a devastating series of events all linked, in his estimation, to a young woman's promiscuity, Horace wants to *keep an eye on* Little Belle, who has already demonstrated promiscuous proclivities of her own. Little Belle, however, will have none of Horace's prying efforts, and the ensuing exchange, like so many of the novel's "dialogues," is a parody of the dialogic, a disruption rather than a model of spoken reciprocity, a final botched cross-examination:

> "Hello. Horace. Is Mamma all right?"
> "Yes. We're all right. I just wanted to tell you . . ."
> "Oh. Good night."
> "Good night. Are you having a good time?"
> "Yes. Yes. I'll write tomorrow. Didn't Mamma get my letters today?"
> "I dont know. I just—"
> "Maybe I forgot to mail it. I wont forget tomorrow, though. I'll write tomorrow. Was that all you wanted?"
> "Yes. Just wanted to tell you . . ."
> He put the receiver back; he heard the wire die. (315–16)

What does Horace want to tell Little Belle? The exemplary tale of the novel's other little belle, Temple Drake? Or merely that he loves her? I like to think that Faulkner's ellipses here disguise what are actually complete sentences, that the absent content of Horace's proposed tale is secondary to the act of telling itself: "I just wanted to tell you . . . *something, anything.*" (Of course he would want to, having told so little to anyone when it really mattered.) But Horace is left talking to the wire, reenacting yet once more the novel's opening scene and its failed pretenses of contact.

Interestingly, in the original text, the entire account of Horace's return to Kinston, including the abortive phone call, is narrated within a letter Horace writes to his sister in Jefferson (SOT 281–83). This early version ironizes Benbow even more; his last halting attempts to speak are paraphrased and circumscribed in the silent spaces of his writing. Benbow's retreat into epistolarity in the original text can only remind us of his world-weary escape into letters at the end of *Flags*.[18] But whichever solipsistic denouement we prefer, Horace is gone for good. He will never return to Yoknapatawpha from Kinston, never again appear in a Faulkner novel. Faulkner's first major lawyer does not so much boldly exit from Yoknapatawpha as fade away into its silent margins, a voice weak and tentative, waiting for a response, an acknowledgment, that will never come. Even when a human life rests on the power of forensic narrative, Horace fails as a storyteller, so his arguments bow before a malevolent rhetoric, an amoral but persuasive theatricality. For this reason Faulkner simply stops telling his story, and Horace must yield his place in the Yoknapatawpha fiction to a man at law whose rhetorical, narrative, and theatrical skills exceed his own: only three months after the publication of *Sanctuary*, a short story entitled "Hair" appeared in *American Mercury*, marking the first appearance of Gavin Stevens, attorney-at-law, on Faulkner's little postage stamp of native soil.

. . . .

CHAPTER TWO

The Emergence of the Lawyer-Citizen:
Gavin Stevens

Sanctuary leaves the reader with little to choose from in the way of positive images of the forensic figure, and in doubt about the relationship between "law and order" and justice in Yoknapatawpha County. If Horace Benbow emerges as an upright, well-intentioned individual, he still lacks the rhetorical, narrative, and listening skills demanded of any effective, responsible courtroom attorney. He may be morally over-qualified for the job of defending an innocent man against a charge of homicide, but he is technically unqualified for it. By contrast, Eustace Graham, Benbow's courtroom antagonist, is a consummate narrator, an attentive listener, a wily rhetorician, a subtle editor of evidentiary material, a forensic thespian, and a lawyer-citizen all too attuned to the provincial interests and values of his community. He certainly shows no scruples about sacrificing a guiltless Lee Goodwin in order to further his own political prospects. A third attorney, the "Memphis jew lawyer" who hovers behind the scenes of the Goodwin trial, is a silent, shadowy puppetmaster impervious to legal or moral strictures, a further, ominous reminder of the law's indifference to, and effacement of, individuals in *Sanctuary*. And it hardly inspires our confidence in the legal system to learn that a lawyer once coerced sexual favors from Ruby Lamar in exchange for legal services he never made good on (S 292), or that one of the most valued clients at Miss Reba's brothel is "the biggest lawyer in Memphis," a two-hundred-and-eighty-pounder who "had his own special bed made and sent down here" (221).

Whether *Sanctuary*'s unblinking anatomy of forensic failure released Faulkner to reassess forensic ethics and competence in a more favorable light, or whether it in fact compelled him to do so, his next move as a writer of forensic fiction was to introduce Gavin Stevens to the Yoknapatawpha chronicle. As an active attorney (one of the most successful in the Faulkner oeuvre), an accomplished storyteller, and an itinerant lawyer-detective, Stevens finds himself intimately involved in the cultural life and *"res in justicii"* of his jurisdiction,[1] which is, appropriately, coextensive with Yoknapatawpha County itself. These attributes make Stevens an almost point-by-point improvement upon the hapless Benbow character.[2]

Where, for example, Benbow is characterized by rhetorical inconsistency and fatal moments of inattention in the courtroom, Stevens in his best moments remains aware of the needs of his courtroom audience and is himself a careful and conscientious listener. He emerges as a flexible, and capable, forensic performer, more comfortable than his predecessor with the courtroom as a site of dynamic, dialogic encounter. Moreover, while Benbow's communicative problems are linked (whether as symptom or cause) to his dissociation from the community and its traditions, Stevens maintains and actively nurtures his relationship to Jefferson and to the southern past. He is an elected official, a thoroughgoing public man, a lawyer-citizen who knows Yoknapatawpha as intimately as he is known there. He is also one of Faulkner's most vehement and credible spokesmen for the lasting influence of history upon the individual and society. And he is capable of criticizing his southern heritage without renouncing it, maintaining an appreciation for the region's peculiar virtues in spite of its peculiar failings.

Stevens's family life, unlike Benbow's, seems to be a source of balance and stability. He too, for instance, follows his father's footsteps into the legal profession, but his decision, unlike Benbow's, is apparently his own. His relationship with his sister Maggie is a close one, but nothing like the jealous and quasi-incestuous intimacy of Horace and Narcissa. His avuncular relationship with young Chick Mallison, played out over the pages of *Intruder in the Dust, Knight's Gambit, The Town,* and *The Mansion,* is so close as to approach a wordless communion at times, a far cry from the practically nonexistent relationship between Horace and his nephew Benbow Sartoris. And when Gavin, in his middle age, does finally wed the sweetheart of his youth, the marriage, as documented in the novella "Knight's Gambit" and in *The Mansion,* seems a basically successful one, a far cry from Horace Ben-

bow's bleak and unfulfilling existence with Belle Mitchell and his stepdaughter Little Belle. For Gavin, fulfilling the familial roles of brother,
uncle, husband, and stepfather—the same roles at which Horace is so
unsuccessful—involves subjecting individual concerns to interpersonal
ones. Each lawyer's role in family life seems to reflect, or perhaps to
prefigure, his role in community life.

Finally, while Horace's actual courtroom experience amounts to little
or nothing before he so ambitiously (or so recklessly) takes on the Goodwin trial,[3] Gavin's professional life centers on litigation. The elected
offices he holds entail frequent appearances in the courtroom, and he
is experienced not only as a public prosecutor but also as a private
defender. (His earliest trial appearance, we learn in the short story
"Tomorrow," is as counsel for the defense [KG 85].) Stevens has the
skill and experience to accept courtroom cases in good conscience, and
he typically has the tenacity to finish them.

Gavin Stevens enters the Yoknapatawpha fiction in a pair of short
stories, "Hair" and "Smoke," which were published in popular American magazines in 1931 and 1932.[4] It is significant that these stories,
which have been largely neglected even by those critics most interested in what Mary Montgomery Dunlap has called "the achievement
of Gavin Stevens," follow hard upon the publication of Sanctuary in
February 1931. It is my contention that "Hair" and "Smoke" should be
read together as consciously paired stories, in which Stevens is painstakingly presented as a proficient storyteller, a working lawyer, and an
active member of the Yoknapatawpha community. As such, he represents a deliberate intertextual reply to the cast of failed, or otherwise
unsuccessful, lawyers in Sanctuary—and in particular to Horace Benbow. Gavin's auspicious debut is tempered somewhat, however, by two
other early appearances, in Light in August (1932) and "Go Down,
Moses" (1941), where his ethics and conduct are subjected to a more
sober, and more ironic, appraisal. Well before the forensic trilogy of
1948–51, these four texts offer us a suggestive glimpse of the wide range
of possibilities represented by the forensic figure as lawyer-citizen.

. . . .

"Hair" is narrated by an unnamed itinerant salesman[5] who becomes
interested in a pair of seemingly unrelated Jefferson mysteries: the
two-week disappearance every April of a local barber known as Hawk-

shaw, and Hawkshaw's unaccountable fascination with Susan Reed, a young orphan girl. Over thirteen years of rounds through northern Mississippi and Alabama, the narrator collects enough local hearsay to piece together the story: Hawkshaw's yearly absences involve ritual returns to the hometown of a young woman who died just before she and Hawkshaw were to be married. Hawkshaw has assumed the mortgage on her home and makes his annual pilgrimages in order to tidy up the house and grounds. When he makes the final mortgage payment on the twenty-fifth anniversary of her death, Hawkshaw is freed of his ritual responsibilities and returns to Jefferson in order to elope suddenly with Susan Reed, who, as it happens, strikingly resembles the dead fiancée. It is Gavin Stevens, in something of a cameo role, who supplies the narrator with the news of the elopement.

"Hair" is a story itself steeped in storytelling, in the oral ambience of a small, Depression-era southern community. The garrulous traveling salesman who narrates the tale is a familiar American type; as he hawks his wares from town to town, he swaps stories with the natives, bringing about a kind of oral cross-pollination as he travels. The discovery of Hawkshaw's past is a direct result of storytelling; most of the important details are not discovered firsthand but rather gleaned by the narrator from local gossip and casual conversation. Further, the narration itself bears the unmistakable signs of oral transmission, making the story live for us as an authentic event of speech, and the resulting vividness and intimacy are real sources of readerly pleasure.[6]

As a character Gavin Stevens seems almost an afterthought in the overall scheme of "Hair." He does reveal Hawkshaw's elopement to the narrator at story's end, but Stevens is by no means alone in knowing about it. In fact, the narrator is just about the only person in town who doesn't know about it (CS 145). If the principal plot elements are just as easily resolved without Stevens, then why is he introduced only a few pages from the tale's conclusion?

He is introduced, it seems to me, precisely in order to establish, for the first time in Faulkner, the credentials of the forensic figure as a skilled, benevolent storyteller. After putting Hawkshaw's story together from the oral fragments he has collected, the narrator of course wants to share his discovery, but, surprisingly, he does not reveal his secret to his friends at the barbershop. Rather, he turns to a single interlocutor, whom he takes pains to defend as an appropriate choice:

I never told anybody except Gavin Stevens. He is the district attorney,
a smart man: not like the usual pedagogue lawyer and office holder.
He went to Harvard, and when my health broke down (I used to be a
bookkeeper in a Gordonville bank and my health broke down and I met
Stevens on a Memphis train when I was coming home from the hospital)
it was him that suggested I try the road and got me my position with this
company. I told him about it two years ago. (144)

Stevens thus enters the Faulkner oeuvre as a sympathetic listener and
a generous man; it is to his intervention that the narrator's good luck in
finding work is attributed. It is then as a gesture of gratitude, a means
of repaying the favor, that the narrator goes to Stevens with the Hawkshaw story: ever the canny salesman, he swaps Gavin stories in return
for the sales job. The choice of gift, as subsequent Stevens fictions will
show, could not be more appropriate.

Gavin's role in "Hair," however, does not end with listening. In the
few pages that remain before story's end, he emerges as a sly storyteller
himself and actually gets the last word in an impromptu competition
with the narrator. By feigning ignorance about the Hawkshaw story,
Stevens is able to turn the narrator's tactic of reconstruction to his
(Gavin's) own advantage, to obtain the information that will give *him*
the whole story first.

When, for example, the narrator returns to Jefferson from the road
and notices "another fellow behind Hawkshaw's chair," he believes he
understands what has happened:

[I]n the afternoon I went to Stevens' office. "I see you've got a new barber
in town," I said.
    "Yes," Stevens said. He looked at me a while, then he said, "You
haven't heard?"
    "Heard what?" I said. Then he quit looking at me.
    "I got your letter," he said, "that Hawkshaw had paid off the mortgage
and painted the house. Tell me about it."
    So I told him. . . . (145)

He looked at me a while. Clearly, in this "confrontation," Stevens knows
something the narrator does not (his cryptic "looking" is mentioned
five times over the course of a few pages), and, just as clearly, it per-
tains to the Hawkshaw "case." It is also clear that the narrator possesses

information (the mortgage, for instance) about which Stevens knows only sketchy details. Stevens naturally wants this information, and he wants to *hear* it in oral form, as a story.[7] Who will go first, however? Which speaker will initiate the exchange of information and thus put his interlocutor, at least temporarily, in the superior position of knowing more than *he* does? If the question seems excessively ingenious, let us remind ourselves that amid Yoknapatawpha's folk economies, such commodities as storytelling skill count for much, and that local raconteurs often engage in informal contests like this one. It is to Gavin's credit not only that he wins this round but also that the narrator is apparently unaware of the victory or even the contest itself. *So I told him:* it is as natural as that, and Stevens learns the details of Hawkshaw's final trip to his former fiancée's hometown.

Hawkshaw's final appearance in Jefferson, however, remains to be accounted for, and an unspoken etiquette among storytellers demands that Stevens now tell what he knows. The narrator mistakenly assumes that Hawkshaw has abandoned his plans to marry Susan Reed because of her promiscuity (it is an established local fact that she "went bad on him"), and that he has left Jefferson to resume the quixotic search for a true love (147). Stevens, however, knows differently, and the coyness with which he plays his final card is an index of how much he enjoys the contest in which he has been engaged.

> "I knew he would be gone [the narrator tells Gavin]. I knew all the time he would move on, once he had that mortgage cleared. Maybe he never knew about the girl anyway. Or likely he knew and didn't care."
>
> "You think he didn't know about her?"
>
> "I don't see how he could have helped it. But I don't know. What do you think?"
>
> "I don't know. I don't think I want to know. I know something so much better than that."
>
> "What's that?" I said. He was looking at me. "You keep on telling me that I haven't heard the news. What is it I haven't heard?"
>
> "About the girl," Stevens said. He looked at me.
>
> "On the night Hawkshaw came back from his last vacation, they were married. He took her with him this time." (147–48)

Thus love conquers all, but the theme of the framing tale asserts itself too: storytelling conquers all; and, make no mistake, in the few lines he

speaks here, Gavin Stevens is a storyteller. He privileges speech, gener-
ously calculates rhetorical effects, makes an emphatic moral point, and
rarely takes his eye (or ear) from his interlocutor. With humor, pathos,
and subtlety, he builds upon and plays off of the tales of his friend and
rival raconteur. He participates actively in Jefferson's oral economy. In
short, he has arrived on the Yoknapatawpha scene.

. . . .

If we are disposed to see in Stevens's rhetorical efforts in "Hair" a
forensic dimension (in his subtle cross-examination of the narrator, for
instance), then we conveniently make the transition to the other story
that introduces him to Yoknapatawpha County, the courtroom narrative "Smoke," in which Stevens displays forensic skills that complement
the storytelling skills we have just encountered in "Hair."

In calling "Smoke" a courtroom narrative, I should explain that the
"trial" is actually an inquest, the "jury" is a grand jury, and the venue
is not the courtroom proper but instead the nearby chambers of one
Judge Dukinfield, a local éminence grise known far and wide for what
the narrator calls "that sort of probity and honor which has never had
time to become confused and self-doubting with too much learning
in the law" (KG 11). Dukinfield, former chancellor of Yoknapatawpha
County, has been shot dead in his office by an unknown assassin who,
incredibly, escapes undetected from a busy courthouse. At the time of
the murder, Dukinfield is deliberating the last will and testament of
Anselm Holland, an outlander who married into land and then held it
in trust for his estranged twin sons. If old Anselm's mysterious death
was also foul play, as Dukinfield's inordinately long deliberation seems
to imply, then the two deaths may be linked, and the primary suspects would be the Holland twins: either Virginius, the even-tempered
elder brother, who drifted away from his father and into partnership
with his cousin Granby Dodge, or violent, vindictive Anselm Jr., the
younger brother, a bootlegger and ex-convict who feuded bitterly with
his father. At the inquest, Gavin Stevens directs the prosecution.

Like "Hair," "Smoke" is narrated not by Stevens himself but by
one of his interlocutors, an anonymous narrator who speaks in the
same first-person plural voice with which Faulkner typically represents
the collective voice of Jefferson.[8] The community perspective is held
together by talk, by gossip and storytelling, speculation and conjec-

ture. It also gives us valuable access to background information. As the plot unfolds, however, and the actual account of the inquest begins, the community perspective narrows in focus, and we realize that our town-narrator is actually a member of the grand jury (17). What we are reading is thus based not on secondhand evidence but on direct observation.

This narrative strategy is not arbitrary. The three-layered perspective (narrator, [as] juror, [as] Jeffersonite) is especially effective as Stevens unwinds his argument during the inquest. As in "Hair," Stevens makes his entrance well into the story (13), and, as in "Hair," this belatedness is linked with wisdom and insight. As lawyer, as storyteller, and as an important source of readerly suspense, Stevens bears a triple responsibility. His modus operandi is to proceed indirectly, coyly, to reveal nothing before its time. For juror and reader alike, this indirection lends a certain baffling quality to Gavin's remarks, to which the narrator attests at the moment he brings Stevens into the story:

> It took Gavin Stevens a long time, that day. . . . [T]he Grand Jury could not tell at first what he was getting at—if any man in that room that day, the jury, the two brothers, the cousin, the old negro, could tell. So at last the Foreman asked him point blank:
> 'Is it your contention, Gavin, that there is a connection between Mr. Holland's will and Judge Dukinfield's murder?'
> 'Yes,' the county attorney said. 'And I'm going to contend more than that.' (13)

Stevens does not indulge in opacity for its own sake, however, for throughout his narration he carefully avoids legal jargon, from which "Smoke" itself is essentially free. Rather, his opacity compels attention, forces the narrator and his fellow jurors to listen carefully, to be drawn in. It whets the interest of the jurors, attunes them to Stevens's rhetoric (the narrator is especially attentive to Gavin's nuances of tone [KG 15]), and prepares them for the story he will tell.

If the jurors and witnesses at the inquest are inclined to attend carefully to Stevens, it is perhaps due to more than their sense of civic duty. For the county attorney's reputation as a storyteller precedes him. Jefferson lore already recognizes in him a rhetorical ability that gives him an almost chameleonic power: "He was a Harvard graduate: a loose-jointed man with a mop of iron-gray hair, who could discuss Einstein with college professors and who spent whole afternoons among the squatting men against the walls of country stores, talking to them in their idiom. He called these his vacations" (16). This is one of the most vivid images in Faulkner's early forensic fiction of the lawyer-citizen as Cincinnatus. It also runs directly counter to the depiction of Horace Benbow in *Sanctuary*. Benbow, we recall, was basically oblivious to the salt of the Yoknapatawpha earth he encountered around the Jefferson town square—some of whom, the novel implies, may have wound up voting against his client at the Goodwin trial. Stevens, however, patrician though he may be, makes time for these people. He is a man thoroughly in his element among the citizenry, and furthermore, as district attorney, it is his job (much as it was the legendary Roman's duty) to protect his fellow citizens against interlopers whose interests run counter to the community's. What is more, Stevens is comfortable at all levels of "idiom," a skill that no doubt serves him well on the hustings as well as in the courtroom. His "vacations" among the plain folk are actually working vacations, investments of his time capable of yielding important dividends. For Stevens, talking with the locals is more than just a source of pleasure. It is a source of information as well, and, as we will discover, one of the crucial lessons of "Smoke" is that such information must be heard, carefully noted, and remembered, that in the relatively stable, closely knit community of Jefferson, no detail is insignificant. *Anything*—a chance remark, a brief anecdote—can eventually serve as evidence for the storytelling lawyer-detective.

Stevens also has a keen sense of the fundamental theatricality of forensic procedure. For instance, note the subtly effective staging of the inquest: conducting it in Dukinfield's chambers can only lend power and immediacy to Gavin's arguments. Nor does the county attorney stop there. The jurors are seated around Dukinfield's desk, among his personal odds and ends, so that their perspective effectively blurs into his: "[W]e sat about the table which had not been disturbed since the day Judge Dukinfield died, upon which still lay the objects which had been, next to the pistol muzzle, his last sight on earth, and with which we were all familiar for years—the papers, the foul inkwell, the stubby pen to which the Judge clung, the small brass box which had been his superfluous paper weight" (17–18). Unlike the typical jury box or courtroom gallery, this seating plan does not sequester the listeners from the space of (represented) events. Rather, it places them in a position of active involvement, from which Gavin can make the jurors see as the judge saw and what the judge saw. It is precisely their proximity to the "superfluous" items on the judge's desk that prepares the jurors to accept one of these items as the clue which will expose Dukinfield's murderer.

Standing above this advantageously situated (and, I might point out, captive) audience, Stevens carefully orchestrates a number of minor climaxes, throughout which the pull of suspense is counterbalanced by the power of closely reasoned forensic argument. The chain of causality must be meticulously forged for reader and juror alike. Interruptions may be tolerated, but they do not change the trajectory of the narration. You will know all in good time, Stevens assures his audience, and for remaining patient, he rewards us with a critical piece of information that the murderer himself has overlooked: old man Holland is allegedly dragged to death behind his horse, after striking it repeatedly with a switch, but this particular horse refuses to bolt under even the most severe switching. Even worse, Judge Dukinfield knows all about the eccentricities of this horse because he is the man who sold it to Holland (18–19).

Small wonder that, in the midst of this emotional and epistemological roller-coaster ride, the narrator and his cohorts have trouble keeping their bearings. They find themselves "in a dreamlike state in which we seemed to know beforehand what was going to happen, aware at the same time that it didn't matter because we should soon wake. It was as though we were outside of time watching events from outside" (21–22). Significantly, detachment and objectivity signal confusion for the jurors; Stevens's aim, as we have already seen, is to keep their perspective a limited, interested one.

The jury is not Gavin's only audience, however, or even his primary one. Readers familiar with the locked-door whodunit will suspect early on that Stevens's labyrinthine rhetoric is actually directed elsewhere, that convincing the jury is secondary to convincing the murderer, leading him to expose himself. The narrator reaches this insight only in retrospect:

> When I look back on it now, I can see that the rest of it should not have taken as long as it did. It seems to me now that we must have known all the time. . . . Because [Stevens] had a plan, and we realized afterward

that, since he could not convict the man, the man himself would have to. And it was unfair, the way he did it; later we told him so ('Ah,' he said. 'But isn't justice always unfair? Isn't it always composed of injustice and luck and platitude in unequal parts?'). (24)

The narrator's editorial comment near the end of the passage, along with Stevens's arch reply, confirms that the rhetorical value of Gavin's performance outweighs its truth value. Gavin's tactics do turn out to be rather unfair. As he pays out the rope with which the murderer will hang himself, Stevens tells the truth but tells it slant. The sheer suasive power of his rhetoric, however, brings the whole truth to light.

Gavin's elaborate bluff hinges on his ability to foreground a pair of important motifs in his story, motifs that Faulkner thus conveniently brings to the attention of his reading audience. First is "the small, curiously chased brass box" that lies innocuously on the judge's desk, a paperweight that, the narrator tells us, is "superfluous" in an office located "where no draft ever blew" (24). By convention, the very inutility of this object alerts the reader of detective fiction to its possible status as clue, but the characters themselves must be similarly alerted if the box is to function convincingly within Stevens's narrative. From the narrator's description of the box, we can infer that everyone present at the inquest recognizes it according to a kind of cultural code; they have heard stories about it and its inappropriateness as a gift. Gavin, then, must take this inconspicuous but familiar object and make it conspicuous somehow, make it signify—literally turn it into a clue.

The second motif, hinted at for the reader's convenience in the story's title, is smoke. As ephemeral as the brass box is substantial, smoke plays an equally important part in Gavin's narrative, and, as a clue-to-be, it too must command special attention. This double emphasis is precisely the point of Gavin's "digressions" in the middle of the inquest. While he continues to puzzle his auditors, his subtle inflections of gesture and intonation register, albeit unconsciously, on them.[9] The narrator's descriptions consistently reveal this influence:

[W]e could not see yet what he was getting at as he began to speak again in that tone—easy, anecdotal, his hand resting on the brass box. . . . He was talking about smoking again, about how a man never really enjoys tobacco until he begins to believe that it is harmful to him, and how non-smokers miss one of the greatest pleasures in life for a man of sensibility:

the knowledge that he is succumbing to a vice which can injure himself alone. (24–25)

Note the way the two motifs dovetail in this portrait of the attorney: his hand rests on the box even as he talks about smoking. Juxtaposing these elements is every bit as important as foregrounding them, and as Gavin's narrative moves onward, the box and the smoke become more and more tightly intertwined. By dissimulation and indirection Gavin remains in control of his audience. In short, he is doing a marvelous acting job.

His finest dramatic monologue follows soon afterward, a masterful exhibition of storytelling (about still more telling, in fact) that trips along anecdotally at first—to the bewilderment of the narrator—but all the while steers us firmly toward revelation.

> Stevens was talking about tobacco again, about smoking. 'I stopped in West's drug store last week for some tobacco, and he told me about a man who was particular about his smoking also. . . . He said he was behind the counter, with the newspaper spread on it, sort of half reading the paper and half keeping the store while the clerk was gone to dinner. And he said he never heard or saw the man at all until he looked up and the man was just across the counter, so close that it made him jump. A smallish man in city clothes, West said, wanting a kind of cigarette that West had never heard of. . . . And he told about the man in his city clothes, with a face like a shaved wax doll, and eyes with a still way of looking and a voice with a still way of talking. . . . "I don't have any calls for them," West said. "What am I trying to do now?" the man said. "Trying to sell you flypaper?" Then the man bought the other package of cigarettes and went out. And West said that he was mad and he was sweating too, like he wanted to vomit, he said.' (26–27)

The intimidating "city man" who so disturbs Dr. West has also been placed at the residence of Virginius Holland and his cousin just before Dukinfield's murder, and when, fortuitously enough, he is arrested for vehicular homicide in the rural community of Batenburg, the local authorities relieve him of a "pistol with [a] silencer on it" (30).

Stevens is now ready to play his hole card. "[T]urning the closed box this way and that way in his hand," he reminds his listeners of " 'the peculiar attribute which this room has. How no draft ever blows in it. How when there has been smoking here on a Saturday, say, the smoke will still be here on Monday morning . . . lying against the baseboard there like a dog asleep, kind of. You've all seen that'" (30). An eyewitness reveals that just such a layer of smoke was there in Dukinfield's office after the murder and that some of this smoke was trapped in the brass box. The effect on the jurors is immediate and electric, but Stevens, ever the thespian, focuses their attention even further, "seem[ing] to watch his hand as it turned the box slowly this way and that" (32). He notes that smoke can linger in a metal box for weeks without dissipating, that Dukinfield's box has not been opened since the murder, and that any smoke that may remain inside can be analyzed and identified. And the Memphis man smoked a strange brand. And the judge didn't smoke at all.[10]

Stevens has proven nothing yet, but this onslaught of speech and gesture proves too much for his most interested listener, who reveals himself as the jury sits stunned. "We did not move," the narrator confesses. "We just sat there and heard the man's urgent stumbling feet on the floor, then we saw him strike the box from Stevens' hand. But we were not particularly watching him, even then. Like him, we watched the box bounce into two pieces as the lid snapped off, and emit a fading vapor which dissolved sluggishly away. As one we leaned across the table and looked down upon the sandy and hopeless mediocrity of Granby Dodge's head as he knelt on the floor and flapped at the fading smoke with his hands" (33). Once Dodge has revealed himself, Stevens can confess his tour de force at the inquest to be a bluff: he has blown his own pipe smoke into the box just before the hearing. "'I was a lot scareder than Granby Dodge. But it was all right. That smoke stayed in that box almost an hour'" (36). This peculiar combination of ratiocination and trickery, however, which may reflect the influence of Poe's detective fiction, is convincing enough to fool the murderer.

With Stevens's performance exposed as a hoax, we are free to see the real hero of the story, and that hero—as in "Hair"—is storytelling itself. As Michael Grimwood has perceptively argued, "Smoke" details the triumph of a tightly knit, rural community over the outside forces of division, violence, and greed,[11] and I would add that this triumph is effected by means of conversation, anecdote, storytelling. These oral elements are actually at cross-purposes with the conventions of detective fiction, for they are decidedly not mysterious and do not require the ingenuity of either detective or reader to bring them to light. Everyone knows them already![12] The timidity of old Holland's horse—its refusal to bolt when switched—is a bit of local lore. The jurors immediately recognize the judge's brass box. The strange still-ness of the air in Dukinfield's leeward office is common knowledge: " 'You've all seen that' " (30).[13] Even Stevens's most important discover-ies have that happenstance quality that violates the murder mystery's verisimilar decorum. One important clue, for instance, is a gift from Granby Dodge, who, in a moment of incredibly bad judgment, sends a man into town to inquire of County Attorney Stevens whether "the way in which a man died could affect the probation of his will." Small wonder, then, if Gavin has had his eye on this man all along. And smaller still if we know, as Gavin knows, that a week after old Anselm's demise, Granby "bought enough rat poison to kill three elephants"—presumably to use on Virginius once the Holland land became legally his. How does Gavin know about the rat poison? He hears about it from the druggist: "West told me" (34). The necessity of listening and remembering in this story cannot be overemphasized. When the smoke settles, property has passed safely and patrilineally from generation to generation, and the interlopers have been detected and jailed. With the help of its Cincinnatus-at-law, Yoknapatawpha has knit itself back together by means of the spoken word.[14]

Furthermore, consider the interlopers themselves. Grimwood has de-scribed them as outlanders, strangers to the pastoral landscape and agrarian values of Yoknapatawpha, undone by their lack of familiarity with the region and its folkways (*Heart in Conflict* 201).[15] The Memphis hit man, for instance, is singled out immediately by his strange brand of "city cigarettes," and later by his reckless driving habits. But Granby Dodge is a native son—a Yoknapatawphan and a farmer to boot. This "sandy, nondescript man whom you would not remember a minute after you looked at his face and then away" (KG 7) would not appear to fit Grimwood's model. What then, besides greed, links Granby with the killer he hires? What indeed but *silence*? In a community where law and social order rest to a significant degree on orality and story-telling, there will be a strong tendency to associate transgression with silence and vice versa. (It was to insure against inflexible applications of this general rule that the Framers added the Fifth Amendment to the Constitution.) Remember that Judge Dukinfield "had been shot neatly once through the bridge of the nose . . . yet *no man about the square that day . . . had heard any sound"* (13; my emphasis). Nor, we remember, was there any sound in the drugstore before the stranger suddenly loomed above Dr. West (27). Is it only a coincidence, then, that Granby Dodge is described as "a man of infrequent speech who in his dealings with men betrayed such an excruciating shyness and lack of confidence that we pitied him . . . dreading even to put him to the agony of saying 'yes' or 'no' to a question" (19). The point is later reiterated: "[W]hen the cousin spoke we could not hear or understand him at once; he had spoken but one time since we had entered the room and Stevens locked the door. His voice was faint; again and without moving he appeared to writhe faintly beneath his clothes. He spoke with that abashed faintness, that excruciating desire for effacement with which we were all familiar" (28). Dodge's desire for self-effacement is ironically what makes him stand out here; his "infrequent speech" is noted and remembered. Does his silence make him suspicious? When, as here, *homo loquens* is the reigning view of humankind, the possibility is a likely one. Perhaps the community, like Stevens, has had its eye on the taciturn figure of Dodge all along.

I have outlined a conventional plot of murder, detection, and justice in "Smoke," and I have traced a subplot of silence and storytelling; but there is a third plot I want to address briefly before leaving this tale, and that is the larger, intertextual story of the Faulknerian man at law. In this respect "Smoke" is a direct reply to *Sanctuary*, a novel published only a year earlier. Gavin Stevens, for instance, displays a rhetorical and theatrical ingenuity that recalls *Sanctuary*'s Eustace Graham, but he acts out of a sense of responsibility and integrity that more nearly characterizes Horace Benbow (or at least Benbow's intentions). If Stevens does not redeem these incomplete precursors outright, he at least represents a positive direction of evolution for the lawyer character in Faulkner's fiction—an evolution toward social involvement and ethical forensic storytelling.

Exhibit B: there is an undeniable similarity between Granby Dodge's Memphis mercenary, "in his city clothes, with a face like a shaved wax doll" (27), and *Sanctuary*'s own Beale Street gangster Popeye, with his citified suit and his face like "a wax doll set too near a hot fire and forgotten" (S 5). If this connection seems tenuous at first, consider in addition the prominent role cigarettes play in delineating each character. Or, most tellingly, compare the murders of Judge Dukinfield in "Smoke" and Tommy, Lee Goodwin's slow-witted but golden-hearted accomplice in *Sanctuary*. In Dukinfield's office, the hit man's silenced pistol makes "less noise than the striking of the match which lighted [his] cigarette" (KG 31). Similarly, to Temple Drake, the shot with which Popeye kills Tommy is "no louder than the striking of a match" (S 107). The point of these analogies seems clear: Gavin Stevens, precisely because, as lawyer-citizen, he is so attentive to his constituents and their stories, gets his hood, connects him conclusively to Dukinfield's murder. By contrast, neither Benbow nor anyone else in *Sanctuary* can bring Popeye to justice (when Popeye does finally go to the gallows, it is ironically for a murder of which he is innocent). Further, if the Jefferson of *Sanctuary* is oppressive in its narrow Puritan morality, the Jefferson of "Smoke" is arguably just as intolerant in its legal purgation of undesirable outside elements—but somehow (perhaps by virtue of the redemptive agrarianism we find throughout the *Knight's Gambit* stories) idyllically so. In each text our impression of the community and our impression of the lawyer figure are mutually dependent.

Finally, since the county attorney and the hired gun are the only characters in the story who actually do smoke, the particular valence that smoke itself assumes for each man is worthy of attention. For the murderer, smoke proves to be the mark that betrays him, a mark, however, that is left behind unnecessarily, indeed almost perversely. The homicide would appear to be flawless. The murderer approaches in silence, undetected even in a busy building, and we know his pistol leaves little or no telltale smoke, since a silencer, like an automobile muffler, works by absorbing the gases released by combustion. But for some unfathomable reason, the man lights a cigarette, finishes it, and "watche[s] the smoke pour slowly across the table and bank up against the wall" (KG 31).

Why would a trained killer do this? Stevens supposes that the man, lulled by "easy money, the easy hicks, before he even drew the pistol," "had guarded so against noise that he forgot about silence" (31), but would a professional commit an act of such oversight and arrogance? The conventions of detective fiction would dictate not—so rusty a villain would pose little challenge to the sleuth or the reader—but what if the act answers to another logic, of a more Freudian order? For is not the silence, along with the methodical, indeed ritual, precision of the hired killer, a form of repression—a way to keep the messy and potentially unruly feelings of guilt, anxiety, self-loathing, and the like, at a safe or at least a manageable distance, while one is about one's work? And doesn't the repressed in fact return through the senseless, superfluous act of smoking the city cigarette over Dukinfield's dead body—a silent form of orality that nonetheless speaks volumes? Is the smoke a kind of confession left behind unconsciously at the scene of an otherwise perfect crime—both an unburdening and a guarantee of exposure and punishment? If so, we can see that the cigarette has become the very opposite of the silencer, fatal to the one who "fires" it. When he lights up, the stranger ironically confirms the prophecy Stevens will make at the inquest, that "a man never really enjoys tobacco until he begins to believe that it is harmful to him," and that "non-smokers miss one of the greatest pleasures in life for a man of sensibility: the knowledge that he is succumbing to a vice which can injure himself alone" (25).

It is the absolute honesty of the smoke he leaves behind that distinguishes the hit man from Gavin Stevens. "Lawyers spend a great deal of their time shovelling smoke," Oliver Wendell Holmes once said,[16] but while Holmes no doubt meant *other* people's smoke (false leads, spurious testimony, useless paperwork, shifty clients), Stevens shovels his own. He talks a great deal about smoking, for instance, but his audience never sees him do it, since his only act of smoking in the entire story goes unwitnessed and is over with before the inquest even begins. To Gavin, smoke is neither a mode of confession nor really even a clue, but a prop, the most important one in the elaborate drama by which, implacable as Eustace Graham over a poker hand, he smokes out Granby Dodge. The *real* smoke, the *real* evidence, has dissipated long before the hearing. Again we are reminded that no one at a legal hearing or inquest enjoys direct access to truth and fact. Rather, what remains in the judge's brass box is pipe smoke, a simulacrum, a fictional representation of reality that Stevens produces literally out of thin air. In short, a smoke screen. Does this smoke screen serve Stevens as an attenuated or an auxiliary form of storytelling? Only, perhaps, in the negative sense of "telling stories," or lying. And yet it is this "lie"—an act of which Horace Benbow, by contrast, is fundamentally incapable—that delivers up a murderer and wins Gavin's case. An untruth that leads us to truth: this is the destiny of rhetoric, the hand-maiden of the lawyer and the measure of his competence from the Ciceronian *weltanschauung* to the Faulknerian one.

. . . .

When Faulkner turns to the larger form of the novel, his ringing en-dorsement of Stevens in the early short stories becomes more equivocal. In *Light in August* (1932), published some six months after "Smoke," Gavin Stevens makes his first appearance in a Faulkner novel. He is only a minor character, however, entering late in the action, in a brief section that exhibits something of the self-contained quality of an in-terpolated short story. Furthermore, District Attorney Stevens does no lawyering in *Light in August*. Thanks to Percy Grimm's enthusiastic brand of vigilante justice, Stevens never gets to prosecute Joe Christmas for the murder of Joanna Burden. Nor does he play the sleuth with the resounding success of the earlier stories. His speculations about the last desperate moments of Joe Christmas are at best shaky, at worst racist and absurd. His conduct as lawyer-citizen is ironized from the start by the questionable moral valence of the community he serves, which is marked by voices of racial hatred and intolerance. Further, Gavin's storytelling skills in *Light in August* meet important, and frustrating, obstacles that render his rhetoric less than fully convincing.

Stevens's appearance in the novel is strictly limited to chapter 19, and he is mentioned only once outside the first section of that chapter (LIA 489–96). With Gavin's abilities as a detective still fresh in our memory from "Smoke," it is not surprising that he is immediately indi-viduated from the shallow and specious theorizing of the town, called upon by the narrative to explain why Joe Christmas would deliberately corner himself in Gail Hightower's house with the law in hot pursuit. This time, however, Gavin's late entrance does not necessarily signal superior insight, as it does in "Smoke." The brief portrait that intro-duces Stevens in *Light in August* ironizes him in the very process of establishing his competence to speak.

> There were many reasons, opinions, as to why [Christmas] had fled to Hightower's house at the last. . . . Some believed it to have been sheer chance; others said that the man had shown wisdom. . . . Gavin Stevens though had a different theory. He is the District Attorney, a Harvard

graduate, a Phi Beta Kappa: a tall, loosejointed man with a constant
cob pipe, with an untidy mop of irongray hair, wearing always loose and
unpressed dark gray clothes. His family is old in Jefferson; his ancestors owned slaves there and his grandfather knew (and also hated, and
publicly congratulated Colonel Sartoris when they died) Miss [Joanna]
Burden's grandfather and brother. He has an easy quiet way with country people, with the voters and the juries; he can be seen now and then
squatting among the overalls on the porches of country stores for a whole
summer afternoon, talking to them in their own idiom about nothing at
all. (489–90)

We recognize parts of this description from the earlier short stories: the
Harvard career, the loose joints, the "irongray hair." The last sentence
of the passage, hinting again at Stevens's role as local Cincinnatus-
at-law, resembles the tribute to Gavin's mastery of Yoknapatawpha
speechways in "Smoke" (KG 16). What is new and significant in this
passage, however, is the hint of Stevens family history, a hint that
threatens to compromise the interpretive authority of this particular
Stevens before he can even offer his theory. The Stevens heritage is an
aristocratic one, which, as always in Faulkner's South, carries with it a
certain ambivalence, the responsibilities and entitlements of noblesse
oblige but also the stigmata of slave ownership and arrogant violence.
In Faulkner's Hawthornean vision, where ancestral sins can and do
visit themselves with regularity upon unlucky descendants, the intolerance and complicity of Grandfather Stevens, who offers his explicit
approbation of a murder committed "over a question of Negro voting"
(LIA 273), cannot but undermine the reliability of the grandson's de-
terministic and racially charged account of Christmas's final moments.

Before Stevens can begin speculating, however, the ground rules
of Faulknerian storytelling require an interlocutor for him, which the
narrative promptly provides in the form of "a college professor from
the neighboring State University, a schoolmate of Stevens' at Harvard,
come to spend a few days of the vacation with his friend"—perhaps
one of those academicians with whom Gavin "could discuss Einstein"
(KG 16). As the professor steps off the train in Jefferson, he is surprised
to see Stevens "engaged with a queer-looking old couple whom he was
putting on the train" (LIA 490). The two old people are the grandpar-
ents of the dead Joe Christmas, the Hineses, whom Stevens is sending

home to nearby Mottstown, with the assurance that he will send their grandson's body after them. Stevens's generous community service here partially obscures the ironic fact that he is serving as undertaker to the same man whom he, as district attorney, would have prosecuted for Joanna Burden's murder, both at a grand jury hearing and almost certainly afterward at a criminal trial. Relieved of this duty, however, by Grimm and his weekend warriors, Gavin channels his forensic habits into a tale for his Harvard friend, a tale that exhibits the conjectural quality and summary manner of a lawyer's closing argument—which, in a sense, it is: the one he will never make against Christmas in the courtroom. "I think I know why it was . . ." (491): the forensic reconstruction of events and motives informs Gavin's commentary throughout the first part of his narration, and the general situation in which he narrates is comfortable and reassuring. His auditor the professor is an encouraging presence, a close friend, an intelligent man of language, and in general not unlike Stevens himself. Moreover, it could be argued that the story, begun on the ride to town and completed on the Stevens veranda, is an expression of southern hospitality, a way for Gavin to acclimate and entertain his guest.

These circumstances lead the reader to anticipate the usual storytelling competence from Stevens, and, as long as he steers his narrative away from racial issues, the district attorney is on solid interpretive ground. His theory that Mrs. Hines advised Christmas to seek out Gail Hightower for help, and thus that Joe's flight to the reverend's house was neither random nor deliberately perverse, makes sense. Cleanth Brooks, among others, has offered a cautious endorsement of it (*The Yoknapatawpha Country* 376). There is also a cautious humility in Gavin's initial remarks. He frequently signals the tentative and conjectural nature of his conclusions with qualifiers such as "I think," "I imagine," "I believe," "very likely," and so on. Later he will drop these marks of contingency and supposition, but as long as he is capable of acknowledging what he does not know, his narration remains credible.

The turning point of Gavin's argument occurs precisely at his moment of greatest humility, as he begins to shift the real focus of his commentary from Mrs. Hines to her grandson. "I dont know what she told him," Stevens freely admits. "I dont believe that any man could reconstruct that scene. I dont think that she knew herself . . . because it had already been written and worded for her. . . . Perhaps that's why

[Joe] believed her at once, without question" (LIA 494). Here the lawyer's interpretive modesty is complicated by the hint of determinism
(it had already been written and worded for her), which only becomes
more exaggerated as Gavin turns his attention to Christmas.

What follows is the first demonstrably incorrect detail of Gavin's narrative. Stevens believes that Mrs. Hines described Reverend Hightower
to her grandson as "a sanctuary which would be inviolable not only to
officers and mobs, but to the very irrevocable past" (LIA 494), and that
this is why Christmas sought out Hightower after escaping from cus-
tody. One thing *Light in August* makes clear, however, is that Hightower
should be the last person one turns to for sanctuary, since he has been
so singularly unsuccessful at finding it for himself. Thus either the advice Christmas allegedly receives is misleading or the allegation itself
is. Does Mrs. Hines wrongly believe in Hightower's invulnerability to
time and violence? Or does Stevens err in his interpretation of the old
woman? The question remains open this time, but the district attorney
will go on to indulge in opinions that are all his own and from which
he cannot be exonerated so easily.

The most notorious of these, of course, is Gavin's elaborate "black
blood/white blood" theory, which reduces Christmas to a kind of living
genetic battleground. As Stevens begins to sort Joe's behavior out into
its "black" and "white" components, the qualifiers begin to drop out of
his narration, as if he here insists on the truth—the inevitability—of
his conclusions.

> "[H]is blood would not be quiet. . . . It would not be either one or the
> other and let his body save itself. Because the black blood drove him first
> to the negro cabin. And then the white blood drove him out of there, as
> it was the black blood which snatched up the pistol and the white blood
> which would not let him fire it. And it was the white blood which sent
> him to the minister. . . . Then *I believe* the white blood deserted him
> for the moment. Just a second, a flicker, allowing the black to rise in
> its final moment and make him turn upon that on which he had pos-
> tulated his hope of salvation. It was the black blood which swept him
> by his own desire beyond the aid of any man, swept him up into that
> ecstasy out of a black jungle where life has already ceased before the
> heart stops and death is desire and fulfillment. And then the black blood
> failed him again, as it must have in crises all his life. He did not kill the

minister. He merely struck him with the pistol and ran on and crouched behind that table and defied the black blood for the last time, as he had been defying it for thirty years." (495–96; I have emphasized the single qualifier.)

This is not simply bad ideology, an anxious response to social conduct that is aggressively uncategorizable, in between, too many things at once. It is also bad rhetoric and as such illustrates the way rhetoric and ideology go hand in hand in *Light in August*. Jefferson's provincial politics, in which community interests not only outweigh but also actively define individual identity, are in large part the function of its talk. As James A. Snead has observed, racial division in Faulkner is depicted as a product of cultural networks of signification that in turn rest heavily on specific linguistic figures. In the passage above, for instance, complex human behavior is immediately reformulated—refigured—as racial behavior, and the person(a) of Joe Christmas is literally rent in two. Though the forensic figure, as a professional rhetorician, is in a position to recognize and even short-circuit the logic that drives this practice, Stevens's remarks reveal that the lawyer-citizen is instead co-opted into it.

It may also be significant that here, for the first time, Faulkner fails to provide a detailed account of how Gavin's interlocutor responds to his narrative (in "Hair" and "Smoke" the narrator-listeners offer unqualified endorsements of Gavin's skill as a storyteller and partner in dialogue). Instead, Gavin's discourse simply ends, and, with no further comment, the text catapults into the riveting, revolting narrative of Percy Grimm. This segue is undeniably ironic: to whom could Stevens yield more appropriately in the text than Grimm, another fatally ironic representative of justice, law, and order, a young avenging fury who eliminates and then emasculates Christmas with the same cold, abstract efficiency with which Stevens rhetorically tears him in two? If Grimm erupts out of Jefferson's latent capacity for physical brutality, Gavin Stevens's morality play (this is judicial theater taken out of the courtroom) mobilizes a psychic violence that springs from the same attitudes of aggression and sensationalism that send Gothic shivers down the spines of the community's white supremacists when Joanna Burden's mutilated body is discovered (LIA 315–18). Up to now, like a Mississippi Antaeus, Stevens has derived his strength as storyteller,

attorney, and sleuth from contact with the local soil, but here, if anything, he is too thoroughly grounded in the narrow values of his constituents. The best of storytellers, like the most responsible of citizens,
knows when to remain within community values and when to challenge or even to transcend them. Stevens, however, in the space of a
single brief narrative, sacrifices a constructive spirit of regionalism to
a constrictive spirit of provincialism.

. . . .

We encounter some of these same provincial attitudes on Gavin's part
in "Go Down, Moses."[17] Once again, as in *Light in August*, Stevens
(who is now depicted as county attorney) performs little forensic activity per se, neglecting his legal business in order to attend personally to what he believes is a more pressing matter in the community.
Again, his detective work is not exactly awe-inspiring, for while he
does locate a missing person in "Go Down, Moses," it is only by means
of a coincidence even more wildly improbable than the wildest accident of "Smoke." Once more he plays undertaker to a killer who has
been repudiated by his community and has died for his crime, and
again that community is characterized by apathy and intolerance.[18]
Again, Stevens seeks a coherent story in the killer's demise and the
suffering of his bereaved survivors, and again he will share this story
with an interlocutor who is himself a man of rhetoric. Again, Stevens's
Yoknapatawpha constituency proves painfully unable to look beyond
racial stereotypes and focus on the human actors involved in the drama
of death and mourning, a blindness from which Gavin, too, suffers.[19] In
this story, however, Stevens eventually achieves a certain integrity that
distinguishes him from many of his fellow Jeffersonites. He achieves
this integrity when he acknowledges his respect and sympathy for a
group of people whose suffering he understands only imperfectly.

As in *Light in August* and the stories before it, Stevens is called
upon in "Go Down, Moses" to solve a mystery. "[A] little old negro
woman" named Mollie Beauchamp commissions Stevens to find her
grandson, Butch Beauchamp, who has been gone from Jefferson for
five years. The introductory sketch of Stevens is by now so familiar
as to be almost formulaic, but, as in *Light in August*, it contains a
new and ambiguous revelation that problematizes the entire description of the "thin, intelligent, unstable face, [the] rumpled linen suit

from whose lapel a Phi Beta Kappa key dangled on a watch chain—
Gavin Stevens, Phi Beta Kappa, Harvard, Ph.D, Heidelberg, whose
office was his hobby, although it made his living for him, and whose
serious vocation was a twenty-two-year-old unfinished translation of
the Old Testament back into classic Greek" (GDM 370–71). The apparently incidental detail of the translation detracts from as much as
it adds to the assessment of Stevens implicit here. Granted that the
translation is evidence of Gavin's facility with language, it is still a
reverse translation, a "dilletantish exercise" that, as Cleanth Brooks
wryly notes, "has no scholarly value" and "amount[s] to a philological
tour de force" (*On the Predilections* 94).[20] As a kind of linguistic retreat,
from an accessible vernacular language into a dead classical one, the
translation project also signals the threat of a social retreat on Stevens's
part, from the public realm of the law office (which is here dismissed
as a mere "hobby") to the monastic realm of the translator. Indeed,
the thought of Yoknapatawpha's leading lawyer-citizen cloistered in
his study, hunched over his desk, poring through Greek dictionaries,
is not that far removed from the image of the reclusive Horace Benbow, Prufrock-at-law, gathering dust along with the fire-proof cabinet
full of wills in the musty office his father has bequeathed him. (One
is tempted to imagine Stevens interpreting these conflicting tendencies in himself: "It was the Cincinnatus blood that drove him to the
law office. And then the Prufrock blood drove him out of there, back
home to the translation, which the Cincinnatus blood would not let
him finish," and so on.)

The translation is also an ideologically loaded project, insofar as
Gavin's Old Testament text contains the narrative (Exodus) that served
African-American culture as a moral and spiritual treatise on the conditions of bondage and slavery (and from which Faulkner took his title
for story and novel alike). That these complex resonances are inten-
tional is confirmed a mere dozen or so lines after this passage, with
Mollie's incantatory insistence that her grandson has been sold into
Egypt and that "Pharaoh got him" (GDM 371). The note of irony introduced by the translation may force us to take a second look at Gavin's
"unstable face"[21] and even to ponder the moral valence of his "prema-
turely *white* hair" (370; my emphasis).

Stevens is of course unaware of these ironies, but he confirms them
almost right away, when he learns that Mollie Beauchamp is the sis-

ter of a local man he has known all his life. Stevens is "not surprised"
to hear this. "They were like that. You could know two of them for
years; they might even have worked for you for years, bearing different
names. Then suddenly you learn by pure chance that they are brothers
or sisters" (371–72). "They" are, of course, "Negroes." Gavin's mental shorthand here verges uncomfortably close to the same process by
which "Negroes" become "Negro" in the mind of an angry mob (see,
for instance, LIA 271). If "they" fail to assume the status of living,
breathing, feeling individuals in Gavin's mind, how effectual can his
action in "their" behalf truly be?

Realizing that he needs "*Something broader, quicker in scope*" than
the local authorities to supply him with information about Butch Beauchamp's whereabouts (GDM 373), Stevens turns unerringly to the
county newspaper editor, Wilmoth. The editor instantaneously provides
Stevens with the information he needs, information that, in what is
arguably our first instance of clear epistemological superiority over
Gavin, we already know: Beauchamp is on death row in Joliet, Illinois,
scheduled to die this very day for the murder of a Chicago policeman
(374). Gavin's "case" is thus solved by the subtly emphasized power of
the press, and the detective story is over. The apparent irrevocability
of Beauchamp's death precludes any real lawyering on Gavin's part,
any last-minute appeals for pardons or reprieves. What does remain,
however, is perhaps a severer test for Stevens, certainly a more human
one: to tell Mollie (but *how much* to tell?) and to console the bereaved.

This test begins immediately upon Gavin's return to his office, where
he finds elderly Miss Worsham, a local spinster who ekes out a living
raising chickens and vegetables with the help of Mollie's brother, Hamp
Worsham, and his wife. Gavin tells Miss Worsham about Beauchamp's
fate, and the two decide together to protect Mollie from this knowledge, to tell her only that her grandson is dead. With a few phone calls
Gavin can insure the town's silent complicity in this scheme, and Miss
Worsham entrusts him with the funeral arrangements. Gavin, however,
complicates this relatively straightforward task with a number of ironic
misprisions. When Miss Worsham feelingly labels Beauchamp's death
"terrible," Stevens, with the rather inhuman voice of abstract justice
and biological determinism, reminds her that the young murderer is "a
bad son of a bad father" who confessed everything and deserves to die.
"It's better this way," he says (375). He plans to have Beauchamp in-

terred in Chicago, until Miss Worsham firmly upbraids him, insisting that Mollie will want to bury her grandson at home. Gavin then, with quite honorable motives, offers a version of the Conradian benevolent lie, grossly understating the burial costs he knows the proud but impoverished Miss Worsham cannot afford to pay. Again, however, the attempt draws a withering rejoinder:

> He looked her straight in the face. He told the lie without batting an eye, quickly and easily. "Ten or twelve dollars will cover it. They will furnish a box and there will be only the transportation."
> "A box?" Again she was looking at him with that expression curious and detached, as though he were a child. "He is her grandson, Mr Stevens. When she took him to raise, she gave him my father's name— Samuel Worsham. Not just a box, Mr Stevens. I understand that can be done by paying so much a month."
> "Not just a box," Stevens said. (376–77)

What these blunders have in common is a startling lack of consideration for the feelings of Beauchamp's survivors, because they are black survivors. Stevens's impulse to keep Mollie in ignorance of her grandson's manner of death is perhaps excusable condescension, but his plans to leave the body in Chicago or to cut costs by burying it in a free "box" are clearly inexcusable and stem no doubt from his failure to assign to blacks the powerful and "natural" emotions of grief and mourning he would instantly attribute to whites in the same predicament. Further, one is hard pressed to imagine Stevens defending an execution as "better this way" were the victim a white man rather than a black one. Here Stevens fails to apprehend fully and consciously what his nephew, in a later novel, will express in poignant litotes: "*You dont have to not be a nigger in order to grieve*" (ID 25). The fact that it is white Miss Worsham who gives him his comeuppance on each of these counts only drives the point further home.

At this point it would be easy to dismiss the county attorney as a self-deceiving paternalist, but "Go Down, Moses" refuses to let Stevens decline into mere two-dimensionality. (This is one reason why the story is an important document in the history of his tenure in Yoknapatawpha.) As if to make amends for his shortcomings in the interview with Miss Worsham, Stevens returns to the newspaper and announces to the editor, "We're bringing him home, Miss Worsham and you and me and some others" (GDM 377). The first-person plural pronoun is important here: an inclusive "we," an active attempt, at a significant cost of time and money, to involve the community in the plight of the Beauchamps and Worshams. I read this altruism as a basically straightforward affair, a gesture of genuine good will on the part of the county attorney. It may be reminiscent of other "tainted payoffs" elsewhere in *Go Down, Moses*, as John Selzer has noted (94), but what does Selzer think Stevens should do? Leave the body in Chicago? Let the financial burden fall on Miss Worsham alone? By so roundly criticizing Stevens's attempt at charity, Selzer seems implicitly to endorse an ethic of renunciation. If so, the example of the last McCaslin, childless, ineffectual Isaac, should demonstrate right away that although involvement always carries the risk of "taint," it is still superior to the moral bankruptcy of renunciation. When, as another critic has observed, "no white McCaslin assists in the burial of their black brother" Samuel (Creighton 147), shouldn't Stevens, who is no relation, be commended rather than criticized for involving himself in the plight of the Beauchamp family? [22] Is his act really devoid of all nobility? He is, after all, willing to put his rekindled sense of moral responsibility ahead of his county attorney business, to the ire of some of his cohorts:

> [D]uring the remainder of that hot and now windless afternoon, while officials from the city hall, and justices of the peace and bailiffs come fifteen and twenty miles from the ends of the county, mounted the stairs to the empty office and called his name and cooled their heels for a while and then went away and returned and sat again, fuming, Stevens passed from store to store and office to office about the square—merchant and clerk, proprietor and employee, doctor dentist lawyer and barber—with his set and rapid speech: "It's to bring a dead nigger home. It's for Miss Worsham. Never mind about a paper to sign: just give me a dollar. Or a half dollar then. Or a quarter then." (GDM 378–79)

What the last sentences of this passage make clear, however, if we read between the lines, is that Jefferson largely ignores the solicitations of the county attorney. The prospect of bringing home an anonymous "dead nigger" obviously fails to inspire anyone. This is why Gavin switches the terms of his appeal to the familiar, and white, figure of Miss Worsham. The donations he requests diminish by halves, down to a mere twenty-five cents, and the tone of the appeal implies that there are few takers (compare Kuyk 174). This from doctors, lawyers, merchants—Yoknapatawpha's patrician class. If the interview with Miss Worsham illustrates the ironic distance between Stevens and the bereaved, the episode around the town square conversely reveals a healthy distance between the active Stevens and the apathetic white professionals and businessmen of Jefferson.

This middle position characterizes Stevens's final appearances in the story. When he visits the mourners at the Worsham place, he is the only person from town to do so, but what he finds there is a circle of suffering and a chorus of grief from which he, despite his best efforts, is excluded. The breakdown in dialogue begins almost immediately. As Gavin goes over funeral details, Mollie and her brother repeat the plaintive "strophe and antistrophe" of Pharaoh and bondage in Egypt, and, as Stevens soon acknowledges, the two discourses never make contact. "*[S]he cant hear me*, he thought. She was not even looking at him. She never had looked at him" (GDM 380; Faulkner's emphasis). The county attorney is badly flustered by this experience and beats a hasty, graceless retreat.

> "I'd better go," Stevens said. He rose quickly. Miss Worsham rose too, but he did not wait for her to precede him. He went down the hall fast, almost running; he did not even know whether she was following him or not. *Soon I will be outside*, he thought. *Then there will be air, space, breath*. . . . He descended the stairs, almost running. It was not far now; now he could smell and feel it: the breathing and simple dark, and now he could manner himself to pause and wait, turning at the door, watching Miss Worsham as she followed him to the door. . . .
>
> "I'm sorry," Stevens said. "I ask you to forgive me. I should have known. I shouldn't have come."
>
> "It's all right," Miss Worsham said. "It's our grief." (380–81; Faulkner's emphasis)

Miss Worsham's first-person plural pronoun devastatingly dismantles Gavin's attempts to enter, as self-appointed community representative, the inner sanctum of mourning. "Our grief" is most emphatically noninclusive. It banishes Stevens, effectively reversing the thrust of his earlier, confident assertion of town support and solidarity, "We're bringing him home." What Gavin sees of pain and loss at the Worsham home leaves him gasping to get outside it. Yet Richard Moreland is

surely right to observe that Gavin's "desperate sense of suffocation and
nausea suggests" not raw horror but "the depth of his own unacknowl-
edged involvement" in Beauchamp's suffering and Mollie's grief. As
such, his "largely unspoken feeling[s]" serve as resources "to be drawn
upon and given new form" (190).

Indeed, the powerful final scene of "Go Down, Moses" reveals that
there are many levels of involvement in the lives of others, and that
Gavin Stevens, despite the flaws we have just seen, is capable of tran-
scending, at least for a time, the cultural boundaries that separate
ideological insiders from ideological outsiders in Jefferson. Faulkner
is at his most imaginative in visualizing and spatializing the various
perspectives on Butch Beauchamp's somber homecoming as a kind of
moral concentricity. When the train arrives bearing the body, two cars
are waiting at the station, their four occupants at the center of the
action: one car contains Mollie and Miss Worsham, the other Gavin
and Wilmoth, the editor. The two cars are flanked by roughly "a dozen"
others, a second, slightly removed group of witnesses. Around or beyond them lies a third level of onlookers, a "number of people, Negroes
and white both . . . idle white men and youths and small boys and probably half a hundred Negroes, men and women too, watching quietly"
in a silence that acknowledges and pays tribute to the bereaved. They,
too, in their modest way, are helping to bring Mollie's Benjamin home.
And as the hearse and two cars circle the town square, a final, outermost circle remains, "the merchants and clerks and barbers and professional men who had given Stevens the dollars and half-dollars and
quarters and the ones who had not, watch[ing] quietly from doors and
windows" in an only halfhearted commiseration that is arguably more
like surveillance (381–82).

There is a further hierarchical articulation of grief in store, however, one that divides the funeral procession itself. As the three vehicles
head out of town toward the cemetery, Gavin and Wilmoth at last reach
the limits of their involvement in the Beauchamp case, and the text
delineates these limits explicitly in a resonant pun.

> When they reached the edge of town the hearse was going quite fast.
> Now they flashed past the metal sign which said Jefferson. *Corporate
> Limit.* and the pavement vanished, slanting away into another long hill,
> becoming gravel. Stevens reached over and cut the switch, so that the

editor's car coasted, slowing as he began to brake it, the hearse and the other car drawing rapidly away now as though in flight, the light and unrained summer dust spurting from beneath the fleeing wheels; soon they were gone. (382–83; my emphasis)

As the corpse speeds away toward its resting place, the corporate limits loom in the foreground. The point is clear: the limitations of individuals like Gavin and Wilmoth are inescapably linked to the corporate limits, the limitations of the community that has incorporated them. Stevens and his friend may be able partially to resist Jefferson's inertia and racial insensitivity,[23] but they cannot transcend the shortcomings of the town perspective altogether. They follow the hearse beyond the town square and its apathy, but not all the way to the country graveyard. The corporate limits represent precisely the midpoint between Yoknapa- tawpha's flawed seat and its redeeming periphery, a not-exactly-golden mean. At the same time, it could be argued that the road sign signi- fies a further "limit" for Gavin and probably the editor too, one that is specifically corporeal, bodily—a function of the two men's white skin. Among the white natives within Jefferson's corporate limits, only Miss Worsham, after all, manages to transcend this particular limitation, to pass beyond the sign (of corporeal difference and distance), to reach the cemetery and the final, tightest circle of grief. As such she may be the exception that confirms the cultural rule represented by the sign, the absurdity that mere epidermal distinctions can all but absolutely prohibit understanding, sympathy, and communication between fellow human beings.

From his literal position in medias res, Gavin pauses for a few, final meditations on Mollie and her grief, meditations that should not, however, be automatically ascribed reliability. *"It doesn't matter to her now,"* Stevens thinks silently. *"Since it had to be and she couldn't stop it, and now that it's all over and done and finished, she doesn't care how he died. She just wanted him home, but she wanted him to come home right. She wanted that casket and those flowers and the hearse and she wanted to ride through town behind it in a car"* (383). Gavin's inter- pretation may seem innocuous enough, but it all revolves around what he means by the word "right."[24] If he means "fairly" or "justly," the interpretation seems in accordance with the dignity Mollie has com- manded throughout the story, but if he means merely "proper" or "correct," he risks another racist misreading (blacks are concerned only with the superficial forms of grief, rather than its profound, protracted, and extremely strenuous demands).[25] Is riding behind the hearse in a car, or having Samuel's obituary printed in the newspaper, really all that important to Mollie, or are more deeply felt factors at work—such as the need to reassert (or simply recover) some small place and role for her exiled grandson in Yoknapatawpha's community and chronicle, not only by burying him in a setting that resonates with family and communal meaning but also by seeing to it that his story joins the stories of other Yoknapatawphans in Wilmoth's paper, the most easily available and widely disseminated forum for those stories? It is hard to decide which opinion Stevens entertains, and on this ironic, mystifying note, he returns to his desk and the story concludes. From solving enigmas, the county attorney has gone on to become one.

Given the connections I have been pursuing between the Faulknerian forensic figure and the raconteur, the reader of "Go Down, Moses" may be struck by a conspicuous absence of storytelling on Stevens's part. The county attorney's most revealing lines in "Go Down, Moses" are addressed to himself, a tendency toward solipsism rather than dialogue that is itself significant. For in "Go Down, Moses," as in *Light in August*, it is the community that must be transcended by individual interpretation and, especially, action. That is, community is basically a positive force among the predominantly homogeneous, agrarian worlds of "Hair" and "Smoke," but when the ruling concern becomes the heterogeneous one of race, as in the two later texts, then Jefferson seems to metamorphose before our eyes (and such shifts in perspective are quite realistic occurrences in moral and social life) into an environment of indifference or outright hostility, and the lawyer-citizen's primary obligation becomes that of questioning rather than enforcing its values. It all depends, in other words, on who the outsider is. Thadious Davis's words of warning about the depiction of community in *Light in August* are especially germane in this regard:

> While the reader may assume the existence of a traditional community in *Light in August* (largely oriented toward rural, agrarian, familial values), the reader perhaps should not automatically assume that its morality is an ideal norm. In the world of Jefferson as much fanaticism and misperception lie within the white community as without. . . .

Faulkner does not uncritically celebrate the community or uphold its standards of religion, race, sex, or ethics.

"In fact," Davis adds, "a major cause of ambiguity in Faulkner may well stem from his own inability to determine exactly how to remain a part of a flawed community while exposing its flaws and questioning the validity of its fundamental assumptions"—exactly the problem that confronts the Cincinnatus-at-law (162).[26] Since Gavin's efforts around the town square to engage the community in dialogue fall largely on deaf ears, perhaps he is his own best audience. (He will not be so unlucky in Faulkner's next novel, though the presence of a disciple will bring its own attendant problems.) Perhaps he understands that the individual is a gateway to the community, that any phylogenetic change there must follow the ontogenetic example of citizens such as himself. "Go Down, Moses" verifies that such a moral education is not without its fits and starts, but it is to Gavin's credit that he applies himself toward establishing a mediatory space of dialogue and inquiry, toward representing the individual and the community without pandering to either the special interest of the former or the provincial failings of the latter. In any case, the space Stevens establishes between himself and the town perspective in "Go Down, Moses," though it does not represent an absolute detachment, is still far more constructive, more viable, than the excessive distance that Horace Benbow, the real solipsist, manages to put between himself and the more frightening Jefferson of *Sanctuary*.

. . . .

Earlier in this chapter, I spoke of Gavin Stevens's storytelling "vacations" among the Yoknapatawpha plain folk as verbal outlays that anticipate and frequently deliver significant returns. This provisional definition can be extended to Faulkner's own portrayal of Stevens in the four texts discussed above. Though Stevens is only a minor character in two of these texts, the attenuated portrait of him that does emerge suggests that he is one of those special investments that Faulkner makes in his vast Mississippi saga, an investment whose yield is not immediate but accretive, growing richer as time passes and fictions accumulate. In Gavin's status as elected official there is perhaps something of both senses of "election": the temporal mandate of his

constituents, and the special approbation of a more shadowy and om-
nipotent figure, an author-creator for whom fiction-making itself was
tantamount to "mov[ing] . . . people around like God" in an apocryphal
county that he called "a cosmos of my own" (Meriwether 255). In this
respect Stevens's characteristic virtues, shortcomings, modes of expression, and other preoccupations in "Hair," "Smoke," *Light in August*,
and "Go Down, Moses" lay the groundwork for the more fully developed depictions of Stevens as lawyer, detective, raconteur, and citizen
in subsequent works such as *Intruder in the Dust*, *Knight's Gambit*, and
Requiem for a Nun. It is to Stevens's role in this forensic trilogy that we
now turn.

CHAPTER THREE

"We're After Just a Murderer, Not a Lawyer":
Gavin Stevens in *Intruder in the Dust*

It is tempting to create a major paradigm shift around Faulkner's "fallow" period between 1942 and 1948, with *Intruder in the Dust* inaugurating a new, "late" phase of the novelist's career, one of public acclaim, financial solvency, and (some might argue) diminished creative vigor.[1] *Intruder*, moreover, seems to signal the emergence of a new side of Faulkner's prose: a pronounced intensification of many of its most idiosyncratic stylistic habits, and at the same time an unexpected eagerness to engage prickly social and political issues in the public voice of a writer whose literary and fiscal fortune was on the mend. It would be unwise, however, to overlook the significant continuities between the two novels that bracket the six silent years. Over and above their general preoccupation with southern race relations, *Go Down, Moses* and *Intruder in the Dust* share specific characters, locations, images, and themes. Keeping the McCaslin story firmly in mind only deepens the experience of reading the later novel.

Intruder opens and closes, for instance, around the same town square where Gavin Stevens encounters such indifference to the suffering of Mollie Beauchamp in the title story of *Go Down, Moses*, an intertextual citation that points forward to the much worse than indifferent reception Jefferson will give Mollie's husband, Lucas Beauchamp, in the pages that follow. Lucas, Molly, and the elderly Miss Worsham appear again in *Intruder*, the latter as Miss Habersham. Moreover, in the early pages of the novel, Charles ("Chick") Mallison, Jr., is invited to go rabbit hunting on the old McCaslin plantation by Carothers Edmonds, the last (and, we may recall from "Delta Autumn," one of the least) of the McCaslin planters. In fact, it has been suggested that Nine Mile Branch, the icy creek into which Chick slips during his hunting expedition, in a symbolic baptism that essentially sets the plot of *Intruder* in motion, is very likely the same creek in which Eunice, a McCaslin slave, drowns herself in *Go Down, Moses*, in what is the first tragic fruit of L. Q. C. McCaslin's aboriginal sins of incest and miscegenation (Sundquist 136). Further, Chick, a southern adolescent struggling against the inertia of his elders to translate moral awareness into moral action, is a direct literary descendant of Isaac McCaslin, the protagonist of *Go Down, Moses*, who also tries, though less successfully, to expiate the sins he discovers in his southern heritage. The consonance between "Mallison" and "McCaslin," "Chick" and "Ike," only underscores the basic resemblance.

That Chick's moral education is ultimately more successful than McCaslin's is due in large part to the influence of Chick's uncle, Gavin Stevens, a final important point of contact between *Go Down, Moses* and *Intruder*. Stevens advances from a minor part in the earlier novel to a major role, though not the central role, in the later one. This role, in fact, and in direct contrast to the role of Horace Benbow in *Flags in the Dust* and *Sanctuary*, was expanded as Faulkner revised the manuscript (Samway, *Faulkner's* Intruder 175). As Stevens's presence begins to loom larger in Yoknapatawpha's theater of justice, we must give him the critical attention he deserves rather than judge him reductively or dismiss him altogether. Once again, as in "Go Down, Moses," his behavior emerges as a complex set of moral responses along a dense spectrum of such responses throughout Yoknapatawpha society. As a lawyer, as a raconteur, as a citizen, and above all as an individual struggling to act wisely and justly, Stevens is a remarkably human character in *Intruder*, one who retains a "capacity to maintain his belief in the ideals of his profession in spite of his repeated mistakes and defeats" (Polk, " 'I Taken an Oath' " 176). The text itself offers a series of conflicting assessments of Stevens, assessments that issue from the fluctuating moods of Chick Mallison, *Intruder*'s central consciousness. One moment, for instance, Chick marvels at his uncle's ability to traffic "not in facts but long since beyond dry statistics into something far more moving because it was truth: which moved the heart and had nothing whatever to do with what mere provable information said" (ID 50), yet later in the novel Chick can come down hard against "his uncle's abnegant and rhetorical self-lacerating" (133). In a sense both descriptions are accurate; Stevens, like almost every one of Faulkner's people, is a living oxymoron, driven by contradictions that Chick must learn to account for and evaluate as he begins to examine Yoknapatawpha critically and to gauge its moral conduct.[2]

Critics of the novel have not always been judicious in their assessments of Stevens. From the earliest reviews and articles on *Intruder* forward, there has been a sizable and not undistinguished contingent of Gavin-bashers, who have lumped Stevens with the novel's villains. Elizabeth Hardwick, writing in *Partisan Review*, ridiculed the "frantic bad taste" of Gavin's "absurd, strident lectures," as if they were Stevens's only contribution to the novel (228). Irving Howe, after omitting Stevens altogether from his favorable review of *Intruder* in *American Mercury*, tempered his admiration for the novel in his book on Faulkner, where he pronounced Stevens "a mere talkative schoolboy" who was one of the novelist's "more tedious characters" (compare "The South and Current Literature" and *William Faulkner* 98–99). More recently, James A. Snead has called the Stevens of *Intruder* a "self-caricature no doubt unintended" on Faulkner's part, suggesting further that Gavin's rhetorical "excesses constitute one of Faulkner's least convincing tonalities and verge on the ridiculous" (217). Joseph Urgo calls Stevens a "blowhard" who "blows dust into the eyes" of the novel's sincere rebels and reformers (88).[3] And Eric Sundquist concurs in deploring Stevens as a "righteous new Southern paternalis[t]" spouting "crude, Tom Sawyerish propaganda" (148–49).

The problem with these comments, despite the modicum of truth in each one, is the distortion they impose upon a novel in which, as Stevens himself well knows, "We're after just a murderer, not a lawyer" (ID 221). Inevitably, the Gavin-bashers center their attacks on Stevens's controversial monologues in the second half of *Intruder*—the long speeches that one puzzled, ambivalent reviewer of the novel called "a kind of counterblast to the anti-lynching bill and to the civil-rights plank in the [1948] Democratic platform" (Wilson, "Faulkner's Reply" 222). In their view Stevens is not allowed a mode of utterance other than this discursive, often bombastic one. While I agree that Gavin's set speeches present problems in both their rhetorical structure and their political content, they should not be lifted entirely out of their contexts and appraised abstractly.[4] Nor are they the sole means by which the county attorney's conduct in the novel should be measured. Stevens is no mere humour character. He is a complicated individual who is, among other things, a lawyer. To do justice to the novel demands doing justice to all sides of his character.

. . . .

Noel Polk has observed of Faulkner's late fiction that "[t]he two chief features of Jefferson, Mississippi's architectural landscape are the courthouse and the jail," dialectical poles that map out "the central axis of [Faulkner's] narrative and thematic concerns" (" 'I Taken an Oath' " 159).[5] In *Intruder*, however, the jail dominates Jefferson's various physical and symbolic landscapes to the almost complete exclusion of the courthouse. While every major character of the novel at some time or another visits the jail, not a single scene in *Intruder* takes place at the courthouse. Moreover, the long sequence of events in which Lucas Beauchamp is accused of murder, apprehended, incarcerated, and eventually exonerated and released, bypasses courthouse and courtroom entirely. Indeed, the courthouse is barely even noted as a geographical landmark. Throughout the novel, the law seems to assume a purely punitive institutional valence.

It should come as no surprise, then, that there is little actual lawyering done in *Intruder*. Early in the novel, Gavin Stevens takes a "case" from Lucas Beauchamp, and at novel's end he accepts two dollars from Lucas for "expenses" he has incurred, but in between, since this "case" never goes before a judge, Stevens has next to nothing to do as an attorney. Even as a private citizen, however, Gavin carries with him the characteristic preoccupations of the forensic figure. His impact upon his nephew, for instance—arguably his most important contribution to the novel—is achieved almost entirely through a novel-long series of anecdotes and ethical cross-examinations. The complex verbal relationship between Stevens and Mallison cannot be characterized exclusively in terms of polemic, bombast, and rhetorical posturing, as the Gavin-bashers would have it. On the contrary, uncle and nephew also enjoy moments of genuine intellectual communion, exciting moments in which Chick partakes of Gavin's deep learning in the lore of Yoknapatawpha and in which, later on, Stevens appreciatively learns from his erstwhile student. While few before have addressed these moments at length, they are crucial elements in Chick's moral education, and they work in at least two additional directions as the novel unfolds: to create a mode of narrative discourse out of which Chick and the reader can arrive at a responsible judgment of Yoknapatawpha County, a mode I call *adversarial,* and to drive Yoknapatawpha toward acknowledging the sorry spectacle of injustice it enacts for itself. Thus Stevens once again illustrates that the Faulknerian forensic figure, in his private as well as public existence, is presented, for better or worse, largely in terms of his competence as a raconteur and citizen.

I repeat: for better *or worse.* One could argue, for instance, that nowhere in the novel are the storyteller's skills more sorely missed than in Gavin's first visit to the jail to see Lucas Beauchamp (ID 58–65). Stevens, whose audience in this scene is literally a captive one, nevertheless ignores Lucas, and as a result their exchanges never approach the reciprocity we expect between the raconteur and his listener or the lawyer and his client. What Lucas gets is less an interview than a lecture, and a most inappropriately timed lecture at that, since a lynching may be imminent. Even as Stevens pleads for information, he never really allows any significant input from his client, interrupting him repeatedly and insisting that he is in charge, in a manner that may remind us of Horace Benbow's absent-minded interviews with Ruby Lamar or Temple Drake.

> 'So you aint going to tell me what you want me to do until after I have agreed to do it,' his uncle said. 'All right,' his uncle said. 'Now I'm going to tell you what to do. Just exactly what happened out there yesterday?'
>
> 'So you don't want the job,' Lucas said. 'You aint said yes or no yet.'
>
> 'No!' his uncle said, too loud, catching himself but already speaking again before he had brought his voice back down to a sort of furious explicit calm: 'Because you aint got any job to offer anybody. You're in jail, depending on the grace of God to keep those damned Gowries from dragging you out of here and hanging you to the first lamp post they come to. Why they ever let you get to town in the first place I still dont understand—'
>
> 'Nemmine that now,' Lucas said. 'What I needs is—'
>
> 'Nemmine that!' his uncle said. 'Tell the Gowries to never mind it when they bust in here tonight.' (61)

The old man, who clearly has something important to tell Stevens, can't get a word in edgewise. What is it that Lucas needs? What does he want to "hire somebody" to do? The county attorney is uninterested in these questions, uninterested for that matter in dialogue with a man whom he has already judged to be guilty. (Imagine the Stevens of "Smoke" refusing to listen in this way!) Lucas will have to turn elsewhere for help.

Chick Mallison, who quietly observes the encounter, likens it to a poker game (ID 61), and the reference may bring to mind the poker-faced district attorney of *Sanctuary*, Eustace Graham, who parlays his experience at cards into ready cash and cutthroat forensic skills. In the jail scene of *Intruder*, however, as Chick realizes, Lucas Beauchamp and not the county attorney holds the cards. Lucas watches Stevens with "a look shrewd secret and intent" (60), carefully weighing Gavin's merits before assuming a silence that signals his lack of confidence in the county attorney. Chick's awareness that there is more between the clipped lines of the interview than his uncle suspects, reveals *him* as the empathetic, attentive listener Lucas seeks, and Chick will later back up this empathy with action. Before the boy can make meaningful contact with the old man, however, the blustering Gavin must retreat from the scene. He does so only after a final failed attempt to harangue the accused:

'Now you listen to me. You'll go before the grand jury tomorrow. They'll indict you. Then if you like I'll have Mr Hampton move you to Mottstown or even further away than that, until court convenes next month. Then you'll plead guilty; I'll persuade the District Attorney to let you do that because you're an old man and you never were in trouble before; I mean as far as the judge and the District Attorney will know since they dont live within fifty miles of Yoknapatawpha County. Then they wont hang you; they'll send you to the penitentiary; you probably wont live long enough to be paroled but at least the Gowries cant get to you there. Do you want me to stay in here with you tonight?'

'I reckon not,' Lucas said. 'They kept me up all last night and I'm gonter try to get some sleep. If you stay here you'll talk till morning.' (64–65)

The comic touch here has a serious subtext: talking all night is within Gavin's competence, but here, anyway, listening is another matter. Stevens's stubborn monologue reflects poorly on him, to say the least.

So does the problematic trio of set speeches that has garnered Stevens such infamy among critics over the years: the "Sambo" speech (149–

50); the "homogeneity" speech (153–56), which is really an extension of
the "Sambo" material; and the italicized "outlander" speech (215–17),
which is quoted only indirectly but which, the text implies, represents
a kind of composite version of remarks Stevens has made to Chick on
countless occasions "since he [Chick] had got big enough to listen and
to understand and to remember" (215). In the first of these speeches,
Stevens attempts to praise the dignity and resilience of the black race.
In the second, he calls for a "confederation" among southerners black
and white against northern federalism and its narrow, legalistic mentality. And in the third, he seeks to defend the South's resistance to
legislated social change against the cynical charges of an imaginary
northern respondent. While each speech could be analyzed separately
and at length, a few select aspects demonstrate the rhetorical and political weaknesses of the group as a whole. If I seem to be arguing against
my own premises here by criticizing Stevens, my intent in examin-
ing these troubled performances (and the earlier one at the jail) is to
differentiate them from the other, more subtle mode of speech that
characterizes Gavin in *Intruder*—the storytelling mode that, as I shall
demonstrate, works itself so deeply into Chick Mallison's consciousness
as to be almost inseparable from his own thoughts.

A number of features distinguish the set speeches from good (or what
Richard Weaver would call ethical) rhetoric. For one thing, they lack
the vivid detail that is the stock in trade of the raconteur. Gavin's abortive panegyric upon "Sambo," for instance, is marred from the start
by the excessive generality of its rhetoric, the tendency to abstraction
by means of which, in the space of only half a page, Stevens can conclude that "no man can stand freedom," solve the political problems
of postwar Europe, and reduce black experience to uniformity with his
unfortunate umbrella term.[6] The easy abstractions recur in the other
two speeches, where the immigrant population of the Northeast becomes "the coastal spew of Europe," the Swiss "are not a people so
much as a neat clean small quite solvent business," southerners are, as
Gavin explains proudly but quite vaguely, "homogeneous" (153),[7] and
labels such as "*Indian and Chinese and Mexican and Carib and Jew*,"
as well as Nazi and Communist (216), are cavalierly bandied about.
Stevens's decision to ignore the ins and outs of the county he knows so
well in favor of unfocused commentary on world events and humanity
at large robs his remarks of an adequate grounding in experience.

Also notably absent from the speeches is any legitimately interactive relationship with the listener, that accommodation of the audience's words and needs that the rhetor ideally seeks. The unfriendly syntax throughout Gavin's orations is only one part of this larger area of difficulty. A cybernetic theorist might complain that the speeches are not interruptible, that they seem preprogrammed, inflexible.[8] The "Sambo" speech never deviates from its appointed course. It runs on, hypotactically and confusingly, neglecting its audience, until it simply ceases, without so much as a period, cut short by a dash as the narrative begins again (150). That is, the performance is interruptible only by a kind of orthographical violence, the kind of violence only the narrator, and not one of Stevens's fellow characters, is capable of. The next long oration presents a similar problem: Stevens's remarks on southern homogeneity come to an obvious end, and the narrative resumes in the next paragraph—but without any quotation mark ever appearing to close off the direct discourse (156). Again, it is as though the narrative itself has censored the county attorney's speech. Perhaps this anomaly is only an editorial or typesetting slip, but when we consider how directly the narrative is grounded in Chick's consciousness and point of view, the censorship makes sense. It is, after all, the kind of abstract provincialism represented in these two speeches that the boy is seeking at precisely this point in the text to censor in himself. Finally, as though to redeem the monologism of his earlier efforts, Gavin appears in his last speech to engage in a dialogue with a hostile northern interlocutor. This narratee, however, is only a trumped-up straw figure more eager to trade insults than ideas, a vessel to be loaded with more Stevens rhetoric:

> when you say Lucas must not wait for . . . tomorrow because that tomorrow will never come because you not only cant you wont then we can only repeat Then you shall not and say to you Come down here and look at us before you make up your mind and you reply No thanks the smell is bad enough from here and we say Surely you will at least look at the dog you plan to housebreak, a people divided at a time when history is still showing us that the anteroom to dissolution is division and you say At least we perish in the name of humanity and we reply When all is stricken but that nominative pronoun and that verb what price Lucas' humanity then (217)

Interruptibility here is a kind of sleight-of-hand trick, the dialogue only thinly disguised monologue. Stevens's imagined opponent, citing the name of humanity, is as abstract as he is, so their debate accomplishes nothing. Once again, the speech does not formally conclude. It simply collapses without benefit of punctuation back into the Roman type of the narrative.

In making the transition from these flawed performances to Gavin's more successful efforts at storytelling, it is only natural to ask how the text distinguishes between the two modes of discourse, and whether it offers any endorsement of one over the other. One way to begin answering these questions is to remind ourselves that *Intruder in the Dust* is, in the most profound sense, the narrative expression of the consciousness of Chick Mallison. The novel's "third-person narrator" demonstrates a strict adherence to Chick's perceptions, memories, beliefs, and values—the kind of unwavering fidelity we normally associate with first-person narrators (see Hart). A great deal of Chick's attention (and thus a great deal of text) is directed toward unfamiliar or disturbing elements that the boy seeks to reconcile with his own experiences and expectations. These experiences and expectations are constantly adjusted, as Chick constitutes and reconstitutes his world, a process faithfully recorded by narrative structure and technique. The novel's hundreds of "*not . . . but . . .*" constructions, for instance, in which a percept or hypothesis is first raised and then rejected in favor of a subsequent, typically more refined impression, dramatize Chick's gradual education structurally as well as thematically, representing it in addition to reporting it. The narrative foreground of *Intruder* is thus dominated by whatever occupies Chick's conscious attention, and this often problematic material, precisely by virtue of its immediate visibility, is subject to review, evaluation, critical scrutiny. As we recede toward the margins of the text, however, we encounter more subtle, indirectly rendered material that Chick tends to accept uncritically, as "what goes without saying" in the various physical and metaphysical landscapes of Yoknapatawpha. This peripheral material frequently provides a much-needed background against which Chick's actions— and the reader's understanding of those actions—can unfold.

One of the most significant features of Gavin's set speeches is their conspicuous foregrounding in the narrative. Of course, quoted speech is almost always set off from the material around it by some means— inverted commas are the most obvious convention, though not the only one, to the reader of English. The self-indulgent Stevens speeches, however, receive additional emphasis. As we have seen, they are highlighted

by deliberately unconventional stylistic features. Each, for instance, begins and/or concludes on an irregular grammatical or orthographical
note, and the third speech further commands our attention by means of
italics. Suspended—indeed, stranded—in the text, readily detachable
from their narrative contexts, the set speeches invite scrutiny in exactly
the manner described above. The amount of negative criticism they
have received here and elsewhere attests to this fact.

We must bear in mind, however, that our scrutiny only exists as a
direct function of Chick's scrutiny—that, according to the narrative
logic that drives *Intruder*, the speeches stand out in the text because
they stand out in his mind. And they stand out in his mind, it is fair
to assume, precisely because they are so troublesome, too troublesome
to be absorbed indiscriminately. The textual emphasis that Gavin's
polemic so often receives is thus an index (lest "expression" seem too
strong) of Chick's reservations about it, and these reservations literally
prefigure our own. The prominence of the set speeches signals anxiety
about them, not confidence in them. They are blocked off in the text
(rather than hidden in it) in order to be judged uncompromisingly. This
is because they seem to need such judgment. In other words, they force
the issue of their own adequacy.

If we merely deem them inadequate, however, and assume that by
doing so we exhaust Gavin's role in *Intruder*, then we neglect an entire
set of episodes throughout the novel in which the county attorney encourages rather than hinders Chick's progress toward maturity. These
latter moments are not highlighted or blocked off in the text. On the
contrary, they are embedded in it, worked almost seamlessly into the
main currents of plot and syntax. They tend to be described indirectly,
in brief passages, rather than represented directly and at length, and
for this reason they are easy to overlook. Most important, they stand
as successful examples of rhetoric that work to countervail the painful
excesses of the set speeches and to constitute a new, encouraging side
of Stevens, a side that more fully rounds him out as a character. With
this in mind, then, consider the import of the following passages, to
which I have added italics with the admittedly paradoxical intent of
emphasizing how subtly, indeed incidentally, the text refers to Stevens.

> Two years ago *his uncle had told him* there was nothing wrong with
> cursing: on the contrary it was not only useful but substituteless but like

everything else valuable it was precious only because the supply was limited and if you wasted it on nothing on its urgent need you might find
yourself bankrupt. (42)

[The jail] was of brick, square, proportioned, with four brick columns
in shallow basrelief across the front and even a brick cornice under the
eaves because it was old, built in a time when people took time to build
even jails with grace and care and *he remembered how his uncle had
told him* that not courthouses nor even churches but jails were the true
records of a county's, a community's history, since not only the cryptic forgotten initials and words and even phrases cries of defiance and
indictment scratched into the walls but the very walls themselves held,
not in solution but in suspension, intact and biding and potent and indestructible, the agonies and shames and griefs with which hearts long
since unmarked and unremembered dust had strained and perhaps
burst. (49–50)

[H]e had stopped the truck was out and had already started to run when
he stopped himself: something of dignity something of pride remembering last night . . . and something of caution too *remembering how his
uncle had said* almost nothing was enough to put a mob in motion so perhaps even a child running toward the jail would have been enough. (137)

They could see the hills now; they were almost there—the long lift of the
first pine ridge standing across half the horizon and beyond it a sense
a feel of others, the mass of them seeming not so much to stand rush
abruptly out of the plateau as to hang suspended over it *as his uncle
had told him* the Scottish highlands did except for this sharpness and
color. (148)

There are over a dozen other moments like these distributed throughout the narrative. The specific quality of the knowledge conveyed
varies widely from passage to passage, running the gamut from general
human truths to specific regional observations and practical advice—
from the ubiquity of human suffering and the power and dignity of
its expression on the walls of the jail (a recurring theme in Faulkner),
to the peculiar volatility of a local lynch mob or the rugged beauty of
the native landscape, to a tongue-in-cheek primer on the nuances of
swearing. But the wisdom that Gavin offers Chick in these scenes—
sometimes gnomic, sometimes profound, sometimes comic, always en-

lightening—stands in stark contrast to the fustian Stevens devotes in his speeches to racial stereotypes, antifederalism, or the tenuous premise of homogeneity.

If, as we have seen, the foregrounding of the set speeches ironizes them, indicates young Mallison's uneasiness with them,[9] then by corollary the most direct endorsement of remarks like Gavin's above is the degree to which Chick has internalized them. These remarks are not held apart for critical review but woven directly into the fabric of Chick's consciousness. The boy has made them part and parcel of his own thought and experience. This is why they can be summarized and paraphrased, rendered in a kind of mental shorthand rather than cited verbatim. In contrast to the set speeches, these remarks directly influence Chick's behavior, forming a background against which the boy struggles to make sense of his world and to act responsibly in it. Again, the passages above serve as examples. Having been alerted to the important place of the jail in the community, Chick pays special attention to the accused murderer housed there, more attention than his uncle does. Similarly, forewarned of the potential explosiveness of the mob, Chick is able to take steps (literally, by tiptoeing) against inciting it and thus endangering Lucas.

The actual utterances that Chick has paraphrased in these scenes are doomed to remain a mystery, but if we take the liberty of reconstructing them speculatively, they suggest features associated throughout this study with storytelling. First of all, they tend to be grounded in a specific place and time, in the ambience of a small southern community during the thirties and forties. Even the weighty remarks on guilt and suffering are substantiated by references to familiar local landmarks such as the jail, the courthouse, and the church. By contrast, the set speeches display either an escapist attitude toward the social and political realities of Yoknapatawpha or, less likely, a marked ignorance of them.

The second feature that Gavin's remarks have in common with storytelling is a more or less explicit community-building function. The wisdom that Gavin shares with Chick in the scenes above is not only specific but also relevant to a young Jeffersonite, pointed in the pragmatic sense of the term explored by William Labov and Gerald Prince.[10] How does the pain and suffering of prison affect a person? When is it appropriate to swear? What kind of people participate in mobs? What is the special character of one's native land? Why do townspeople build their houses so close together? (See ID 47 for the rather bemused answer to that one.) However innocuous they may seem, these are questions that Chick must learn to answer as he matures, questions that subtly introduce him to the concerns of adult society. By instructing Chick in these communal matters, Stevens is educating him in the root sense,[11] while the sledgehammer didacticism of the set speeches verges uncomfortably on brainwashing—and fails precisely as a result.

Finally, this material suggests storytelling in the power and efficiency with which it communicates itself to its audience. Gavin's remarks above do not encounter the critical resistance that limits the effectiveness of the set speeches. They are verbal gifts rather than verbal assaults, designed to please and instruct the listener rather than to obliterate or indoctrinate him. This makes them so thoroughly assimilable that they almost disappear into Chick's own thoughts. To the extent, in other words, that Stevens accommodates and encourages the active participation of his listener as a partner in an interactive circuit of loving exchange, Chick can literally make his uncle's remarks his own, and this is precisely what he does. Wesley Morris has noted an impulse in the novel "to disrupt monologic authoritarianism with the insistence of dialogue," an impulse, however, with which he fails to credit Stevens (231). But the verbal performances I am reconstructing here are dialogically inflected. Handed down anecdotally from generation to generation, passed along to Stevens and then in turn to his nephew, these stories are the product of many voices, and thus the property of no single voice. By simply existing, and perpetuating themselves, they militate against the authoritarianism Morris condemns. The label *story*, then, is not applied arbitrarily to the moments examined here. The wisdom Chick gleans from his uncle is not the result of more specious and sanctimonious polemic. Rather, the distinctive effects Gavin's words have this time around reveal them as the work of the raconteur.

. . . .

Once we have balanced our image of Stevens the demagogue with Stevens the raconteur, we can see his storytelling at work behind some of the most important moments in *Intruder*. In fact, Chick draws on Gavin-inspired wisdom in one of the novel's earliest scenes, the boy's

first encounter with Lucas Beauchamp. After slipping off a log into the
icy Nine Mile Branch, Chick flounders there until he hears "a voice"
ordering his friends to let him fend for himself in the water. As he
climbs out of the creek and up the bank, Chick encounters the source
of the mysterious voice, and the narrative follows the boy's gaze in a
cinematic pan upward:

> he saw two feet in gum boots which were neither Edmonds' boy's nor
> Aleck Sander's and then the legs, the overalls rising out of them and
> he climbed on and stood up and saw a Negro man with an axe on his
> shoulder, in a heavy sheeplined coat and a broad pale felt hat such as his
> grandfather had used to wear, looking at him and that was when he saw
> Lucas Beauchamp for the first time that he remembered or rather for the
> first time because you didn't forget Lucas Beauchamp. (6)

The import of this short scene, however, goes beyond the cinemato-
graphic. Documented here in meticulous detail is a process that is gen-
uinely epistemological. We witness the coalescence of discrete percep-
tual stimuli into a cognitive whole, in a manner that suggests Gestalt
psychology: "feet," "legs," and "overalls" become "a Negro man," and
then this anonymous man, with the addition of an axe, a coat, and a
hat, somehow emerges as Lucas Beauchamp. It is the second part of
this process that is the more puzzling: most of us can cognitively as-
semble a man out of his constituent parts, but how does Chick know
that the man who stands before him, a man he has never met and
probably never even seen before, is Beauchamp? What catalyzes his
re-cognition? The answer involves a story.

> Edmonds' boy said something to the man, speaking a name: something
> Mister Lucas: and then he knew who the man was, remembering the
> rest of the story which was a piece, a fragment of the country's chronicle
> *which few if any knew better than his uncle:* how the man was son of one
> of old Carothers McCaslin's, Edmonds' great grandfather's, slaves who
> had been not just old Carothers' slave but his son too. (7; my emphasis)

The Yoknapatawpha chronicle alluded to here is of course an oral, not
a written, text, the composite of countless acts of individual memory
and transmission. It is reasonable, however, to conclude that Gavin
Stevens would not be mentioned here were he not the source for this
particular fragment of it. The story he tells Chick—a story, one might

add, straight out of *Go Down, Moses*—enables the act by which young Mallison constitutes the old man. The boy can then go on to remember "the rest of [it], the legend: how Edmonds' father had deeded to his Negro first cousin and his heirs in perpetuity the house and the ten acres of land it sat in—an oblong of earth set forever in the middle of the two-thousand-acre plantation like a postage stamp in the center of an envelope" (8).

Another fragment of the county chronicle helps Chick recognize Lucas's wife, in a scene that to a striking degree mimics (or continues) the one above. Lucas leads the soaking-wet boy and his hunting partners back to the Beauchamp cabin, where Chick immediately sees a "clay-daubed fieldstone chimney in which a halfburned backlog glowed and smoldered in the gray ashes and beside it in a rocking chair something which he thought was a child until he saw the face, and then he did pause long enough to look at her *because he was about to remember something his uncle had told him* about or at least in regard to Lucas Beauchamp" (10, my emphasis). Whereas Chick first becomes conscious of Lucas as "a voice," the boy's initial impression here is only of an ill-defined "something." What Chick is "about to remember," however, allows him to identify the "tiny old almost doll-sized" figure gradually taking shape before him as Molly Beauchamp, wife of Lucas, native of Jefferson, cohort of Chick's grandmother, and (in an earlier context) client of Gavin Stevens. It is rather ironic that the threat of paternalism in Chick (who sees a black woman as "something like a child") is actually short-circuited (at least in this instance) by the humanizing Stevens story—by the very man who is so often castigated for trying to force-feed provincial paternalism to his nephew.

Over the four-year history of his relationship with Lucas, Chick hears a number of local stories and anecdotes that complicate his picture of Beauchamp and sometimes help him resolve the old man's puzzling behavior (see 18–19, 27–28). The composite portrait of Lucas that emerges from these accounts is one of solitary pride and dignity, but Beauchamp's most utterly human moment in *Intruder* would escape Chick completely but for another story attributed specifically to Gavin Stevens. One day, Lucas walks past Chick on the town square without acknowledging or apparently even recognizing him, leading Chick to believe that the old man has finally forgiven the debt he rang up at the Beauchamp cabin. The reason for Lucas's indifference, however, is not that the old man has finally terminated their little game of gift-giving, one-upmanship, and mutual obligation.[12] It is rather, as the boy learns a year later from another of his uncle's stories, that Lucas has been rocked to his very foundation by the death of his wife. *That was why he didn't see me*, Chick tells himself, "thinking with a kind of amazement: *He was grieving. You dont have to not be a nigger in order to grieve*" (25; Fáulkner's emphasis). Here Chick's obligation to Lucas takes on a new resonance. The boy has learned that grief and suffering, so often in Faulkner "the index of a person's essential humanity" (Bassett, "Gradual Progress" 214), are not the prerogative of whites alone. Mallison will draw on this wisdom when Lucas's time of real need arrives. To point out Stevens's role in this episode is not to exaggerate his importance, but merely to note that, once again, one of his timely stories underlies and in part enables his nephew's growth.

These stories also loom behind some of Chick's most skillful sleuthing. The detective plot of *Intruder* revolves around the boy's efforts to prove that Beauchamp's "fawty-one Colt" pistol did not in fact kill Vinson Gowrie. Sent to the Gowrie burial ground by the imprisoned Lucas to exhume the body and check the bullet wound, Chick, along with Aleck Sander and Miss Habersham, finds that Vinson's corpse has been removed from its grave and another substituted in its place. This corpse Chick somewhat squeamishly identifies as Jake Montgomery, "a shoestring timber buyer from over in Crossman County" (104), with an ease that seems not to have caught the attention of the many critics who have complained about Faulkner's strained corpse-switching trick in this scene. No one to my knowledge, in fact, has bothered to ask how a sixteen-year-old town boy, who spends most of his spare time at his uncle's law office, can possibly recognize, at a moment's notice, in the dark of night, and in the most incongruous situation imaginable, the dead face of an obscure, itinerant working man who is not even from Yoknapatawpha but from a neighboring county. Chick's powers of perception and recognition seem almost superhuman here, but they should not merely be dismissed as implausible. Instead, they vividly demonstrate that Chick's mastery of Yoknapatawpha lore extends even to its census, through the accretion of interwoven stories and anecdotes. If there is no direct textual evidence of further Stevens stories behind this scene, I can see no more likely source for Chick's thumbnail biography of Montgomery than the county attorney.

Then there is the matter of the murder weapon itself. After Vinson's body is finally exhumed from quicksand, where it has been hurriedly dumped by the murderer after one of the bizarre grave robberies, the sheriff reveals the murder weapon to be a German Luger automatic, thereby exonerating Beauchamp and implicating Crawford Gowrie, the victim's brother and the owner of the Luger. Chick is in a position to recognize both weapon and owner immediately, because he has, only a few pages earlier, remembered an anecdote involving both of them, an oral fragment from among the many out of which the boy constructs for himself an impromptu Gowrie genealogy. By now, the source of this information should hardly come as a shock.

> Crawford . . . had been drafted on the second day of November 1918 and on the night of the tenth (with a bad luck in guessing which, *his uncle said*, should not happen to any man—a point of view in which in fact his federal captors themselves seemed to concur since his term in the Leavenworth prison had been only one year) had deserted and lived for almost eighteen months in a series of caves and tunnels in the hills within fifteen miles of the federal courthouse in Jefferson until he was captured at last after something very like a pitched battle (though luckily for him nobody was seriously hurt) during which he made good his cave for thirty-odd hours armed with (and, *his uncle said*, a certain consistency and fitness here: a deserter from the United States army defending his freedom from the United States government with a piece of armature captured from the enemy whom he had refused to fight) an automatic pistol which one of the McCallum boys had taken from a captured German officer and traded shortly after he got home for a brace of Gowrie foxhounds. (164–65; my emphasis)

The Jake Montgomery episode appears more and more plausible after feats of recall like this one. Chick, it seems, can summon detailed portraits of his fellow Yoknapatawphans almost at will, but he compiles these portraits out of a communal matrix of narrative to which his uncle is a leading contributor. Gavin's anecdotes not only help to bring the murder mystery to a close. They also lead Chick to a deeper awareness of the painful implications of fratricide, implications that include the still-bitter regional memory of the South's instigating role in America's great fratricidal conflict and that, as we will see, many Yoknapatawphans are still unready to acknowledge.

By the same token, when it comes to winning freedom for Lucas
Beauchamp, Stevens makes a more significant contribution as the hidden oracle behind Chick's detective work than he does as Beauchamp's
defense counsel. As raconteur, Stevens literally and almost single-
handedly creates Yoknapatawpha County for his nephew—its history,
legend, folklore, genealogy, landscape, local color, population, politics,
and sociology—and this legacy is necessary, if not sufficient, capital
against which Chick draws in his struggle to embrace the peculiar
virtues of his native region and to reject its provincial vices. If the
metaphor of creation here seems unwarranted, too cosmological in its
implications, I would defend its appropriateness by citing an important
passage from chapter 7 of the novel, a passage that, in the vivid sweep
of its imagery and the almost biblical sonority of its language, evokes
a world as if at its genesis. Just before the climax of *Intruder*, on his
way for the second time to Caledonia Chapel cemetery, Chick surveys
the entire county spread out before him, "the earth which had bred
his bones and those of his fathers for six generations," in a powerful,
panoramic moment of vision. As his uncle's car creeps "up and onto
the last crest, the plateau" where the Gowries bury their dead, Chick
sees

> his whole native land, his home . . . unfolding beneath him like a map
> in one slow soundless explosion: to the east ridge on green ridge tum-
> bling away toward Alabama and to the west and south the checkered
> fields and the woods flowing on into the blue and gauzed horizon be-
> yond which lay at last like a cloud the long wall of the levee and the
> great River itself flowing not merely from the north but out of the North
> circumscribing and outland—the umbilicus of America joining the soil
> which was his home to the parent which three generations ago it had
> failed in blood to repudiate; by turning his head he could see the faint
> stain of smoke which was town ten miles away and merely by looking
> ahead he could see the long reach of rich bottom land marked off into
> the big holdings, the plantations (one of which was Edmonds' where the
> present Edmonds and Lucas both had been born, stemming from the
> same grandfather) along their own little river (though even in his grand-
> father's memory steamboats had navigated it) and then the dense line of
> river jungle itself: and beyond that stretching away east and north and
> west not merely to where the ultimate headlands frowned back to back

upon the waste of the two oceans and the long barrier of Canada but to
the uttermost rim of earth itself, the North. (151–52)

Note how richly verbal and visual motifs intertwine here, as individual
features of the prospect, like plantations and rivers, immediately sprout
minor anecdotes of their own, little pictures spinning off a dozen or
a hundred words.[13] This great patchwork quilt of a landscape, though
"soundless" itself, is the visual equivalent—indeed the embodiment—
of all that Gavin has orally brought to life for Chick in his Yoknapatawpha tales and legends. Put simply, it is what the composite story that
is Yoknapatawpha looks like, and as such it stands as a tribute to the art
of storytelling. Let us not forget, moreover, that Stevens has literally as
well as figuratively driven the boy to this moment. Thanks to his uncle,
Chick can see his native land (and, we may infer, its inhabitants) anew,
from a wider, deeper, more mature perspective. This perspective in turn
informs mature action, action that might have remained unfocused
were it not directed within a meaningful context generated intersub-
jectively. All in all, Gavin's spoken stories and anecdotes instruct Chick
in communal values and assumptions even as they sometimes kindle
in him an urge to challenge these values and assumptions.[14]

   This is to say that the "rhetorical" Stevens whom Olga W. Vickery (in
one of the few early articles on Stevens still capable of provoking serious scholarly discussion) criticized for his use of language in *Intruder*
"as a buttress which threatens to imprison him even while it protects,"
already participates in the kind of "moral dialectic" for which Vickery
praises him in *Requiem for a Nun* ("Gavin Stevens" 2, 4).[15] The importance of distinguishing *Intruder*'s "two Gavins"—the overwrought
rhetor and the understated raconteur, whose discourse is not necessarily incompatible with dialectic—and of noting the linguistic basis of
this distinction, cannot be overemphasized.

   Keeping this in mind allows us to refine even the more insightful
critical comments on Stevens's dual role in the novel. Walter Taylor,
for instance, bisects Gavin into "a guide for Chick" and "a theorist
who could prophesy the future of [the] redeemed South as it took its
rightful place in the nation again" (156). Likewise, Vickery argues that
the Stevens character "divides neatly" into "the man" on one hand, a
"living, visible occupant of space . . . immersed in the flux of events,"
and "the voice" on the other, "the invisible embodiment of the rational

intellect" that plagues the set speeches ("Gavin Stevens" 1–2). These categories rest on an unstated opposition between (politically effectual) action and (politically futile) speech: guides and men accomplish something, theorists and voices do not. But in *Intruder*, guide and theorist, man and voice alike share a common linguistic existence. They are really *all* voices. The real issue is their use of language. As guide/man, Stevens relies on storytelling and anecdote, as theorist/voice on polemic. In *Intruder*, the question is not whether to use words, since language cannot be escaped, but how to use them, what to use them for. "Here," Morris observes, "one cannot say that language makes no contact with life" (225), but one must still decide what kind of contact it will make.

Why are speech and storytelling such important features of *Intruder*'s world? The reaction of Yoknapatawpha's white and black elements to the prospect of a Beauchamp lynching offers the beginnings of an answer. These passages are characterized by uneasy extremes of sound and silence that cry out for the conciliatory powers of story. We may remember, from the fate of Lee Goodwin in *Sanctuary*, the strange, thick, almost tangible silence that often in Faulkner accompanies the act of lynching itself. It does not bode well for Lucas, then, when, early in the novel, an ominous white welcoming committee gathers on the streets of Jefferson in eager, silent anticipation of his arrival at the jail. As Chick Mallison notes right away, the reticence of this "crowd which made no sound" (ID 43) signals its volatility and its purpose. "[S]uddenly the empty street was full of men. Yet there were not many of them, not two dozen, some suddenly *and quietly* from nowhere. Yet they seemed to fill it, block it, render it suddenly interdict as though not that nobody could pass them, pass through it, use it as a street but that nobody would dare, would even approach near enough to essay the gambit as people stay well away from a sign saying High Voltage or Explosive" (42; my emphasis). The town offers no outright approval of this mob-in-embryo and its pernicious silence, but Jefferson's own tight-lipped stance toward it indicates acquiescence and thus complicity. Likewise, the night Lucas is jailed, the night he is most likely to be lynched, the Square seems empty, but, as Chick later recalls, Jefferson "was not dead nor even abandoned but only withdrawn giving room to do what homely thing must be done in its own homely way" (214).

[I]t was not empty at all: a Sunday night but with more than Sunday
night's quiet, the sort of quiet in fact that no night had any business with
and of all nights Sunday night never . . . a sense not of waiting but of
incrementation, not of people—women and old folks and children—
but of men not so much grim as grave and not so much tense as quiet,
sitting quietly and not even talking much in back rooms and not just the
bath-cabinets and johns behind the barbershop and the shed behind the
poolhall stacked with soft drink cases and littered with empty whiskey
bottles but the stock-rooms of stores and garages and behind the drawn
shades of the offices themselves whose owners even the proprietors of the
stores and garages conceded to belong not to a trade but a profession, not
waiting for an event a moment in time to come to them but for a moment
in time when in almost volitionless concord they themselves would create
the event, preside at and even serve an instant which was . . . simply the
continuation of the one when the bullet struck Vinson Gowrie. (213–14)

The volatility first assigned to the mob alone now extends to the whole
town, and the passage makes clear that all levels of white male society
are implicated in Beauchamp's fate.

A pervasive silence also infects the black population, but with a different, though no less disturbing, valence. Here silence signals how
effectively white tyranny subjugates the black community. It is a product of terrorism. A black man whom we have first encountered as a
"voice" is accused of the most heinous of crimes, but when mute white
might makes right in Yoknapatawpha, this voice is not allowed to speak
in its own defense. Its silence, however, will be interpreted with pleasure by the white population as a sign of guilt. Given this double bind,
there seems little for the county's black residents to do other than to
wait out the cycle of injustice and cruelty and to avoid further needless
suffering, so, all over the county, in houses and cabins, black families
sit "quietly in the dark," "waiting for what sound what murmur of fury
and death to breathe the spring dark" (85). Similarly, the black inmates at the jail make "no sound of any sort" (56), huddling in their
cells "within elbow's touch whether they were actually touching or not
and certainly quiet, not laughing tonight nor talking either, sitting in
the dark and watching the top of the stairs because this would not be
the first time when to mobs of white men not only all black cats were

gray but they didn't always bother to count them either" (51). Even
in broad daylight two black convicts sit "quiet and motionless" in the
sheriff's car, all too aware of the white mob's indiscriminate thirst for
black blood (139). The quiet endurance depicted in these scenes, which
almost never fails to elicit Faulkner's admiration, is a stern rebuke to
the complicitous overtones of white silence.

No less threatening than this white silence is what we may call, acknowledging the cybernetic implications, the white noise of the mob.
Of course, even innocent gatherings of the Yoknapatawpha plain folk
are attended by a certain, healthy degree of noise and confusion. On
the most ordinary Saturday, after all, the throngs of squaregoers are
subjected to "the motion and the noise" of "radios and . . . automobiles," "jukeboxes" and "bellowing amplifiers," until "nowhere inside
the town's uttermost ultimate corporate rim should man woman or
child citizen or guest or stranger be threatened with one second of
silence" (237–38). In the lynch mob, however, we see a darker side
to this confusion, a "moil and mass of movement" that communicates
its desires not in language but in a kind of primal throb that bristles
with hostility, "one dense pulse and hum filling the Square" (135). This
is literally white noise, jamming communication and thereby preventing the emergence of critical voices that might question or otherwise
impede the unfolding drama of communal violence and retribution.
When individual voices do emerge from this background drone, they
tend merely to babble: "[A] car rushed from nowhere and circled the
Square; a voice, a young man's voice squalled from it—no words, not
even a shout: a squall significant and meaningless—and the car rushed
on around the Square, completing the circle back to nowhere and died
away" (49). Or they seethe with hatred, in a rhetoric so impoverished
that it can only repeat the same grating themes:

> 'They won't do nothing today. They're burying Vinson this afternoon and
> to burn a nigger right while the funeral's going on wouldn't be respectful
> to Vinson.'
>   'That's so. It'll probably be tonight.'
>   'On Sunday night?'
>   'Is that the Gowries' fault? Lucas ought to thought of that before he
> picked out Saturday to kill Vinson on.'

'I don't know about that. [Sheriff] Hope Hampton's going to be a hard
man to take a prisoner away from too.'

'A nigger murderer? Who in this county or state either is going to help
him protect a nigger that shoots white men in the back?'

'Or the South either.'

'Yes. Or the South either.'

This grim humor is all too common among Yoknapatawpha's white
natives, and Chick Mallison has "heard it all before" (40; compare 44–
45, 47–48, 80, 89). Even Gavin Stevens's polemical excesses of speech
may be preferable to the "paucity," as Faulkner calls it, of the mob vocabulary. As Morris demonstrates, this linguistic poverty "is the very
force of communal bonding" in *Intruder*, "reduc[ing] familiar reality . . .
to comfortable predictability" by forcibly excluding the eccentric along
with anything else not immediately convertible to short, handy formulas (224). As such it not only menaces Lucas but also exerts an "extraor-
dinary pressure" on Chick, Gavin, and all the other members of the
"discursive community," a pressure to acquiesce and to conform (222).

The effect of the mob's rhetorical tactics—silence one moment, babel
the next—is thus to subvert the possibilities of the kind of meaningful
discourse that might promote better understanding among Yoknapatawpha's black and white residents. This subversion is necessary at a
deep psychological level. The lynch rhetoric addresses itself to a fictive
but socially *speakable* (that is, conceivable) crime, a race murder per-
petrated by a member of the *wrong* (that is, the other) race. The white
mind of Yoknapatawpha is ready to acknowledge Beauchamp's act as
understandable "nigger" behavior, and to make the proper white response accordingly, with glares, hisses, invective, sick jokes, and finally
a bonfire of gasoline. On this view, the "nigger murderer" and the lynch
mob alike are only following the rules of a time-honored game (see ID
48–49). But Beauchamp is not the murderer, and there are hints in the
text that, early on, Beat Four may be aware of his innocence. If this is
true, then the fictive account of Vinson Gowrie's death that is allowed
to circulate throughout the county serves as a cover story, masking the
unspoken, and literally *unspeakable*, crime at the core of the novel,
Crawford Gowrie's act of fratricide.[16] This act did not happen. It cannot have happened. It must not be *said* to have happened. Even Miss

Habersham, one of the county's more liberal white minds, shudders to think of it: "He put his brother in quicksand" (231). The resonance of fratricide hits Yoknapatawpha too close to home, implicating it in universal (all murder is fratricidal) and regional (the Civil War was fratricidal) contexts of violence. Thus the white vigilantes, plotting the death of a black man whom they are incapable of recognizing as their brother, stand doubly implicated. Lucas they are ready to roast as a scapegoat offered against their own collective guilt, but Crawford, too uncomfortably like themselves, they can only repudiate.

Exposing the mob's hypocrisy and saving Beauchamp's life, however, are both contingent on unearthing the real crime,[17] naming the real murderer, and making the fact of Beauchamp's innocence "hearable over the demanding voices of societal expectation and individual desire" (Gwin 95)—in short, on speaking the unspeakable. This is where the novel's storytellers come in. The lynch rhetoric attempts to smother the hard fact of fratricide beneath oppressive layers of silence and cacophony, but Chick, Miss Habersham, Aleck Sander, Stevens, and, to some extent, Lucas himself, together overcome these obstacles and tell a story that forces Yoknapatawpha County, at least for a moment, to take stock of itself. They dare to speak of fratricide, to say, "It happened." *Intruder*'s modicum of social change thus rests upon a series of speech acts, in a way that challenges invidious distinctions between language and action. Storytelling is a form of moral action that can raise as well as reflect the consciousness of its audience. It can save lives.

. . . .

If the trial at which Gavin Stevens might have practiced his craft as a forensic storyteller in *Intruder* never materializes, this is not to say that the novel entirely begs the questions of law, judgment, and other forensic matters. *Intruder* does, however, tend to relocate these usually institutional issues at the level of individual action and decision-making. It is not difficult, for instance, to detect a pronounced forensic dimension in scenes such as the long passage, late in the novel, where Gavin and Chick try to figure out why the mob runs away after Beauchamp is exonerated (196–206). As this scene gradually unfolds, with Stevens's long periods punctuated by his nephew's blunt objections and interjections, it begins to suggest the structure of courtroom encounter, pushing the text toward what I would call an adversarial mode of discourse.

Rather than Lucas Beauchamp or Crawford Gowrie, however, it is the mob, and by extension all of Jefferson and Yoknapatawpha County, that is put on trial during these adversarial exchanges. Stevens claims that the crowd withdraws in frantic repudiation of the Gowrie fratricide, thus acknowledging as the first principle of all human conduct the injunction not to kill "thy mother's child" (200; emphasis removed). Chick, on the other hand, fears that the mob runs in order to duck the consequences of its terrible misjudgment of Beauchamp. He takes his uncle to task on this point.

> 'So for a lot of Gowries and Workitts to burn Lucas Beauchamp to
> death with gasoline for something he didn't even do is one thing but for
> a Gowrie to murder his brother is another.'
> 'Yes,' his uncle said.
> 'You cant say that,' he said. (ID 200)

Chick's short rebuttal is rhetorically effective. Its concision connotes moral conviction. It is ironic to see Lucas Beauchamp's hired advocate arguing here in support of Beauchamp's would-be lynchers, but Stevens's intent in this trial-of-sorts is to defend the mob. By contrast, Chick plays a dual role, for if his cynical assessment of the mob seems "prosecutorial," as it were, he also—since the narrative viewpoint of the novel works to render all "verdicts" finally his—presides as judge and jury over the exchanges with Gavin.[18]

His decision, let there be no doubt, goes against the mob. Chick's words communicate his own position firmly: " 'They ran,' " he says, "calm and completely final, not even contemptuous" (204). Having pronounced his deeply flawed fellow countrymen guilty of bigotry and hypocrisy, however, the boy must also decide whether to treat them with contempt or with clemency. This question is at the heart of all acts of judgment, and young Mallison faces it squarely, thanks in part to his uncle. Gavin Stevens's pleas on behalf of the mob, though they do not clear it of the charges Chick brings against it, appear to have this ultimately beneficial effect: as pleas above all for leniency, they steer his nephew away from a self-righteous repudiation of his peers toward an acceptance of their flaws as symptomatic of human fallibility in general. This acceptance, however, is not to be mistaken for an endorsement or an excuse. The text forcefully depicts it as a "fierce desire" on Chick's part that his fellow Yoknapatawphans "should be perfect because they were his and he was theirs," a

> furious intolerance of any one single jot or tittle less than absolute perfection—that furious almost instinctive leap and spring to defend them from anyone anywhere so that he might excoriate them himself without mercy since they were his own and he wanted no more save to stand with them unalterable and impregnable: one shame if shame must be, one expiation since expiation must surely be but above all one unalterable durable impregnable one: one people one heart one land. (ID 209–10)

Phrases like "furious intolerance" and "without mercy" may obscure the fact that Chick elects to retain his place in the community, leading from within in the tradition of Cincinnatus and the Cincinnatus-at-law. Rather than lecture to Yoknapatawpha from some Archimedean point of moral superiority, he will converse with it, argue with it, perhaps even redeem it, from the inside.[19] This inclination toward tolerance seems inspired at least in part by his uncle's ability to empathize with even the more culpable members of the community—an ability (one is tempted to say, a negative capability) that is a prerequisite for lawyers, who typically represent a range of clients and interests.[20]

These issues acquire a larger resonance when we remind ourselves that Chick has struggled against the desire to repudiate from the very beginning of *Intruder*. It could be argued, for instance, that the novel's opening scene presents Chick as an incipient member of the mob rather than its prime antagonist. Recall that, on the "Sunday morning when the sheriff reached the jail with Lucas Beauchamp," Chick "was there, waiting. *He was the first one*, standing lounging trying to look occupied or at least innocent, under the shed in front of the closed blacksmith's shop across the street from the jail *where his uncle would be less likely to see him* if or rather when he crossed the Square toward the postoffice for the eleven oclock mail" (3; my emphasis). Is this behavior conscientious, suspicious, or merely ambivalent? What exactly is Chick "the first one" *of* or *to do*? The first person at all to await Beauchamp's arrival—a harbinger of Chick's leadership later in the novel? Or, more ominously, the first member of the gathering crowd that will menace Beauchamp in front of the jail and afterward? Further, why is Chick hiding from his uncle? Because Gavin, fearing for his nephew's safety, might order him home? Or because Chick shares the budding mob's hostility toward Lucas and is ashamed lest his uncle discover this fact? Which way is Chick leaning here? There is just enough uncertainty on this issue to problematize Chick's relation to the mob and thus to problematize in turn any opinions he may later offer about it.

On several other early occasions, Chick is tempted to disavow the debt he incurred at Lucas Beauchamp's cabin and declare himself "free" of the old man. Even after Beauchamp's arrest, when the stakes have been raised substantially, Chick plans to saddle his horse and ride directly away from town until he knows that the seemingly inevitable lynching is done (35, 41, 67, 137–38). That he rides his horse instead to the Gowrie burial ground, in acknowledgment of his responsibility to Lucas, only confirms his disdain for the mob, whose ostensible repudiation of Crawford Gowrie masks a deeper unwillingness to ask forgiveness from Lucas for its mistaken appraisal of him. In contrast to Chick, that is, the mob owes a debt to Beauchamp it does not make good on.

To repudiate the mob, however, would only be to repeat its error, the error Chick has earlier resisted. With help from his uncle, he resists it again.[21] The adversarial struggle to understand the events around the town square thus works ultimately to everyone's benefit, as Vickery notes: "[t]he reconciliation of the ideas of uncle and nephew comes when each admits the justice and cogency of the other's position." While Stevens "is forced to recognize that his defense of the South rests necessarily on the actions of Chick, Miss Habersham, and Aleck Sander, all of whom have defied and so transcended and revivified the social norm," Mallison comes to understand "that his moral impulses must be exercised within the social framework" (*The Novels of William Faulkner* 143). And the members of the mob, despite their culpability, are to be neither repudiated nor banished.

. . . .

The latent forensic dimension of Chick's and Gavin's adversarial debate in chapter 9 cannot altogether offset the virtual absence from *Intruder* of forensic procedure. The reader of this novel enters a world of crime and punishment, accusation and acquittal, but also a world devoid of trial. The Beauchamp trial, of course, never materializes, but neither does a Gowrie trial, since Crawford, in a handy bit of poetic justice, commits suicide with the murder weapon. In both instances the

scales of justice are squared by events that take place outside the courtroom. The absence of any kind of institutional context for law insures
the malfunction, or the outright disappearance, of judicial theater, the
cultural spectacle of courtroom performance by means of which communities enact, sanction, and celebrate their history, their values, and
their promised continuity. "It is the function of this drama," writes
legal scholar Milner Ball, "to provide an image of legitimate society"
as well as "a continuous way of saying . . . 'what the law is' " (62). One
important corollary of this is that in every act of courtroom litigation,
the entire community is in a sense also on trial.

The image of Yoknapatawpha society that emerges from *Intruder*'s
judicial theater is not a flattering one. For most of the novel, the town
square serves as an arena for a communal performance that is typical
of what Ball calls judicial "saturnalia," which arises when legal procedure degenerates into "an extravagant entertainment or orgy . . . in
which all are participants." Saturnalian "mob scenes and the gathering and release of passion" threaten to "overrun reasoned deliberation
and reduce the potential for protecting defendants' rights" (56). This
is more or less what happens in *Intruder*, whose would-be lynch mob
hijacks due process in the name of a thinly disguised vigilantism, never
even allowing the Beauchamp case to reach its proper courtroom setting. This mob script would carry the day but for the intervention of
Chick Mallison and his cohorts, who have a different kind of judicial
theater, and an altogether different notion of justice, in mind.

Appropriately, the text articulates these two positions by means of
a series of theatrical metaphors. Among "the amphitheatric lightless
stores" of the town square (ID 49), outside the "lighted stage" of the
jailhouse (83), men and women (but "not one child") gather to await
the performance of a lynching, which it is the duty of the Gowries to
initiate but in which, once it has begun, even the spectators plan to join
in saturnalian fashion. Faulkner explicitly compares this moment to
"the before-curtain in a theater," only to revise the theatrical analogy a
few lines later in a specifically forensic direction: "no crowd now waiting for the curtain to rise on a stage's illusion but rather the one in
the courtroom waiting for the sheriff's officer to cry Oyez Oyez Oyez
This honorable court" (136–37)—though this mockery of judicial theater is scheduled to take place in front of the courthouse rather than

inside it. Meanwhile, the distinctions continue to blur between actors and onlookers in the spectacle.

The next time we visit Jefferson, however, things are different. Vinson Gowrie's body has been exhumed, Crawford Gowrie has been implicated in his brother's murder, and Lucas has been exonerated. As a result, the terms of the drama played out around the amphitheatrical square have altered significantly. What had threatened to become a misguided revenge tragedy has yielded to low farce, in which the fleeing mob dubiously assumes the leading role. On every side of Chick Mallison, the principal witness to this spectacle of shame, are faces in flight and automobiles roaring away frantically, "crossing the mouth of the alley *like across a stage.*" Again Faulkner repeats the comparison, drives it home: "[A]nother turn to the left into the next cross street and there they were again fleeing *across that proscenium* too unbroken and breakless" (185–86; my emphasis). Note how the theatrical metaphors in this passage have shifted subtly from the earlier one: no longer before the stage, as bloodthirsty audience, the mob is now onstage, fully in view, on trial, if you will. It has replaced Lucas as the central object of communal inspection. Worst of all, it can no longer guard its anonymity, so it simply flees. In renouncing Crawford Gowrie and his abominable act, however, it also repudiates its own existence, its own narrowly averted fratricidal design against Lucas.

Indeed, as Morris has brilliantly explained, the inability of white Yoknapatawphans to see a lynching as a fratricide—to see a black man as a brother—not only enables their violence against him but also exposes Yoknapatawpha as a community in which the transition, explored by Freud in *Totem and Taboo*, from the primal horde to more modern and inclusive modes of social organization, is still largely incomplete (231–34). In *Intruder*, that is, the specific taboo against fratricide (the fundamental social law of the fraternal clan) has not yet been universalized into an injunction against murder generally, or into the positive corollary of this injunction, the ideal of equal protection under the law (a founding principle of modern social existence). When the word "brother" can be understood as a social term as well as an exclusively familial or genetic one, there will no longer be any difference in Yoknapatawpha's eyes between the act that the mob wishes to perform upon Lucas Beauchamp and the act that Crawford Gowrie does perform upon his brother Vinson. Yoknapatawphans will no longer be separated into "murderable" (others) and "unmurderable" (brothers). This utopian moment, however, hovers somewhere in a very indefinite future. As Gavin Stevens wryly observes, "it wont be next Tuesday." But even so, Chick and his cohorts have still made a tentative first step toward universalizing and enriching the concept of brotherhood in Yoknapatawpha.

The closest thing to a healthy sense of judicial theater that emerges in *Intruder* is the therapeutic action of Chick Mallison and his saving remnant, who like the mob also work outside the law and the courtroom, but with the happy result of healing, at least for the time being, a community that cannot or will not heal itself. Once again, the text explicitly figures this performance in dramatic terms. After the mob has vacated the square, the stage is Chick's for the taking, the drama his to complete. Prompted by "cues" from his uncle, he soon resumes "his unfinished part in it" (197), walking the streets of Jefferson as if to reclaim that disputed territory from the enemy. As he does so, Chick experiences a mixture of pride, dominion, and finality, "like the actor looking from wings or perhaps empty balcony down upon the waiting stage vacant yet garnished and empty yet, nevertheless where in a moment now he will walk and posture in the last act's absolute cynosure, himself in himself nothing and maybe no world-beater of a play either but at least his to finish it, round it and put it away intact and unassailable, complete" (211). If, in making the Beauchamp interlude "his to finish," Chick appears to have supplanted not only Beat Four but also his storytelling uncle, it is only as the apprentice supplants the mentor who has taught him all he knows.

. . . .

The menacing crowd of would-be vigilantes that Chick helps to humble is reminiscent of the even more volatile *posse comitatus* that takes justice into its own hands at the Lee Goodwin trial in *Sanctuary*. In both novels the mob members are depicted as the violent alter egos of the plain folk who routinely mill about the town square on weekends and stock-auction days (compare ID 135–36 and 235–38 with S 107–8 and 273–74). But *Sanctuary*'s mob makes good on its threat to lynch an innocent man, while *Intruder*'s planned lynching is averted. This contrast in turn reflects upon the lawyer characters depicted in the two novels. *Sanctuary*'s Horace Benbow is powerless to stop the mob's violent miscarriage of justice, while *Intruder*'s Gavin Stevens, thanks in large part to his nephew and tutee, is not. Rather than face up to his ineffectuality—or, perhaps, as a way of admitting it—Benbow retires to Kinston, where we lose sight of him permanently. Like every other important character in *Sanctuary*, he is ultimately exiled from Jefferson. Stevens, on the other hand, remains in his town square office as *Intruder* comes to a close, still at the center of community life. Chick Mallison is also there, an exemplary member of the community he almost repudiated: a Cincinnatus-at-large joining the Cincinnatus-at-law. So is Lucas Beauchamp, the falsely accused "criminal" who, unlike Lee Goodwin, is reintegrated into the community, where he can continue to illustrate and inculcate "the non-negotiable responsibilities of human interchange" to Chick, Gavin, and other Yoknapatawphans, to teach them all "what a receipt is" (Gwin 96). *Intruder*'s relatively happy ending affirms the power of storytelling and responsible citizenship to create and sustain the conditions that make judicial theater and moral conduct possible. Viewed against the inarticulate Benbow's pervasive problems with language, the achievement of Gavin Stevens—and the nephew who takes after him—is not least of all the victory of a lawyer-citizen and raconteur over the divisive forces of "injustice and outrage and dishonor and shame" he encounters all too often in those around him and even, in weaker moments, in himself.

. . . .

CHAPTER FOUR

Colloquial Detection; or, "Discovering It by Accident" in *Knight's Gambit*

At the center of Faulkner's forensic trilogy, *Knight's Gambit* (1949) is the only full-length Faulkner work in which Yoknapatawpha's best-known lawyer-citizen is unequivocally the central character. The presence of Gavin Stevens in the six whodunits (the title story, in which a murder is averted, might be more aptly labeled a "who-tried-it") supplies the volume with a basic unity and coherence, "an integrated form of its own" (SL 266) reinforced by the presence of the structural and generic conventions of detective fiction in each tale. Recent critical work has revealed even deeper, more sophisticated themes underlying and unifying the collection. All six stories, for instance, are driven by agrarian values that emphasize the importance of land, family, and community, values endangered by hostile, invading outlanders, whose threat is in turn ultimately neutralized by the local detective figure.[1] Indeed, as Michael Grimwood has demonstrated, it is quite often the would-be interloper's ignorance of some slice of rural arcana that allows him to be intercepted by Gavin Stevens and other knowing agrarian insiders (*Heart in Conflict* 201–2). In one story everything rests on the relatively simple matter of mixing a toddy, in another on running a trotline for catfish, in a third, on an exotic brand of "city cigarette," and in yet another, on local hearsay about a killer stallion.

Knight's Gambit asks new questions of Gavin Stevens, develops new sides of his character, and pursues the links among storytelling, forensic work, responsible citizenship, and detection in Yoknapatawpha County. In this anthology-novel[2] the narrative, rhetorical, social, and even theatrical skills that are the stock in trade of the Faulknerian forensic figure turn out to be prerequisites for competent sleuthing in and around Jefferson. By virtue of these skills, Gavin Stevens emerges as suited to detective work in a way that Horace Benbow, so abysmal a failure at both investigation and litigation in *Sanctuary*, never was. The modus operandi of Detective Stevens in this volume, however, is not exactly conventional.[5]

Stevens of course has already played a prominent part in the gripping crime plot of *Intruder in the Dust*, but it would be misleading to call his role there that of a detective. That title is more appropriately reserved for Chick Mallison, Aleck Sander, and Miss Habersham, the unlikely trio whose midnight heroics at Caledonia Chapel cemetery set the wheels of discovery and justice in motion. *Intruder* could not iterate more clearly that, in a social climate dominated and indeed terrorized by white hegemony, the call to detection assumes a distinct moral valence. Exhuming the bigotry, hypocrisy, violence, and other taboos buried beneath the oppressive white surface of things is certainly an epistemological quest for Chick and his fellow reformers, as are all forays into detection, but it is also an ethical one; and insofar as Gavin Stevens declines to participate in this effort—and continues to decline until Lucas Beauchamp's innocence is undeniable—he is guilty of a damaging irresponsibility, or even apathy. What redeems Stevens, as I argue in chapter 3, is his storytelling. If he cannot rouse himself to action quickly enough to suit Chick Mallison or the reader, the lifetime of local apocrypha he passes on to his nephew, in the form of story, legend, and anecdote, has its own latent ethos, and this solid grounding in Yoknapatawpha lore helps trigger the boy's moral awakening.

Knight's Gambit, however, finds Chick Mallison in an ancillary role (in the four stories in which he appears) and Gavin Stevens firmly at center stage. Stevens fares well as an amateur sleuth and agent of justice in these tales, solving—or at least re-solving—all six of his cases. Yet some readers have been left with the nagging feeling that Gavin's victories are not really earned, that there is an annoying tendency throughout *Knight's Gambit* for important leads to drop more or less unsolicited into his lap, thus absolving him at once of the ratiocinative ingenuity we tend to expect from the heroes and heroines of conventional detective fiction, and of the more mundane behind-the-scenes labors of the ordinary gumshoe. William C. Doster has complained of *Knight's Gambit* that Stevens ferrets out felons "without any of the difficult leg work which goes along with routine police activity," letting others like Chick Mallison run his errands for him while he "sits in the ivory tower of his study, thinking, thinking, thinking and talking, talking, talking" (191–92). Even an admiring critic observes of the story "Monk" that "as a detective" Stevens "discovers nothing; he stumbles across the truth by accident," "a gross infringement" of the rules of detective fiction (Gidley 105–6).

Nor is this observation true of "Monk" alone. In "Smoke," we recall from chapter 2, the county attorney receives his most important information from a casual tête-à-tête with a garrulous pharmacist. In "Tomorrow," Stevens requires only a pair of porchside chats with cooperative country folk to figure out why a jury remains inexplicably hung. The murder plot of "Knight's Gambit" is exposed as a result of a chance encounter around the town square. "Hand upon the Waters," a more conventional detective tale in which Stevens exhibits keen powers of observation and deduction, is nonetheless set in motion by a sentimental, and rather coincidental, impulse to attend a rural funeral. Even "An Error in Chemistry," which won second prize in a mystery magazine contest as a "story of almost pure detection" (quoted in Gidley 110), hinges upon an unlucky accident that exposes the villain.

If detective skill is no more than a happy facility for being in the right place at the right time, if luck and coincidence (and an unprotesting errand boy) are the major forces behind the unraveling of mystery, then the value of the individual stories is compromised and the integrity of the volume threatened. Precisely this reservation may have prompted Irving Howe's complaint that "the detective apparatus gets in the way of Faulkner's meaning" ("Minor Faulkner" 473), or Edmund Wilson's assessment of the detective plots as "implausible and, for Faulkner, a little cheap" ("Faulkner and Henley" 58), or Ruth Chapin's rather ambivalent remarks on the "special circumstantial knowledge" that wraps up each case (20).

One cannot deny the truth of these allegations, but one can choose to assign a different valence to them. The trouble with the contempt of critics such as Doster for Stevens and his "talking, talking, talking" is not that this description of Gavin's working habits is wrong per se, but that the conclusions drawn from it (that a "talking" detective is necessarily inferior to an "active" one who does "leg work," and that for this reason Stevens, despite his successes, deserves no respect) rest upon subjective assumptions about the relative value of speech versus other modes of action, assumptions that are open to debate and that in the context of *Knight's Gambit* are simply misguided. One of the central premises of this entire study is that the tired "speech-action" dichotomy is irrelevant and indeed invidious when applied to the professional and personal activity of lawyers, who act principally by talking and writing. For the litigator such as Gavin Stevens especially, speech is profoundly performative, the prevailing instrument of forensic power. Men and women at law, after all, daily find themselves in situations where spoken words and stories have the most immediate, palpable impact upon the lives of clients, antagonists, and other fellow citizens.

Nor should we necessarily expect (or desire) this state of things to change when the lawyer turns to detection. Here, too, the lawyer's facility with language, rather than an impediment, proves to be an ally. What is Doster's mythical "leg work" anyway but the largely verbal task of corroborating existing accounts of the facts and soliciting new stories and interlocutors—that is, a means of pursuing dialogue? (Perhaps "ear work" would be a more accurate, if slightly belabored, term.) For that matter, don't the sudden flashes of deductive genius we value so highly in our fictional and real-life detectives usually depart from quite ordinary premises, premises themselves generated by the patient, labor-intensive, socratic task of talking, talking, talking—asking trenchant questions, then listening carefully for the many levels of meaning behind answers? In a recent interview, filmmaker and former private investigator Errol Morris, who wrote and directed the award-winning documentary *The Thin Blue Line* (1988), confessed that what made him a good detective, indeed "what good detectives are all about," is "the ability to get people to talk to you and to listen to what they have to say" (Dennison 10). Approaching the issue in this way, one can begin to understand the ways in which litigation and detection are actually quite complementary practices.

Such anyway is the case with *Knight's Gambit*, a volume in which the poetics of detection, along with the particular work ethic of County Attorney Stevens, revolves less around the power of ratiocination than the power of conversation, the reciprocal give and take that ranges from interrogation to full-blown storytelling. Here the law office is no mere ivory tower where Prufrocks-at-law find shelter from the untidy business of reality. Rather, as if deliberately to refute this allegation,

Faulkner opens *Knight's Gambit* with a story in which reality marches obtrusively into the law office, revealing it as an important locus of detection in its own right. In "Smoke," the chambers of Judge Dukinfield (himself a lawyer-detective investigating a suspicious will) become the scene of a murder and also the site of an inquest, conducted by Gavin Stevens before a grand jury. In this emblematic fashion, Faulkner prepares us from the outset to accept the lawyer-detective as a figure who uses language to enter and order his world rather than to retreat from it. That language is capable of both functions is a point too often overlooked in Faulkner criticism, where Faulkner's intellectual, moralistic, and other essentially verbal characters are frequently condemned across the board, in a kind of knee-jerk reaction denying words any validity as praxis.[4] Not all words are empty, however, and few knew better than Faulkner their creative and performative values.

Seen in this light, as the result of accomplished linguistic performances, the "accidental" discoveries of Gavin Stevens command new respect. To dismiss them as chance is to downplay the hand Stevens has in his own luck. For even the anecdotal evidence that descends upon Gavin as if by special dispensation is meaningless unless recognized as significant by the lawyer-detective and incorporated within the larger rhetorical framework of the case. The acts of listening and remembering are thus at the heart of what I call *colloquial detection*, as practiced in the *Knight's Gambit* stories: in any tightly knit community, such as Jefferson and its environs, where information tends to circulate orally, it is expedient to note and remember as much as possible of what one (over)hears, since hindsight not infrequently converts this circumstantial material into the stuff of evidence. Thus in using the term *colloquial* I mean to emphasize at least two of its senses. First, many of the most important instances of detection arise out of encounters among the plain folk characterized by the kind of informality we call colloquial. Second, Stevens typically solicits and receives information by means of colloquy, or conversation, itself. The most elementary plot summary I can think of that still does justice to the *Knight's Gambit* tales is the following: Stevens hears stories, and he uses them to solve crimes. What this simple narrative omits (and thus assumes) is the sophisticated ability on Gavin's part to make sometimes fragmentary and often unmemorable moments of casual discourse signify as clues. And this peculiar gift is the product at least in part of Gavin's lifelong traffic in stories at every level of Yoknapatawpha society, from "discuss[ing] Einstein with college professors" to "spen[ding] whole afternoons among the squatting men against the walls of country stores, talking to them in their idiom" (KG 16). Colloquial detection thus emerges both as a mode and as a product of conscientious involvement in community life. As such, it could be argued that the Cincinnatus paradigm informs the conduct of the Yoknapatawpha sleuth as well as the Yoknapatawpha lawyer.

In "Smoke" (1932), for instance, a story that I discuss at length in chapter 2, we encounter a textbook exercise in colloquial detection. On a routine visit to the local drugstore for some pipe tobacco, Gavin Stevens happens to hear a chilling story involving Dr. West (the druggist) and a silent, dangerous-looking stranger who smokes a little-known brand of "city cigarettes" (26–27). It may be on the same visit that West tells Stevens that a local farmer named Granby Dodge has recently "bought enough rat poison to kill three elephants" (34). And from another interlocutor Stevens learns that the roadster belonging to West's eerie customer has been seen at Dodge's farm (28). From these hints Stevens fills in the blanks: Dodge has murdered old Anselm Holland, hired the city stranger to kill the probate judge when the latter grows suspicious, and bought the rat poison to use on the heir to the Holland land, Virginius Holland, whose will names his cousin Granby as beneficiary and executor (33–34). By revealing this information at the inquest into Dukinfield's murder, in the form of a carefully crafted, suspenseful, dramatic story, Stevens leads Dodge to expose himself.

Grimwood claims that "Smoke" is a parable of the triumph of agrarian solidarity over grasping exogenous forces which threaten "the hereditary transmission of property" (*Heart in Conflict* 198; and see 195–203 generally). There is an equally important tension at work in the story between speech and silence, a tension that amounts to a structural opposition. The Memphis hit man, for example, is characterized above all by his stealth. Dr. West mentions his "still way of talking" (KG 27), and if the narrator is to be believed, this hired thug is the first person ever to slip into Judge Dukinfield's chambers without rousing the perpetually dozing janitor stationed just outside the judge's door (14). Likewise, Granby Dodge is described as "a man of infrequent speech" (19), faint of voice and overcome by an "excruciating desire for effacement" (28) in his rare moments of discourse. Ironically, however, these silent accomplices find in the end that their reticence works against them. For in the colloquial environment of Yoknapatawpha, silence aggressively advertises difference, thereby engendering profound, visceral suspicion. West's reaction to the Memphis hood is a case in point. What especially disturbs the good doctor is the fact that "he never heard or saw the man at all until he looked up and the man was just across the counter, so close that it made him jump" (27). But West's instinctive decision to make this encounter the subject of a conversation, and to choose Stevens as his interlocutor, proves a most effective means of neutralizing the stranger's threat. The moral is clear: the spoken word circumvents the silent avatars of rapacity and violence, and the task of keeping peace in the polis falls to storytellers and colloquial detectives.

Nor do the lawyer-detective's responsibilities end here. There is no doubt a certain aesthetic pleasure that comes from weaving together the strands of information one gleans colloquially into narratives of guilt and transgression. This pleasure closely approximates that of the literary creator or even the *bricoleur*[5]—since crimes, "constructed" by criminals, can only be re-constructed (or, on rarer and more fortunate occasions, de-constructed) by the would-be sleuth, out of whatever fragments of evidence are available. This private satisfaction must be matched, however, with a willingness to turn one's stories to public use, to speak out against the guilty and, perhaps even more important, to speak on behalf of the innocent, the victimized, the falsely accused. For in the oral economy of Yoknapatawpha County, as in the courtroom itself, inarticulateness is a handicap conceivably even more damaging than actual guilt. Here is where the courtroom lawyer's experience as an advocate must supplement the detective's investigative talents. The courtroom is by definition that forum where all members of a society are guaranteed the right to tell their stories: "draw near and you shall be heard," goes the cry of *oyez* that opens court sessions. As a litigator, Gavin Stevens is trained to be a custodian of that right. And to his credit, his acts of advocacy are not confined to the courtroom. In story after story, Stevens offers his voice in service of the voiceless, the muted, the marginal, and the inarticulate. By discovering and telling their stories, Stevens exonerates, vindicates, or simply protects these characters, though there are times when his real goal is merely to understand them.

Faulkner also stresses the importance of colloquial detection by negative example. *Knight's Gambit* features a number of parodic inversions of the lawyer-detective. These pathological figures are not lawyers themselves, nor detectives, but rhetors who deliberately exploit their communicative skills for subversive or even destructive ends. They, and not Gavin Stevens, are the real demagogues in this volume. Bill Terrel, the convicted murderer who is the principal villain of "Monk," is perhaps the most glaring example of these malevolent raconteurs. Terrel is elected to speak for his fellow inmates at a meeting of the Pardon Board, in a parody of forensic advocacy. But, as Gavin Stevens discovers, Terrel is also capable of a more malignant strain of discourse, whose imagery of freedom and tilling the soil so beguiles poor Monk Odlethrop that Monk, who had been happy enough in prison, murders his only real friend (and Terrel's bitter enemy), the warden, in a quixotic attempt to "go out into the free world, and farm" (49). In best demagogic fashion, that is, Terrel's populist rhetoric simultaneously conceals and serves his ruthless self-interest. Another one of the volume's rhetoricians-gone-wrong, Joel Flint of "An Error in Chemistry," authors a scheme of murder and fraud that hinges upon impersonation and persuasion. Flint, a former escape artist whose stage name was Signor Canova, correctly perceives himself as the antitype of Gavin Stevens, since the lawyer, in the courtroom at least, is also something of an illusionist, an exponent of verisimilitude. Out of vanity and bravura, then, Flint engineers a climactic showdown with Stevens, who ultimately sees through his performance. By concocting false stories and scenarios or imposing incriminating fictions upon innocent scapegoats, characters such as Terrel and Flint/Canova serve their own corrupt ends while directing suspicion away from themselves. It is up to the lawyer-detective to expose and counter the threat of these figures by penetrating to the real stories behind their convincing distortions.

Moreover, we should not overlook the fact that the lawyer-protagonist of *Knight's Gambit* happens to be an elected official as well as a detective. ("Tomorrow," which documents the first case Stevens ever argues, is the exception that proves the rule.) His actions are thus inscribed inescapably in a public context. Not that the prosecutor's public persona necessarily compromises the detective's effectiveness, for Gavin is in no sense a *private* investigator. It can be argued, in fact, that his ability to canvass his constituents for information as well as for votes is one of the major sources of his effectiveness.

There are, however, other difficulties that attend Gavin's particular form of public service. As county attorney, he owes his allegiance to two masters, the law he has sworn to uphold and the people who have elected him. This double allegiance has been implicit in American rhetoric from the earliest days of the republic, when Thomas Paine asserted that "in America the law is king" and the Framers almost simultaneously declared the people sovereign. These closely related principles are not altogether free from tension, however, and the stories of *Knight's Gambit* acknowledge as much in several instances where the law threatens the rights and interests of individuals.

Monk Odlethrop, for instance, is sentenced to life in prison for a murder he did not commit, then hanged for another killing of which he is at most the unwitting instrument. Similarly, Jackson Fentry of "Tomorrow" is stripped of his foster son by the boy's uncles because, as a bystander tells poor Fentry, "They got the law" on their side (KG 102).[6] Cases like these demand of the lawyer-detective a readiness to resist the dominion of the symbolic order, to bend, overrule, or otherwise look past the law in order to avert or amend injustice. Once again Gavin Stevens, who understands that a lawyer must be as "interested in justice and human beings" as he is in his lawbooks (KG 111), is the man for the job. Stevens is willing when necessary to let his empathy and intuition outweigh a strict adherence to procedural rules. On this view law is less a reified code of conduct than the living action of a community and its members, a cultural conversation that takes place not in the courts alone but along folkways and speechways, the vital lines of contact that at once constitute and perpetuate social life. The loss of this larger perspective is one of the attendant dangers of the specialization and compartmentalization that have come to dominate the practice of law over the last century. Stevens, however, largely avoids this danger. He manages to observe the spirit as well as the letter of the law in Yoknapatawpha, as we shall see in more detail in the following analyses.

. . . .

No less exemplary than "Smoke" as a narrative of colloquial detection, and much more so as a narrative of advocacy, is the second story in *Knight's Gambit*, "Monk" (1937). The title character, Monk Odlethrop, is "a moron, almost a cretin" (KG 39) who comes to Jefferson from the pine hills of eastern Yoknapatawpha. After seven years in Jefferson, Monk is convicted of a murder he did not commit and sent to prison for life. Five years later, another man confesses to the crime, and Gavin

Stevens secures a pardon for Monk from the governor. Monk, however, does not want to leave prison. He seems to have found a sense of belonging there that was missing from his life in Jefferson, and Stevens honors his desire to stay. Within a week, however, Monk, "apparently leading an abortive jailbreak" and in the presence of fifty witnesses, kills the warden whom he had formerly loved and served with "doglike devotion" (47). The act seems utterly inexplicable, as does the condemned Monk's final, incredible non sequitur from the scaffold:

> He walked up . . . and stood where they told him to stand and held his
> head docilely (and without being asked) to one side so they could knot
> the rope comfortably, his face still serene, still exalted, and wearing that
> expression of someone waiting his chance to speak, until they stood
> back. He evidently took that to be his signal, because he said, 'I have
> sinned against God and man and now I have done paid it out with my
> suffering. And now—' they say he said this part loud, his voice clear and
> serene. The words must have sounded quite loud to him and irrefutable,
> and his heart uplifted, because he was talking inside the black cap now.
> 'And now I am going out into the free world, and farm.' (49)

Stevens fears that the key which links these events may never be found, but three years later he "discover[s] it by accident" (50), in the story's central episode of colloquial detective work. Stevens is a delegate sent to observe a meeting of the prison Pardon Board presided over by the state's corrupt governor, who is unapologetically selling pardons in exchange for political support (51). One of the inmates up for pardon, Bill Terrel, speaks on behalf of the entire prison population, but his pleas before the board echo almost exactly Monk's cryptic speech from the gallows. Instantly Stevens realizes that Terrel has somehow manipulated Monk with these words into killing Warden Gambrell. Stevens extracts the truth from Terrel in a private conference, thus confirming his suspicions. The story ends with rather cold comfort: Gavin cannot overturn the governor's self-serving decision to free Terrel, but he can use his knowledge of Terrel's complicity in the Gambrell murder as leverage against the convict, insuring his good behavior after his release.

It is worth mentioning that public service fosters detection in "Monk," in precisely the manner I have discussed earlier in this chap-

ter. In assuming the role of delegate, Stevens places himself in a position to (over)hear Terrel's speech. He thus furthers his own efforts
to link the incongruities of the Gambrell murder in a meaningful
way. Even more specifically, the lawyer's vision informs "Monk" on a
number of levels. Consider the story's opening paragraph, narrated by
Chick Mallison:

> I will have to try to tell about Monk. I mean, actually try—a deliberate
> attempt to bridge the inconsistencies in his brief and sordid and un-
> original history, to make something out of it, not only with the nebulous
> tools of supposition and inference and invention, but to employ these
> nebulous tools upon the nebulous and inexplicable material which he left
> behind him. Because it is only in literature that the paradoxical and even
> mutually negativing anecdotes in the history of a human heart can be
> juxtaposed and annealed by art into verisimilitude and credibility. (39)

Edmond L. Volpe has pointed out the affinities between storytelling and
detection in this passage ("Faulkner's 'Monk'" 87–88).[7] In addition,
however, we should not neglect the *forensic* dimension of the practices
described by Chick. It is not "only in literature" but in litigation as
well that inconsistencies must be bridged, that supposition, inference,
and invention must be employed to "make something out of" the inexplicable material of the past, and that "anecdotes in the history of a
human heart" are annealed into verisimilar stories. And just as rhetorical ability is perhaps the essential measure of courtroom competence in
Faulkner's world, it may be that forensic experience can in turn make
one a better storyteller. If this is so, Faulkner's choice of narrators for
"Monk" becomes especially significant. It is, after all, a lawyer, Gavin
Stevens, who supplies our narrator, Chick Mallison, with the main subject matter of his tale, and perhaps the shape and style of the story
as well. Further, the fact that Chick himself works in his uncle's law
office and is familiar with the Mississippi reports (55) indicates that
he entertains ambitions of practicing law and following in his uncle's
footsteps. As the collaborative effort of a working lawyer and a forensic
apprentice, then, "Monk" not only interrogates (at the level of theme)
the lawyer's rhetorical skills, it is also (at the level of structure) the
product of those skills.[8]

   If Chick seeks primarily to bridge the epistemological gaps that separate him from his subject, Monk Odlethrop's primary goal is to bridge

social ones. Throughout the story, this isolated individual engages in a series of frustrated attempts to connect himself with others. His early history reveals a gradual progress townward from the thinly populated pine hills to the east, and once he reaches Jefferson, he seems eager to be assimilated there, dressing in "cheap, bright town clothes" and "talkative when anyone would listen" (43). He enters the community, however, in only the most attenuated, strictly corporeal sense, and when he is found standing over a murdered man with a pistol in his hand, Jefferson immediately fabricates a narrative of his guilt, reading the murder as a last, misguided effort at assimilation by a man whose "imperfect connection between sense and ratiocination" (43) leaves him unable to comprehend societal rules. Thus he is allowed to enter that society only in a transgressive, indeed antisocial, role: as a murderer. It is, Chick explains, "as though the sound of the shot had broken the barrier behind which he had lived for twenty-five years and . . . he had now crossed the chasm into the world of living men by means of the dead body at his feet" (44). He is therefore assigned the fate of all such threats to society, to be "more completely removed and insulated from the world than any nun" (50). No sooner does he enter the community than he is forced to leave it.

In prison Monk comes across a rather different means of articulating his desire for connectedness, as evidenced by his final agrarian vision of free men working the soil together. This vision Volpe takes at face value as the central message of the story ("Faulkner's 'Monk' " 89–90), a reading that is to some extent supported by Chick Mallison, who believes that at his death Monk "establish[ed] at last that contact with the old, fecund, ponderable, travailing earth" he had been more or less instinctively seeking all his life (KG 44–45). The theory is an attractive one, since *Knight's Gambit* often alludes to the almost mystical power the land exerts over the simple farmer. But there are a number of ironies that limit our ability to accept the agrarian vision as ultimately a redemptive one for Monk. For one thing, as Chick realizes, Monk the agrarian has never practiced what he preaches. He doesn't know very much about farming, has no experience at it to speak of, and "could not have wanted to do it himself before, or he would have, since he could have found chances enough" in the cotton fields of Parchman farm (49).[9] Rather, as Gavin Stevens learns, the agrarian vision is foisted on Monk by Terrel, who has never farmed either. Monk's gallows homily thus emerges as a rhetorical ploy designed by Terrel to promote his own self-serving desire for freedom (Warden Gambrell has repeatedly blocked his parole). Further, we should not forget that Monk's ostensible desire to connect himself with the soil goes hand in hand with an equal desire "to bridge the hitherto abyss between himself and the living world, the world of living men" (40). Terrel's brand of agrarianism runs directly counter to both of these desires, cutting Monk and the warden off forever from the soil and from the world of the living. Any attempt to read Monk's speech uncritically or prescriptively runs into these problems.

But Monk, I think, knows better than Jefferson or Edmond Volpe that neither murder nor last-minute agrarian proselytizing will gain him acceptance in the human community. Rather, he intuitively realizes that it is above all language, and especially story, that connects individuals in the way he seeks. Storytelling, in fact, is just about the only such mode of connection with which Monk has ever had any experience. This experience dates from a childhood episode that is in many ways the story's primal scene.

> He had been to school in the country, for one year . . . but he did not
> stay. Perhaps even the first-grade work in a country school was too much
> for him. He told my uncle about it when the matter of his pardon came
> up. He did not remember just when, nor where the school was, nor why
> he had quit. But he did remember being there, because he had liked
> it. All he could remember was how they would all read together out of
> the books. He did not know what they were reading, because he did not
> know what the book said; he could not even write his name now. But he
> said it was fine to hold the book and hear all the voices together and then
> to feel (he said he could not hear his own voice) his voice too, along with
> the others, by the way his throat would buzz, he called it. (45–46)

This scene dramatizes at the most visceral, somatic, "buzzing" level the potential for story to transcend and eradicate social differences (the differences that mark the handicapped and the mentally impaired, for instance) and to incorporate even social outcasts into a community of "the book," one literally (if only briefly) constituted by and in the narrative act. From this brief moment of union onward, *telling*—a Benjy Compson-like "trying to say"—characterizes all of Monk's efforts to participate in group life. It is not so much the substance of what he says as the saying itself—and the hearing, the feeling of his voice among "all the voices together"—that represents the means of winning membership in a social world.

Once we have recognized this fact, some of Monk's most perverse behavior suddenly begins to make sense. His arrest for the first murder is, as he sees it, a welcome event. His guilt or innocence is a moot issue, for the immediate opportunity to address an audience outweighs the potential danger of an unjust conviction. The forum is what's important to him. Thus his incredible, utterly vague testimony against himself, testimony intended not as confession but simply, and far more urgently, as communication:

> Monk did not for a moment deny that he had killed the deceased. They could not keep him from affirming or even reiterating it, in fact. He was neither confessing nor boasting. It was almost as though he were trying to make a speech, to the people who held him beside the body until the deputy got there, to the deputy and to the jailor and to the other prisoners . . . and to the J.P. who arraigned him and the lawyer appointed by the Court and to the Court and the jury. Even an hour after the killing he could not seem to remember where it had happened; he could not even remember the man whom he affirmed that he had killed; he named as his victim (this on suggestion, prompting) several men who were alive, and even one who was present in the J.P.'s office at the time. But he never denied that he had killed somebody. It was not insistence; it was just a serene reiteration of the fact in that voice bright, eager, and sympathetic while he tried to make his speech, trying to tell them something of which they could make neither head nor tail and to which they refused to listen. (39–40)

Thus also his non sequiturish announcement, as the murder indictment is read against him, that "My name ain't Monk; it's Stonewall Jackson Odlethrop" (45). And thus his unlikely swan song on the scaffold. There, however, Monk's last words, which "must have sounded quite loud to him and irrefutable," are ironically muffled by the black hood that covers his head (49). These final garbled syllables become emblematic of all Monk's efforts to enter society via language. His life, with its parodic elements of confession, silence, and isolation, illuminates the rich array of connotations behind his nickname.

Since the unfortunate Odlethrop is too inarticulate to control his own stories, he is subject to (as well as the subject of) the stories of others. He thus becomes the principal victim of a narrative tyranny that pervades "Monk." From his earliest appearance in Jefferson, stories are imposed upon Monk almost at will. "[H]alf-rumored information about his origin" and upbringing begins to trickle in from the pine hills, tales of his noble grandmother, his shiftless father, and his "hard, bright, metallic" city woman of a mother (41), and further tales of the death of the grandmother and Monk's subsequent sojourn with an old bootlegger named Fraser (42–43). On reinspection, the first murder case emerges as a paradigm of narrative tyranny. The actual murderer is one of the dead man's companions on the night of the shooting, who creates a scapegoat by sheer narrative fiat: it is only on his death-bed that this man confesses to "fir[ing] the shot and thrust[ing] the pistol into Monk's hand, *telling Monk to look at what he had done*" and to offering perjured testimony against Monk (46; my emphasis). Institutions as well as individuals get into the act. The state of Mississippi's indictment against Monk (45) is a compact narrative document that bristles with presumptuous editorializing about Monk's state of mind. The ascription of malice aforethought to a moron seems particularly egregious.[10] Similarly, the Gambrell murder becomes front-page fodder for the Memphis papers (47), but the press seems content to grab its flashy headlines and retreat, leaving the larger context of the crime unexplored. Gambrell's murder, as we have already seen, is the product of Terrel's subtle narrative coercion, storytelling that kills rather than anneals. Terrel's confession to Gavin Stevens reveals with chilling clarity the power of his homely rhetoric.

'I told him [Monk]. I said here we all were, pore ignorant country folks that hadn't had no chance. That God had made to live outdoors in the free world and farm His land for Him; only we were pore and ignorant and didn't know it, and the rich folks wouldn't tell us until it was too late. That we were pore ignorant country folks that never saw a train before, getting on the train and nobody caring to tell us where to get off and farm in the free world like God wanted us to do, and that he [the warden] was the one that held us back, kept us locked up outen the free world to laugh at us agin the wishes of God. But I never told him [Monk] to do it. I just said, "And now we can't never get out because we ain't got no pistol. But if somebody had a pistol we would walk out into the free

world and farm it, because that's what God aimed for us to do and that's
what we want to do. Ain't that what we want to do?" and he said, "Yes.
That's it. That's what it is." And I said, "Only we ain't got nara pistol."
And he said, "I can get a pistol." ' (57–58)

Thus the trap of language snaps shut, and Monk, so desperate to be
integrated into *any* story, becomes the perfect dupe for this one.

Here, then, if ever there was one, is a man in need of advocacy. The
young, untested public defender who represents Monk at the first murder trial lacks the presence of mind even to plead mental incompetence
for his client. So the role of advocate devolves upon Yoknapatawpha's
public prosecutor, who, as in *Intruder in the Dust*, finds himself defending (though not in court) an innocent suspect. Gavin's support first
manifests itself in his efforts to gain a pardon for Monk, efforts that
are frustrated only by Monk's own decision to remain in the penitentiary (a decision that, incidentally, Stevens insists the prison officials
respect, thus signaling his own willingness to grant Monk full human
dignity and autonomy). Furthermore, while no one else appears to be
disturbed by the stubborn refusal of the events surrounding Warden
Gambrell's murder to "add up," Gavin continues to brood over the case
until the Pardon Board hearing, when the pieces finally fall into place.
During the gripping interview with Terrel, Stevens is still in some sense
speaking for Monk—representing his interests, protecting his memory, and ultimately clearing his name. And when he asks the governor
to deny Terrel's request for pardon, Stevens is similarly pleading in
Monk's behalf.

These efforts, of course, meet with mixed results: the governor refuses to hear Gavin out, Terrel goes free, and Odlethrop is not around
to enjoy being (partially) vindicated. The triumph of colloquial detection in "Monk" thus assumes a rather pyrrhic cast. Still, by breaking
through to the story behind the story, Gavin does to some extent res-
cue Monk from the posthumous ignominy to which society typically
condemns its murderers. Gavin's Monk is no inscrutable sociopath. He
is, to quote one of Faulkner's favorite writers, "one of us"—poor and
ignorant, innocent, wanting to belong, susceptible to the same kind of
demagoguery inside the penitentiary that the governor practices outside it. By passing Monk's story along to Chick Mallison, who in turn
hands it along to the reader, Gavin secures the sympathy of a small

but select audience for his friend. Such sympathy may be the most important example of advocacy at work in the story.

Moreover, in eliciting our sympathy for Monk, Gavin and Chick challenge us to back up that sympathy with action, to pore over the details of Monk's "brief and sordid and unoriginal history" in our own effort to discover new and deeper meaning there. Consider, for instance, the name with which Monk so puzzlingly rechristens himself at his trial: Stonewall Jackson Odlethrop. Only by acknowledging with Gavin that Monk is one of us can we fully appreciate the enormity of his tragedy: to be first betrayed and then destroyed by the very people to whom he so desperately wants to be connected. More martyr, in other words, than monk. No wonder then that he prophetically names himself after the greatest martyr of the Lost Cause, a man shot from the saddle by his own soldiers after being mistakenly identified as an enemy, a hostile invader. Whether the allusion is conscious, intuitive, or even arbitrary, the point is clear: is Stonewall Jackson's death really any more costly, his tragedy any more senseless, than Monk's own?

The gallows scene also repays closer scrutiny. It is entirely plausible that Monk, who actually has killed someone this time, would accept his punishment unprotestingly. Instead, he picks this moment to make the most memorable speech of his life, a speech in which he quotes verbatim the man who, whether Monk realizes it or not, has talked him into killing Warden Gambrell. In a wonderful bit of delayed irony, this act seals Terrel's doom. With his final words Monk leaves behind the clue that exposes the man responsible for Gambrell's death and for Monk's own. That clue merely awaits the right detective to discover it by accident.

The colloquial lawyer-detective emerges from "Monk" as the single ray of light in a legal system shot through with incompetence and abuse. He refuses to be an uncritical representative of that system. Compare Gavin Stevens, for instance, with Monk's first lawyer. That the latter, a "young man just admitted to the bar," is handed a murder case for what may be his very first trial, seems a dangerous indiscretion on the part of the judge who appoints him. It is also significant that the prosecutor at the trial is "a young District Attorney who had his eye on Congress" (39), a description that calls to mind *Sanctuary*'s Eustace Graham and the peculiar combination of malevolent rhetoric and Machiavellian forensics he stands for. The Pardon Board hearing is a further travesty of justice. The "puppet Board" itself, as Chick calls it, is basically a stacked jury, the governor a parodic judge whose rulings further his own political ends, as he quite candidly admits to Stevens (54).

How to contain such endemic corruption? Stevens is on the right track when he threatens to turn the governor's words against him, to repeat them in a public context—that is, to do precisely what Monk did to Terrel. The governor, however, will not be intimidated. As he claims, the votes he stands to lose from such allegations are votes he never had in the first place. But if Gavin cannot contain the governor's threat, he can at least contain Terrel's. First, Stevens silently allows Terrel to believe that his vote can block Terrel's pardon. Next, he trades this vote back to the convict for the inside account of Gambrell's death, which he then uses as leverage against Terrel. Unlike the governor, Terrel capitulates to the threat. Here, as in Poe's "Purloined Letter," silence supplants story, and the most effective form of information turns out to be withheld information. Stevens may take the law into his own hands, but his act seems necessary if the many miscarriages of justice in "Monk" are to be even partially redeemed. Here the lawyer-citizen's obligation to protect individual liberty, dignity, and expression (even Monk's homely form of it) overrides his allegiance to the formal institutions and representatives of law.

. . . .

Improbably enough, Stonewall Jackson Odlethrop finds a namesake in "Tomorrow" (1940), the fourth story of *Knight's Gambit*. Like Monk, Stonewall Jackson Fentry also hails from the Yoknapatawpha pine hills, is also cruelly mistreated by the legal system, and also, as we might by now anticipate, finds an advocate in Gavin Stevens. It should further be noted that "Tomorrow" contains the purest, most sustained examples of colloquial detection in all of *Knight's Gambit*. Nowhere in the volume is the art of listening emphasized more.

The story unfolds in two stages, the first of which finds Gavin Stevens back at work in the courtroom. Like Monk's young public defender, Stevens takes on a murder trial for his very first case out of law school. The case conforms to the agrarian paradigm Grimwood has described as common to all the *Knight's Gambit* stories. A threatening outlander "appear[s] overnight from nowhere" in the remote enclave of French-

man's Bend: Buck Thorpe, "a brawler" and "a gambler," as well as a
bootlegger and cattle thief. Even worse in this homogeneous farming
community, Thorpe is "kinless" (86). Moreover, he is one of the parodic, destructive rhetor figures described earlier in this chapter. With his
"daring and glib tongue," and with an obvious eye on her inheritance,
he seduces the daughter of a prosperous local farmer named Bookwright. As the daughter prepares to elope, however, there is a confrontation between Bookwright and Thorpe, and the former kills the latter
in what seems to be self-defense. When the village subsequently learns
that Thorpe was already married at the time of his death, Bookwright
becomes an even more sympathetic figure. (Note how this emerging
community narrative legitimates violence against the outlander, and in
service of sexual orthodoxy.) Few believe Bookwright will come to trial
at all, and even when he is indicted for murder, his acquittal seems a
certainty.

Gavin's defense of Bookwright gives him the opportunity to make
an eloquent speech before the jury of farmers and storekeepers, and
it also gives Chick Mallison, who is once again our narrator, an occasion to pay tribute to his uncle's forensic acumen: "although he had
been talking to them for only a year, he could already talk so that
all the people in our country—the Negroes, the hill people, the rich
flatland plantation owners—understood what he said" (87). With this
accommodating rhetoric Gavin presents himself to the jurors as one of
their own, and his strategy is to present Bookwright the same way, as
a "human being" who was "faced by a problem" and who "solved that
problem to the best of his ability and beliefs, asking help of no one,
and then abode by his decision and his act" (87–88). The assistant district attorney who prosecutes the case essentially concedes it, offering
in place of a closing statement only a Eustace Graham–like bow. The
gallery awaits the inevitable "not guilty" verdict.

Thus far "Tomorrow" holds little if any mystery. We know who killed
Thorpe, and we know his motive. The mystery arrives with the news
that Gavin's jury is hung by a single man. Acknowledging that "justice
is accomplished lots of times by methods that won't bear looking at"
(88–89), Gavin sends Chick to spy on the jury, which is sequestered in
the back room of a boarding house. From his perch in a mulberry tree,
Chick learns that the dissenting juror is a "little, worn, dried-out hill
man" named Jackson Fentry. ("I remembered all their names," Chick
explains, "because Uncle Gavin said that to be a successful lawyer and

politician in our country you did not need a silver tongue nor even an intelligence; you needed only an infallible memory for names" [89].) Fentry acknowledges that Thorpe was no good, that he would have remorselessly ruined a young girl, and that Bookwright was clearly defending himself. But he stubbornly refuses to retract his guilty vote. "I can't help it," he says. "I ain't going to vote Mr. Bookwright free" (89). The judge dismisses the deadlocked jury and orders a retrial in the spring term of court.

With the hung jury we enter the second part of the story, where the detective work begins. With Chick in tow, Stevens heads for the pine hills to learn what he can about Fentry's past, on the off chance that history might hold the key to fathoming the juror's animosity toward Bookwright. This intelligence-gathering operation is entirely colloquial. Even at this early point in his career, the lawyer-citizen is recognized and well-liked by the country folk, and in his presence they are forthcoming with their stories, a fact demonstrated by the following exchange between Gavin and one of Fentry's neighbors. Note the almost biblical parataxis of the final two sentences:

> [T]he man rose from the gallery and came down to the gate.
> 'Howdy, Mr. Stevens,' he said. 'So Jackson Fentry hung your jury for you.'
> 'Howdy, Mr. Pruitt,' Uncle Gavin said. 'It looks like he did. Tell me.'
> And Pruitt told him. . . . (91)

Stevens implores, Pruitt tells. This is the kind of supposedly unearned windfall that irks those readers of *Knight's Gambit* who expect conventional rather than colloquial techniques of detection. These readers should remind themselves that hill people like Pruitt don't spill their guts to every stranger who darkens their doorstep. One must gain their trust in order to overcome their characteristic reticence, and Stevens inspires such trust. "It was as if people looked at his face," Chick remarks, "and knew that what he asked was not just for his own curiosity or his own selfish using" (91).

Gavin and Chick join their host and his mother on the gallery (a proverbial site of southern storytelling), where the Pruitts, "talking in rotation," collaboratively unfold the Fentry story (91–97). Jackson worked the Fentry land with his father for twenty-five years. He then took a job on wages at a Frenchman's Bend sawmill, where he stayed for two and a half years. When he returned to the pine hills, he brought

a baby boy with him—the issue, Jackson claimed, of his marriage to a
woman "from downstate" who later died in childbirth. Fentry worked
the land and raised the boy, whom he named Jackson and Longstreet
Fentry, until one morning a few summers later both he and the child
were gone. Finally, five years afterward, Jackson reappeared on the
farm without the child, whose existence he has thereafter refused to acknowledge. As the long tale unwinds, Stevens attends eagerly to every
detail, by turns hurrying the Pruitts onward and urging them to linger
over particularly significant moments. Further, as we have seen elsewhere in Faulkner, the entire storytelling scenario takes its place within
a larger context of southern hospitality. The Fentry history, in a way, is a
gift from the Pruitts to their visitors from town, and when the telling is
over, Gavin and Chick are invited to share a meal with their hosts (97).

Fentry's absences from the family farm, however, still remain to be
accounted for, so Stevens politely declines the invitation. Instead, he
and Chick head south toward Frenchman's Bend, where the events at
the Pruitts' more or less repeat themselves.

> So we sat on the gallery of the locked and deserted store while the
> cicadas shrilled and rattled in the trees and the lightning bugs blinked
> and drifted above the dusty road, and [Isham] Quick told it . . . talking in
> a lazy sardonic voice, like he had all night to tell it in and it would take
> all night to tell it. But it wasn't that long. It wasn't long enough for what
> was in it. But Uncle Gavin says it don't take many words to tell the sum
> of any human experience; that somebody has already done it in eight:
> He was born, he suffered and he died. (97–98)

The porchside seat, the affable, forthright host, the attentive guests, the
moving subject matter, the willingness to let the tale unfold in its own
way, at its own pace—here once more are the ingredients of effective
storytelling. Once again Stevens punctuates the story with his timely
interjections, and again, when all is said, comes the call to communion
over supper (104).

From Quick, whose family employed Fentry at the sawmill, Stevens
hears a chain of events that recalls the Lena Grove–Byron Bunch plot
of *Light in August*: when a pregnant young woman shows up alone
at the sawmill, Fentry is immediately smitten with her, takes her in,
offers to marry her, is rejected, and assists at the birth of her child,
an event that the woman, unlike Lena, does not survive. Three summers later, the woman's brothers, the Thorpes, show up at Frenchman's

Bend with a "paper all wrote out and stamped and sealed and regular" (100), in search of their nephew. Quick accompanies them to the pine hills, where they take the child away from the heartbroken Fentry, who has no one to advocate for him against the Thorpes and their legalistic document. Cheated in this way by the symbolic order, Jackson disappears for five years, and little Jackson and Longstreet Fentry becomes Buck Thorpe, the man Bookwright has killed.

Stevens has set out on his expedition to the pine hills and Frenchman's Bend as Bookwright's advocate, but he returns to Jefferson as equally Jackson Fentry's. The stories he has heard in the country bring out the many similarities between Bookwright and Fentry: proud, self-sufficient men, farmers, fathers who do their best to protect their children, and victims of injustice. Fentry's insistence on hanging Gavin's jury is, Stevens now realizes, consistent with his human dignity—his personal counteroffensive against the order of law and culture that has mistreated him. He too is one of us. "Of course he wasn't going to vote Bookwright free," Gavin now understands, and when young Chick begs to differ, the boy draws a stern rebuke.

> 'I would have,' I said. 'I would have freed him. Because Buck Thorpe was bad. He—'
> 'No, you wouldn't,' Uncle Gavin said. . . . 'It wasn't Buck Thorpe, the adult, the man. He would have shot that man as quick as Bookwright did, if he had been in Bookwright's place. It was because somewhere in that debased and brutalized flesh which Bookwright slew there still remained, not the spirit maybe, but at least the memory, of that little boy, that Jackson and Longstreet Fentry, even though the man the boy had become didn't know it, and only Fentry did. And you wouldn't have freed him either. Don't ever forget that. Never.' (104–5)

That Chick closes his story with these lines rather than his own more skeptical ones is a sign that his uncle's generous spirit has passed on to him, to be passed on in turn to the reader. As in "Monk," this channel of sympathy creates new advocates for the casualties of the legal system.

. . . .

"Hand upon the Waters" (1939) and "An Error in Chemistry" (1946), the third and fifth stories, respectively, of *Knight's Gambit*, depend more intimately on conventional ratiocinative modes of detection than on colloquial ones. Interestingly, however, ratiocination in the two stories is attended by an increased risk of physical, indeed life-threatening, injury to the detective. Thus even these apparently exceptional stories demonstrate the general rule that Stevens works most effectively (and safely) in the volume when he works colloquially.

In "Hand," Lonnie Grinnup, the last surviving descendant of one of the county's trio of founding figures, is found drowned on his own trotline in the Yoknapatawpha River. Though the inquest is out of his jurisdiction, County Attorney Stevens attends anyway, in homage to the now-extinct Grenier line. As he lingers at the inquest, what he learns from the two witnesses who found Grinnup's body arouses his suspicion that Lonnie's death was no accident. Stevens soon discovers that a local farmer, Tyler Ballenbaugh, has for eleven years paid the premiums on a hefty life insurance policy for Grinnup, with himself as beneficiary. Tyler, a wagering man, considers the policy an expedient gamble (he is betting he will outlive Lonnie), but his miscreant brother Boyd decides to improve the odds by murdering Grinnup. When Stevens discovers the brothers covering their tracks at Lonnie's riverside shack, Boyd turns on Tyler and then on Gavin, only to be attacked himself by Joe, the deaf-mute orphan who has lived with and idolized Lonnie for more than a decade. Joe is evidently familiar with the concept of poetic justice, for Boyd's corpse is found dangling from Lonnie's trotline the next day. The stroke of deductive genius that breaks open the case concerns a paddle found in Grinnup's boat: since country folk like Lonnie run their trotlines by hand, the superfluous paddle must have been left in the boat by someone other than he: the murderer (81).

"An Error in Chemistry" is a bit more baroque. Joel Flint, a Yankee "outlander" and former carnival man with a cold contempt for southern ways, marries the "dim-witted spinster" daughter of old Wesley Pritchel, whose "good though small farm" is the site of a clay pit coveted by the highway industry (one of the closet villains of the story). Two years later, after killing his wife with a shotgun (whether accidentally or deliberately he will not say), Flint turns himself in to the sheriff, and Pritchel locks himself in his room, half in aggrieved outrage, half in fear that Flint will return for him. Within hours Flint escapes from the Jefferson jail and apparently flees the county. After Mrs. Flint's funeral, Pritchel suddenly emerges from his room, now willing to sell his land to a group of northern entrepreneurs whose offers he has previously spurned. Pritchel rather contemptuously summons Gavin and the sheriff to witness the sale, which, he claims, will fund his efforts to track Flint down and bring him to justice. As he mixes a farewell round of cold toddies, however, Pritchel stirs the sugar directly into the raw whiskey, rather than dissolving it in the water first. Instantly detecting this gross infringement of southern decorum, Gavin, Chick, and the sheriff pounce on "Pritchel," who is really, of course, Flint in disguise. They find the real Pritchel buried in the stable, disfigured and disguised to look like Flint, head "pillowed carefully" on "a big ledger" filled with clippings chronicling Flint's career as Signor Canova, a circus illusionist ("He Disappears While You Watch Him") now long past his prime (128). The Pritchel affair was to be at once Flint/Canova's comeback and the capstone to his career, his greatest vanishing act.

Both of these stories address the forensic issue of advocacy—one in a straightforward manner, one negatively. In "Hand," as soon as Stevens determines that Lonnie Grinnup has been murdered, he becomes the dead man's advocate, and when he tracks down Boyd and Tyler Ballenbaugh, it is Grinnup's name that he invokes in demanding justice (77). Just as much as Lonnie, however, the deaf-mute Joe finds an advocate in Stevens. Throughout the story, Joe's efforts to express himself fall on uncomprehending ears, but his vengeance upon Boyd Ballenbaugh, which saves the lives of Gavin and Tyler, is most articulate in speaking for him. In return, Gavin feigns ignorance before the sheriff as to how Boyd got on the trotline. This version of the Conradian lie that saves is intended to protect Joe. Here the act of advocacy entails knowing what not to say about the party in whose behalf one acts.

In "Error," the figure of the advocate is parodied in Joel Flint, who does not actually advocate so much as impersonate. Flint speaks with the voice of old Pritchel, rather than for that voice. He traffics in verisimilitude, as courtroom advocates do, but he does so purely for his own material gain. It is thus appropriate that the story's other, more magnanimous exponent of verisimilitude and advocacy, Gavin Stevens, is on hand when Flint finally "misspeaks," as it were—in a slip of the toddy rather than a slip of the tongue.

Both stories also contain examples of colloquial detective work, though this work is ultimately subservient to deduction. When Stevens arrives at the Grinnup inquest in "Hand," he finds a number of friendly constituents gathered there, most of whom he knows personally. "Better still, they knew him, voting for him year after year and calling him by his given name even though they did not quite understand him" (67). This is the kind of gathering that often results in colloquial information for the county attorney, and the inquest proves no exception. After he pays his last respects to Lonnie, something compels Stevens to stay on at the hearing. He listens carefully to the witnesses, and a brief chat with one of them when the inquest is over yields the disturbing detail about Lonnie's paddle that sets Gavin's investigation in motion.

"Error," on the other hand, features a series of important conversations between Stevens and his friend the sheriff, during which these two detectives attempt to talk their way through the gaps and enigmas that riddle their case. Like Quentin and Shreve in *Absalom, Absalom!*, they are engaged in conjectural narration, the halting, intuitive, collaborative reconstruction of agency and motive.[11] If Flint deliberately murdered his wife, why would he do this before she had inherited the Pritchel land from her father? And why would Flint so aggressively want to be locked up? Not because he is afraid of Pritchel—if anything the reverse is true. Perhaps the story is not over with Flint's incarceration—perhaps, Gavin offers, "what has already happened is not finished yet" (116). Flint's escape confirms this conjecture: he went to jail "[s]o he could escape from it" (118). This reciprocal process of proposing and modifying explanations leads Gavin and the sheriff dialectically toward better and better accounts, but never all the way to a definitive version. This version emerges only after an "accidental" encounter with an insurance adjustor leads Gavin, Chick, and the sheriff back to Pritchel's house, where they witness the (literal) mix-up with the toddy. As in "Hand," that is, the colloquial elements of the story are secondary, a mere prelude to ratiocinative detective work.

The fruits of ratiocination in "Hand" and "Error," however, are problematic. Stevens of course gets his man in each story, but it may be more than merely coincidental that the two cases in which deductive logic plays a primary role are also the only cases in *Knight's Gambit* in which the detective is assaulted. At the conclusion of "Hand," in fact, Stevens is almost killed. A bullet from Boyd Ballenbaugh's pistol leaves him with "a crease in [his] skull you could hide a cigar in" (80). Deductive logic thus quite literally leaves its mark upon the county attorney, and were it not for the intervention of Joe, other, fatal marks would have followed. Similarly, when Flint realizes he has given himself away in "Error," he hurls a heavy whiskey glass at the advancing Stevens, narrowly missing his head. It then takes the combined forces of Gavin, Chick, and the sheriff to wrestle the slippery impostor into submission. In both stories, then, using one's head seems to place that very head in jeopardy.

Why is ratiocination depicted as a potentially dangerous act in *Knight's Gambit?* One answer might be that it tends to be an act one performs alone: an individual, observing a case, reasons his or her way from a premise to a conclusion. This underlying individualist ethos contrasts sharply with the more communitarian principles that inform colloquial detection in Faulkner's world: sharing stories, mutual give and take, attending to the words, wisdom, and needs of others, and speaking out on their behalf. Even when justice is not the product of the legal system in *Knight's Gambit*, it is still almost unfailingly the product of teamwork. While individuals fall prey to interlopers, communities resist them. This is the point, I think, behind Joe's timely appearance in "Hand" and the assistance provided by Chick and the sheriff at the conclusion of "Error": whatever his deductive skill, the detective who frequents Yoknapatawpha's agrarian circles needs allies to help him meet both the narrative and the physical demands of his work. There is little room for "soliloquial" detection in a colloquial world.

. . . .

The final three stories of the volume trace the emergence of Chick Mallison as a sleuth in his own right. In "Tomorrow," we recall, Chick goes along as Gavin's sidekick on the trip to the pine hills and French-man's Bend, but at the end of the story the boy must be talked out of his condescending view of Jackson Fentry and talked into seeing the Fentry story sympathetically, as Gavin sees it. In "An Error in Chem-istry," however, Chick detects Joel Flint's fatal miscue at exactly the same moment Gavin does, and he helps his uncle subdue the villain. "Knight's Gambit" (1949) marks Chick's most decisive performance as colloquial detective. In this 110-page novella, it is Chick who discovers the clue that allows his uncle to prevent a murder, and, in keeping with the volume's peculiar logic of detection, he discovers this clue by accident.

"Knight's Gambit" is oddly bifurcated between detective story and love story, and this division has important consequences for the characterization of Gavin Stevens. The plot is set in motion by a series of romantic conflicts and complications. The Harriss children, Max and his unnamed sister, try to enlist Stevens in their effort to run Captain Gualdres, their dashing Argentinean house guest, out of town. The sister loves Gualdres but fears he may be after her widowed mother's fortune. When Stevens refuses to take the case, Max storms away, threatening violence against the captain. Further pleading by the sister persuades Stevens that the boy's threats are serious, so Gavin agrees to keep an eye on him. The next day, Max roars out of town in his roadster, so conspicuously as to convince Gavin that he is establishing an alibi. This conviction turns out to be correct, but for now, Gavin concedes, he can only wait for Max's next move.

From a chance conversation with a Yoknapatawpha horse trader named McCallum, Chick learns that next move. McCallum is the owner of a killer stallion whose "hatred for anything walking upright on two legs" (200) is something of a local legend, and he has just sold the stallion to Max, who then, in a move that is the literal opposite of chivalry, orders it delivered to the Harriss stables. Chick passes this information on to Gavin, and the two, along with McCallum, rush to the Harriss place in time to intercept Captain Gualdres before he goes down to the stables for what would have been the last of his nightly rides. While Gualdres looks on, the stallion explodes out of its stall, screaming and bent on violence (much like Max himself). Foul play is thus averted, and the next day, which happens to be Saturday, December 6, 1941, Stevens, rather than having Max arrested, pressures him into enlisting in the army. He also learns that Captain Gualdres and the Harriss daughter have married.

The detective plot thus happily resolved, we now learn the full extent of Gavin's participation in the love plot. Early in the novella, the narrator devotes a very long digression (142–73) to the history of the enigmatic Mrs. Harriss, a circumstantial history comprised of local gossip and conjecture: her girlhood in Yoknapatawpha (in "Knight's Gambit" we learn neither her first nor her maiden name); her mysterious engagement, later broken, to an unknown local suitor; her marriage to Harriss, a New Orleans bootlegger improbably devoted to her; the transformation, under Harriss's direction, of her father's "once-simple country house" into a grand simulacrum of southern opulence; her travels in Europe with her daughter and son; the husband's murder (making the widow "Mrs. Heiress," as it were); her inheritance of his untold fortune; her subsequent trip to South America with the children; her return with Gualdres; and the captain's rumored designs upon her wealth. Once Gavin insures, however, that Gualdres no longer contends for the hand of Mrs. Harriss, he reveals himself to Chick as the mysterious suitor from the widow's past (228–35). She has gotten away from him once, thanks to his own immaturity (see the differing accounts of the breakup on 235–37 and 243–45), so he is not about to let a second chance go by. In the short final section of the novella (239–46), set in 1942, we learn that Gavin has indeed made good on his pledge, and that Chick has a new aunt.

There is a further sense in which *Knight's Gambit*, like *Intruder in the Dust*, is a narrative of Chick Mallison's education. As in *Intruder*, the story's third-person narration is strictly limited to Chick's point of view, so we are subject at all times to his observations and interpretations. From his uncle, Chick learns the value of wisdom, courage, humility, and especially love. From the negative examples of Max Harriss, he learns the bitter consequences of youthful indiscretion (a lesson backed up by his uncle's early history as a suitor). Moreover, Chick learns a great deal in "Knight's Gambit" about the techniques of colloquial detection.

The story of the Harriss affair, for example, which verges at times on legend, is the property of the entire community, particularly "the spinster aunts who watched by hearsay and supposition (and maybe hope) from their front galleries" (154) for each new development "as you watch the unfolding story in the magazine installments" (148). By means of their gossip, the spinster aunts perpetuate a form of surveillance that is at once social and oral, and in this respect they are not unlike Chick's bachelor uncle, the colloquial detective. Or consider the searching conversations between Gavin and Chick in section two of the novella (173–77, 191–95), exchanges reminiscent of those between Gavin and the sheriff in "An Error in Chemistry." Working together, uncle and nephew expose the flaws in a number of misleading cover stories offered up by Max Harriss and his sister and arrive at a composite account, a more convincing version of the state of affairs in the Harriss household. Once again, collaborative, conjectural narration figures prominently in successful sleuthing.

In this context, it is no doubt significant that the dialogues between

Chick and Gavin take place over their nightly chess match, for if chess is a kind of conversation between players who share a language (the rules), then colloquial detection is conversely a kind of game in which the responses themselves are verbal, conversational.[12] A language game, Wittgenstein would say. And since, according to Gavin, "all human passion and hope and folly can be mirrored and then proved" in this particular game (192), we could say that Chick's lessons in chess and detection go hand in hand with a lesson in life itself. On a number of levels, then, he is being instructed in how to *move*.

"Life is motion," Faulkner never tired of repeating. To him the act of moving constituted a refusal to succumb to stasis and death. Yet a move also refers to a single diachronic moment of certain games—chess being only one example. The tension between the kinetic and ludic senses of the word "move" is present almost every time the word appears in "Knight's Gambit," obviating easy distinctions between games like chess and the larger game of detection, as in the following passage: " 'Yes,' his uncle said. . . . '[T]hey have both decided to try something else, and I dont like it. Because they are dangerous. Dangerous not because they are stupid . . . [b]ut because they have never had anybody to tell them they are young and stupid whom they had enough respect for or fear of to believe.—Move' " (175). Gavin's last word indicates of course that it is Chick's turn to move a chess piece. But the injunction to "Move" also means, "You play detective now. Respond to my hypothesis. Keep the story, the language game of conjecture, going." [13]

Chick soon enjoys an opportunity to put these lessons to good use. When Stevens retires to his sitting room to work on his translation (a pet project, we recall, from "Go Down, Moses"), he is effectively conceding that Max's plans remain a mystery to him, and Chick is left to himself for the evening. In contrast to his solitary, sedentary uncle, Chick plays the peripatetic, wandering into town for a movie. On his way home, he drops by a diner on the square, where the clue he has not even been seeking drops right into his lap. The text leaves no doubt how accidental the discovery is:

> So he went to the show. *And if he hadn't gone to the show*, he wouldn't
> have been passing the Allnite Inn where he could see, recognise the
> empty horse-van at the curb before it with the empty chains and shackles
> looped through the sideplanks, and, turning his head toward the win-

dow, Mr McCallum himself at the counter, eating, the heavy white-oak cudgel leaning against the counter beside him. *And if he hadn't had fourteen minutes* yet before the week-night hour (except Saturday or unless there was a party) when he was supposed to be back home and indoors, he wouldn't have entered the Inn and asked Mr McCallum who had bought the horse. (206; my emphasis)

Accidental, yes, but also colloquial. A less gregarious individual might have merely waved through the window at McCallum and arrived home fourteen minutes early. But Chick, well versed in Gavin's methods of detection, proves an admirable stand-in for his uncle.

In the county attorney's defense, it should be said that once he learns Max has bought the killer stallion, he immediately leaps into motion. The paragraphs that describe the trip out to the Harriss estate bristle with action verbs: "His uncle was up too now, snatching off the eyeshade and flinging it away and kicked the chair backward and snatched his coat and vest from the other chair" (209). Again Gavin demonstrates how, when the occasion demands, to move. And when Gavin arrives at the Harriss place, his bilingual exchange with Captain Gualdres (212–21) is an extremely tactful rhetorical performance, as is his poker-faced showdown in his office with an unrepentant Max Harriss the next day (222–26). All of this is only to say that Stevens is here, as elsewhere in *Knight's Gambit*, a capable man of action. But his retreat to the sitting room and the translation is nonetheless a disturbing moment, arguably the only moment in the entire volume where William Doster's objection to Stevens as an ivory tower figure seems justified. The translation can of course be viewed as further proof of Gavin's linguistic facility, but the peculiar backward-looking nature of the project (to render the Old Testament back into "classic Greek") makes for an irony that undermines this position.[14]

The Cincinnatus paradigm provides a useful contrast here. When summoned to defend his people from an invading army, the fabled Roman turned away from his plow and answered the call. In "Go Down, Moses," we may recall, the plow of Cincinnatus becomes the translation project of Gavin Stevens, a project described with some irony early in the story but never mentioned again—as though to emphasize that its hermetic siren song never seriously tempts Stevens away from his responsibilities as a lawyer-citizen. Confronted by an impend-

ing crisis in the community in "Knight's Gambit," however, Stevens
initially ignores the crisis, "retiring" to the appropriately named
"sittingroom" to work on his "Translation" (it is now capitalized, reified,
fetishized). Locked in the room like the corpse in a whodunit (even
as Max Harriss threatens to turn Captain Gualdres into one), Stevens
uncharacteristically fails to translate private existence into the public sphere, shutting himself off from "man woman [or] child, client
well-wisher or friend" (207) and turning away from the very real
"scoundrels and felons" lurking outside in the community to the safely
literary ones of the Old Testament (205).

From the very beginning, in fact, Stevens has tried to avoid involvement in the Harriss affair. As if to indicate his essentially static posture
at the outset of the story, his case must literally intrude upon him, burst
into his house in the dark of night—twice—in order to gain his full
attention. And he explicitly refuses the role of lawyer-detective until
the second appearance of the Harriss girl, who manages finally to coax
him into accepting it (138). Indeed, it may well be that Chick Mallison,
who is not only an apprentice-at-law (202) but also a soldier-citizen-
in-training (cadet lieutenant colonel at the local academy [195–96]),
comes closest to fulfilling the Cincinnatus ideal in "Knight's Gambit."
The story's World War II context, it seems to me, only heightens the
resonance of the Cincinnatus legend. A crisis of epic proportions, after
all, is brewing beyond the local boundaries of Yoknapatawpha, but
rather than intervene in this crisis directly, Jefferson's leading lawyer-
citizen sends Max Harriss off to enlist (224–25). By story's end, in fact,
Chick and Captain Gualdres have also joined the war effort, while
Stevens can get no further than the train station. Here Faulkner's own
frustration at not being allowed a more active role in the war effort
than that of local air-raid warden clearly informs his depiction of the
county attorney. If, that is, Faulkner felt that in wartime his role as
artist-citizen paled in comparison to the much more crucial and dangerous exploits of America's young soldier-citizens abroad, something
of that pain and disappointment may well have carried over into the
portrait of a similarly diminished lawyer-citizen in "Knight's Gambit."

Throughout the tale, in fact, there is an ambivalence about the characterization of Gavin Stevens that is simply not present in the other
stories of the volume. This ambivalence is related, whether as symptom or cause, to the contradictory demands placed on Gavin by the

two plots in which he is involved: the detective story and the love story. Man at law and man in love, he is really two characters in one.

Once again the Cincinnatus legend proves instructive. The story illustrates the same diametrical opposition between love and duty that bifurcates the plot of "Knight's Gambit." When crisis arises, Cincinnatus must leave not only his plow and farm but also his wife behind. In Livy, she is the one who hands Cincinnatus the toga symbolizing his public identity and responsibility. When peace and order reign once again in Rome, he can return to her side. Matters of the state and matters of the hearth are thus assigned completely different spheres, in what is no doubt a kind of patriarchal fantasy (men can inhabit both realms equally [though not at the same time], women only the latter realm).

"Knight's Gambit" tries to resolve this opposition by making the resolution of the love plot a direct consequence of the resolution of the crime plot. Stevens wins the girl precisely by virtue of wrapping up his case. He simultaneously neutralizes Max Harriss's design against Gualdres and the Captain's own possible designs upon Gavin's romantic interest, Mrs. Harriss. One result of this is that the love plot continues on after the detective plot is completed, creating the impression that the former somehow frames, encapsulates the latter—an impression only heightened when we recall that the mystery plot begins with a baroque, deliberately misleading account of romantic rivalry. Indeed, Faulkner himself seems to have thought of "Knight's Gambit" first and foremost as a romance. "It is a love story," he wrote his editor, Saxe Commins, while still at work on the tale, "in which Stevens prevents a crime (murder) not for justice but to gain (he is now fifty plus) the childhood sweetheart which he lost 20 years ago" (SL 280). If romance seems to supplant even justice among Stevens's priorities, perhaps this is why it gets the first and last word in the story.

The plot can thus in some sense accommodate romance and detection, but the characterization of Gavin Stevens is another matter. In Stevens himself the lover and the lawyer-detective coexist only uneasily. The two roles are never completely reconciled. It is instructive to contrast these personae on a number of different levels. The lawyer-detective, for instance, is a pragmatist. He trusts his methods and even bends the law when it suits his purposes (he does not, for example, press charges against Max Harriss, who has attempted murder). The lover, on the other hand, is more of an idealist. He envisions the woman he loves as "a child playing in a windless and timeless garden," and he elsewhere invokes images of stillness, spring, flowers, and the past in order to describe her (see KG 232–35 in particular). Furthermore, the lawyer-detective solves enigmas. Throughout the volume, there is little in Yoknapatawpha County that remains unknown to him. The lover, however, as Grimwood has noted, *is* an enigma. Unknown to the community, Stevens is the mysterious suitor from Mrs. Harriss's past (*Heart in Conflict* 188, 210). And while the lawyer-detective is a master of language (or, in this story, a master of languages), whose "terse glib succinct sentence[s] sometimes less than two words long" are capable of blasting Chick out of the room (208),[15] the lover is characterized by silence, an "incredible taciturnity" (142) that directly contradicts the rules of colloquial detection. A visit from his sweetheart's son and daughter, for instance, is enough to leave Gavin uncharacteristically speechless, as his puzzled nephew observes.

> [T]wo strangers had burst not only into his home but into his private sitting room, and delivered first a peremptory command and then a threat and then burst out again, and his uncle had sat calmly back to an interrupted chess game and an interrupted pipe and completed a planned move as though he had not only not noticed any interruption but hadn't actually been interrupted. This, in the face of what should have supplied his uncle with food and scope for garrulity for the rest of the night. . . . (141–42)

And whenever anyone broaches the subject of Mrs. Harriss or her early history, the normally loquacious Gavin clams up.

> He—his uncle—was home again [from Heidelberg] now, for good this time, and his sister and mother, Charles's mother and grandmother (and all the other women he couldn't help but listen to probably) had told him about the marriage and about the other shadowy betrothal too. Which itself should have unbraked his uncle's tongue when the violation of his home didn't, for the very reason that it was not merely no concern of his but so little concerned with any reality at all that there would have been nothing in it anywhere to confound or restrict him. (147)

> [Mrs. Harriss] was gone, running from what, the town maybe thought it knew. But hunting for what or if hunting for anything, this time not even

> his uncle, who always had something to say (and something that quite
> often made sense) about anything which wasn't particularly his business,
> didn't know or at least didn't say. (154)

> [H]e would watch his uncle sitting even then, holding one of the letters
> his mother had received [from Mrs. Harriss], incorrigible and bachelor,
> faced for the only time in his life with something on which he apparently
> had nothing to say. . . . (160)

In these passages, Gavin is less the story's leading agent of interpretation than a principal object of interpretation.

Finally, the lawyer-detective is an active, crusading public figure,
a member of the community, a Cincinnatus-at-law, while the lover
is private and retiring, drawn to the *hortus conclusus* of his sweetheart's windless garden. While the former, that is, is a figure on the
move, and moreover an instructor in the art of motion, the latter fetishizes motionlessness. One critic has perceptively noted that the young
girl with whom Stevens is so smitten is merely a "static image," that
what Stevens thinks of as love should be redefined as a sentimental
"longing for retreat . . . into an idealized, static child's world of make-
believe" (Volpe, "Faulkner's 'Knight's Gambit' " 232–33).[16] As I see it,
the Translation must be interpreted in this context, as further evidence
of Gavin-the-lover's propensity for escape—especially when we realize
that the project is itself a substitute for (indeed a symbol of) the lost
girl, a transitional diversion Stevens takes up in order to ease the pain
of his broken engagement, after he has "proved himself unworthy or
incapable of love" (Dunlap, "William Faulkner's 'Knight's Gambit' "
233).[17] The girl and the translation are Gavin's only true loves.

"Knight's Gambit," therefore, with its intertwined plots and Janus-
faced hero, affords us a unique place from which to survey Faulkner's
Gavin Stevens fiction. On the one hand, the detective plot broaches
issues that locate the novella in a line of forensic fictions spanning two
decades, fictions that include *Intruder in the Dust*, "Go, Down Moses,"
"Hair," the cameo appearance in *Light in August*, and the other five
stories in the *Knight's Gambit* volume. On the other hand, the love plot
anticipates Gavin's role in a pair of novels from the fifties, *The Town*
and *The Mansion*—a connection Millgate has noted (*The Achievement*
270).[18] In these novels, as in parts of "Knight's Gambit," Stevens can
be annoyingly weak, escapist, idealistic, and by turns silent and bom-

bastic.[19] He also deviates in important ways from the paradigm of the Cincinnatus-at-law, bearing an uncomfortable resemblance on occasion to his ineffectual, Prufrockian predecessor-at-law, Horace Benbow. Moreover, the Cincinnatus paradigm itself comes under revision in the Snopes volumes, where, along with V. K. Ratliff, the lawyer-citizen mounts a campaign against a clan of invaders whose values are not as alien as he would like to believe—who, as it happens, are no poorer sons-of-bitches than Stevens and Ratliff themselves.

We are a bit premature, however, in announcing the demise, or even the decline, of Lawyer Stevens, for one of his most important forensic performances still awaits us. It is to this powerful, socratic performance, in *Requiem for a Nun*, that we turn in chapter 5.

. . . .

CHAPTER FIVE

Maieutic Forensics; or, *Requiem for a Nun* and the Talking Cure

As Faulkner originally conceived of it, *Requiem for a Nun* would have rounded out an interconnected group of forensic fictions from the early thirties, the texts that chart the transition from Horace Benbow to Gavin Stevens in Yoknapatawpha's theater of justice: *Sanctuary*, "Hair," "Smoke," and *Light in August*.[1] In December 1933, at his home in Oxford, Faulkner made two attempts to begin a new manuscript he entitled "Requiem for a Nun." The shorter of two handwritten openings bearing this title, which were discovered at Rowan Oak in 1970, is a two-paragraph meditation on the Jefferson jail, narrated from the point of view of an unnamed character about to enter the building. This attempt was probably abandoned in favor of the second, longer opening, set in the office of a lawyer named Stevens. In this five-paragraph text, Stevens questions a black couple about an attack the woman has recently suffered, apparently at the hands of another woman. Stevens has sent for the couple himself, hoping that the dispute can be settled without a trial. This opening too was soon discarded by the author, or at least set aside for the time being (see FAB 825–26).[2]

What the early *Requiem* might have become had Faulkner pressed on in the thirties we will never know. Within two months he was hard at work on *Absalom, Absalom!*, which proved a more than worthy distraction. More than a decade and a half would pass before Faulkner once again took up the *Requiem* project in February 1950. This time the manuscript emerged as "an interesting experiment in form," "a story told in seven play-scenes" over three acts, with "three introductory chapters," narrative prologues "which hold the 3 acts together" (SL 305). The dramatic sections, in which Albert Camus heard the accents of an authentic idiom for modern tragedy,[3] reintroduce us to a pair of characters from *Sanctuary*, Temple Drake and Gowan Stevens, eight years after their luckless lost weekend at the old Frenchman place. Married now, a fashionable Jefferson couple with two children, Temple and Gowan seem to have expiated their terrible past, until their baby girl is smothered to death in her crib by Nancy Mannigoe, a former drug addict and inmate of Miss Reba's Memphis brothel whom Temple has hired as a nursemaid and confidante. Nancy is sentenced to hang, but, late in the first act, Gavin Stevens, uncle to the bereaved and (implausible as it may seem) defense counsel to the accused, senses that Temple is in some unexplained way involved in her child's death and persuades her to go before the governor and plead for Nancy's pardon. Although Gavin suspects that the governor will reject Temple's pleas—the Law must extract its pound of flesh from Nancy—he believes that "get[ting] it told, breathed aloud, into words, sound" (RFN 78) will prove therapeutic for Temple and also, perhaps, for Gowan, who, concealed in the governor's office by a trick of the stage, witnesses his wife's confession. In the final act, set at the Jefferson jail, the two women finally confront each other, and Temple is left to wonder how she can go on living with her guilt and anguish. While no easy answers await her questions, she seems resolved to make meaningful the pain she has endured and also in part caused.

What the 1933 *Requiem* fragments have in common with the published novel of 1951, besides a title, are an interest in the symbolic potential of the jail as a local landmark, and, perhaps more interesting, the presence of Gavin Stevens. (It is tempting to surmise that Stevens is also the unnamed focal character of the shorter fragment.) Though Faulkner envisioned *Requiem* from the start as a novel "about a nigger woman" (SL 75), it is only Stevens, rather than Nancy Mannigoe (or for that matter Temple Drake), who specifically figures in the project from its inception to its completion. The Gavin Stevens of the 1933 false starts is no mere plot device. He is a lawyer in search of a story, a man involving himself on behalf of others, and even this sketchy outline is enough to suggest the Stevens we find in the published text and elsewhere in Faulkner, the lawyer-citizen and raconteur.

The eighteen-year gap between the inception and publication of *Requiem* placed the novel in an even more prominent position among Faulkner's forensic fictions, as the anchor volume of the forensic trilogy beginning with *Intruder in the Dust* (1948) and *Knight's Gambit* (1949).

Over these three volumes Faulkner conducts his most sustained inter-rogation of the lawyer as rhetor and citizen, whether inside or (more often) outside the courtroom. While *Intruder* centers on Stevens talk-ing (in both the long-winded polemic that ironizes him as a character and the storytelling mode that embeds itself so subtly in his nephew's memory as to become inseparable from the boy's own thoughts) and *Knight's Gambit* emphasizes the act of listening (the patient gather-ing of colloquial information that enables the lawyer-detective to re-pel alien incursions against the agrarian community), *Requiem* focuses upon the socratic activity of *teaching to speak*, as Gavin, in a kind of ex post facto cross-examination, struggles to elicit from Temple Drake Stevens the untold story behind the death of her child, to lead her toward wisdom but also toward expiation—or, as one of Faulkner's fel-low cartographers of the psyche would have put it, toward a talking cure. So compelling in fact is the urge to "get it told, breathed aloud" in *Requiem* that the teller-hearer relationship is foregrounded time and time again in the novel,[4] along different but complementary lines of imagery: the forensic imagery of client and counsel, the theatrical imagery of actor and audience, the religious imagery of penitent and priest, and the therapeutic imagery of analysand and analyst.[5] At one point or another, the gripping encounters between Temple and Gavin suggest each one of these configurations.

Any attempt to analyze the performance of the forensic figure in *Re-quiem*, however, or the maieutic he attempts to practice there, must reckon with Gavin's relentless insistence that Temple air her secrets, relive her past. Does his tenacity reveal a genuine concern for Temple's welfare, or, as an early reviewer wrote, a "cruelly inquisitorial" desire to abuse her (Hicks 22)? Is the "bereaved mamma," as Temple at one point calls herself, best served by being left to suffer silently and alone, a martyr to her own fiercely individualistic ethos? Or by being urged to enter a community of sufferers by means of the interpersonal act of confession? Does her silence signify gritty endurance or the worst kind of escapism? And to what degree is she herself involved in the tragedy that strikes her family?

Furthermore, how much of Temple's story does Stevens know in ad-vance, before he hears it from her? Clearly, if Temple's decision to unburden herself before Gavin and the governor is not arrived at freely, the therapeutic value of her confession is nil. Does Stevens coerce Temple into telling all by leading her to believe he already knows all (a

posture that makes it extremely difficult for her to hold back)? He de-
clares himself innocent of any such foreknowledge, and, when pushed
by Temple, he even swears an oath to this effect. Is he lying? (Would he
lie? we might well ask. Would this character swear to a deliberate false-
hood?) Has he, by bribery, intimidation, or simple request, obtained
damaging information from Nancy?

There is also the question of how responsibly Defense Attorney
Stevens serves his client. Late in the first act, it is suggested that Nancy
might have fared better at her trial with a plea of insanity than with
the not guilty plea she does enter. Should Stevens have pled Nancy
insane? More to the point, is Nancy insane? Or is she responsible for
her actions—guilty of killing the child? Should Gavin perhaps have
pled her guilty, throwing her upon the mercy of the court? The issue in
turn suggests a larger one: how effective is the criminal justice system
as a public forum—as judicial theater—in which individual citizens
can tell their stories and give meaning and context to their actions?
What sort of stories are told about Nancy at her trial? What sort are
repressed? What sort of story does the legal system allow her to tell?
For that matter, what does a plea of guilty signify in Yoknapatawpha's
judicial theater? A plea of not guilty? An insanity plea? I address all of
these questions in the pages ahead.

The constant circulation of intratextual energy between the narrative and dramatic sections of the novel has been demonstrated in detail
by Noel Polk, in his book-length study of *Requiem*, and by Richard
Moreland, who sees the prologues as "extended stage directions" detailing "not the mere costumes, lighting, and layout of the stage" but
also "larger social contexts and longer historical backgrounds" (195).
The introductory meditations have much to teach us about the genesis and subsequent history of the law in Yoknapatawpha County. It is
in the dramatic sections, however, where Gavin Stevens resides, that
we see the forensic figure at work. Throughout the discussion that follows, then, the play-scenes command the larger part of my attention.
In keeping with the novel's own purgative spirit, this is intended as a
confession rather than a disclaimer.

. . . .

In the three pages of act 1, scene 1, the courtroom and the stage dovetail as nowhere else in Faulkner, and for this reason alone these pages

warrant special attention. The scene is the very incarnation of judicial theater as Milner Ball has defined it. The explicit theatricality of courtroom architecture and the explicit drama of courtroom procedure are made manifest from the moment the stage lights come up and the opening curtain begins to rise:

MAN'S VOICE (*behind the curtain*): Let the prisoner stand.

> The curtain rises, symbolising the rising of the prisoner in the dock, and revealing a section of the courtroom. It does not occupy the whole stage, but only the upper left half, leaving the other half and the bottom of the stage in darkness, so that the visible scene is not only spotlighted but elevated slightly too, a further symbolism which will be clearer when Act II opens—the symbolism of the elevated tribunal of justice of which this, a county court, is only the intermediate, not the highest, stage. (RFN 43)

With its solemn jussive, the hidden voice appears to speak the scene into being, in an act of fiat that recalls the founding and naming of Jefferson itself, as recounted in the prologue (28). That the rising curtain somehow "symbolizes" the rising prisoner is a kind of Brechtian effect that only reemphasizes the many links between the outward form and the inward content of this intensely self-conscious scene, as do the pun that the spotlighted and elevated section of the courtroom depicted here is only a "stage," and our realization that the figures we are watching before us—"the judge, officers, the opposing lawyers, the jury" (43), along with the accused—are actors in a play as well as characters participating in a trial.[6] Moreover, that a rising curtain can somehow "symbolize" a rising prisoner suggests that this prisoner's role in the courtroom drama is already ominously "symbolic," that Yoknapatawpha has made her into a symbol of social transgression and uncanny difference that must be aggressively contained and explained. In such a scenario, what threatens to be lost, or actively suppressed, is a host of alternative personae—less overtly symbolic, and also perhaps less amenable to conventional juridical interpretation—through which "the prisoner" might have spoken in the courtroom. Though the text will in fact list a number of these other personae, these other potential voices—field hand, cook, "drunkard," "casual prostitute," wife (44)—they are all effectively silenced in the courtroom scene. Only a murderess is allowed to remain.

What would at first seem to be missing from the courtroom set is a
gallery, but this role has been reserved for the theatrical audience itself.
Whether we are attending an actual performance of *Requiem for a Nun*
(an adapted version of the play did run briefly in New York and Paris
in the fifties) or simply reading the novel, our point of view is that of
an imaginary spectator, seated in front of the action, and later in the
scene, a stage direction will allude specifically to "the invisible spectators in the room" (45), calling for an audible response on their (our)
part. All in all, it would be difficult to illustrate more vividly the fact
that litigation, like drama itself, is a spectacle enacted by and before
the people, and as such the responsibility of those people.

The action remains suspended during the next two paragraphs of
stage directions, while a pair of characters is introduced and then described in detail. One of these characters is the defense attorney,

> Gavin Stevens, about fifty. He looks more like a poet than a lawyer and
> actually is: a bachelor, descendant of one of the pioneer Yoknapatawpha
> County families, Harvard and Heidelberg educated, and returned to his
> native soil to be a sort of bucolic Cincinnatus, champion not so much of
> truth as of justice, or of justice as he sees it, constantly involving him-
> self, often for no pay, in affairs of equity and passion and even crime too
> among his people, white and Negro both, sometimes directly contrary
> to his office of County Attorney which he has held for years, as is the
> present business. (43)

There are a number of features worth noting in this sketch. First of all,
Gavin's "poet" side connotes a healthy respect for language as a creative, evocative, and coercive force, a respect that complements rather
than undermines his forensic side. Any suggestion of the tendency
toward withdrawal that we find in many actual and would-be artists in
Faulkner's fiction is countered by the reference to Stevens's habitual
and often charitable involvement in the affairs of others. Moreover,
Stevens's pioneer forebears link him to the communal origins of Jefferson (as documented in the first prologue), and his long pedigree suggests an awareness of the past and its instructive value for the present.
Such attentiveness to community and tradition is a trademark of the
lawyer-citizen—hence the direct allusion to Stevens as a Cincinnatus
figure, the most explicit such reference anywhere in Faulkner (see also
184). In this context, Gavin's concern for "his people" signifies partici-

pation in and guardianship of the community more than any strictly proprietary interest in it. Finally, that Stevens is capable of acting "contrary to his office," when he is convinced that the interests of justice dictate such a move, should not be construed as a sign of inconsistency or irresponsibility. Rather, it is a sign of profound responsibility. Stevens is bound less by his office than by his conscience. Willing to resist the dictates of the symbolic order, he puts the concrete human needs of others before impersonal rules whenever the two are in conflict—a fact that would seem to redeem Gavin from the charge of abstraction so often leveled against him. All in all, "the only direct authorial characterization of Stevens in the novel" (Polk, *Faulkner's* Requiem 61) seems to present a lawyer-citizen who basically upholds the virtues of his ancestors and the ideals of his vocation rather than one who falls away from them.[7]

The next paragraph offers a portrait of Gavin's client that is just as rich in its implications.

> The prisoner is standing. She is the only one standing in the room—a Negress, quite black, about thirty—that is, she could be almost anything between twenty and forty—with a calm impenetrable almost bemused face, the tallest, highest there with all eyes on her but she herself not looking at any of them, but looking out and up as though at some distant corner of the room, as though she were alone in it. She is—or until recently, two months ago to be exact—a domestic servant, nurse to two white children, the second of whom, an infant, she smothered in its cradle two months ago, for which act she is now on trial for her life. (RFN 43–44)

The narrator[8] makes it clear beyond doubt that Nancy did smother Temple's daughter; in *Requiem*, as so often in Faulkner, motive rather than agency is the crucial element of mystery. The most significant aspect of the passage, however, is the relentless isolation and objectification of Nancy Mannigoe throughout the courtroom proceeding. Everything about the scene singles her out as an object of inspection and, it is implied, revulsion. She alone is on her feet as the passage begins, and throughout the scene she conducts herself as if in total solitude. Motionless, gazing at no one in particular, she is the focus of every gaze around her. "There is a dead silence in the room while everybody watches her" (44). Here we see an institution that evolved specifically in order to affirm, in moments of particular social and moral stress, the individual's membership in her community and to provide a forum for her stories ironically accomplishing the exact opposite effect, for it could not be clearer that the Yoknapatawpha County courtroom is a place of silencing and alienation. It is easy, of course, to understand why this is the case: an object, after all, is easier to dismiss as alien, anomalous, mad, inhuman—and easier to kill—than a person is. The silent complicity of the reader—as theatrical spectator and/or courtroom gallerygoer—only makes Nancy's alienation more complete.

As the scene continues, this ocular tyranny is supplemented by the same kind of narrative tyranny at work in "Monk," a story discussed in chapter 4. As the judge, before sentencing Nancy, rereads the original indictment against her, the simple legal language of this statement works to oppress as well as to clarify. Concealed beneath its logic of compression is a second logic of omission. The jury may indeed have ruled that Nancy "did on the ninth day of September, wilfully and with malice aforethought kill and murder the infant child of Mr and Mrs Gowan Stevens in the town of Jefferson and the county of Yoknapatawpha" (44). But the complex story that the events of September ninth might have told—a story that, indeed, it will take the rest of this novel to recount and interpret—is sacrificed to the terse, formulaic official narrative of the state of Mississippi. The act depicted in the indictment is one that literally has no meaning, no satisfactory context, only a consequence (this is precisely what seems so insane about it). And the specific rhetorical details of the indictment only make the role it imposes upon Nancy more objectionable. For example, to say that she "wilfully" killed the Stevens baby is true enough, but—and this may seem paradoxical—to ascribe malice to the act is to take interpretive liberties that the novel ultimately does not permit. Similarly, the phrase "kill and murder" should alert us immediately to the fact that there is a world of difference between killing and murdering, though the two verbs are used in the indictment as if they were synonyms.[9] This is a damning example of the law's tendency to employ rhetorical techniques such as synonymy, repetition, and redundancy in service of a mythical comprehensivity and universality, which work in turn to consolidate the law's political authority and cultural legitimacy (Jacobson 167–68). Whether "kill" or "murder" more accurately describes Nancy's act is an important issue that should be discussed and debated at length, not glossed over by a spurious redundancy. This sort of authoritarian, punitive discourse also characterizes the death sentence (RFN 45). The overall effect of both pronouncements is to isolate Nancy as utterly as she has been isolated by the stares of the spectators. Having designated her the sole cause of the infant's death and the sole victim of punishment for that death, the state can safely dispose of Nancy and resume its business, freeing itself of one more aberrant pathogen and absolving itself of any responsibility for the disease. From Nancy's point of view, and no doubt her attorney's as well, to plead guilty to the prosecution's charge would have been tacitly to endorse its rhetorical bullying, and to underwrite the abuse of state power at its most myopic.

The state's practice of singling out targets for accusation and condemnation runs directly counter to the novel's most insistent message: the inescapable connectedness of human events and the complicity of human actors across history and society. Contemporary reviewers such as Anthony West and Robert Penn Warren were already well aware of these themes. Writing in the *New Yorker*, West to his distaste found the novel's cast of characters to be "brutishly and incredibly entangled" (114), while in the *New York Times*, Warren wrote more admiringly of *Requiem*'s "massive coilings of human motive" and the "interpenetration of past and present" in the novel (1). More recently, Warren Beck has cited "ethical entanglement" as the "unifying factor" in *Requiem* (*Faulkner* 627), and Doreen Fowler has argued for "continuance, connectivity, and eternal accountability" as the novel's reigning concerns ("Time and Punishment" 255). The dramatic and narrative sections of the novel bear witness to the fact that no individual lives in isolation— be that isolation temporal, from his or her own past acts, or social, from other human beings. Social institutions such as courts of law should conduct themselves so as to affirm rather than deny this connectedness, and one way to begin doing this is to grant litigants the status of speaking subjects rather than silent, or *spoken*, objects.

Nancy's response to her (mis)treatment in the courtroom is rather surprising. "[Q]uite loud in the silence [the stage directions tell us], to no one, quite calm, not moving," she responds to the death sentence pronounced against her by saying simply, "Yes, Lord." With these brief words, she affirms her culpability in the death of the baby girl and accepts her fate, but in a way that short-circuits (and puts in its place) the unfeelingly efficient protocol of the judicial ceremony. If the court insists on objectifying her with its discourse, in other words, Nancy will subvert that discourse. By going over the head of the presiding judge and invoking a higher one (another of the "invisible spectators" at the trial), Nancy signals the irrelevance of the court's alienating practices, the radically "intermediate" nature of its authority and rhetoric, and her own disdain for its procedures. The corporeal witnesses, of course, are outraged, and their reaction recalls a similar one at the Lee Goodwin trial in *Sanctuary*: "There is a gasp, a sound, from the invisible spectators in the room, of shock at this unheard-of violation of procedure: the beginning of something which might be consternation and even uproar, in the midst of, or rather above which, Nancy herself does not move" (45). Meanwhile, the theatrical machinery reoccupies the foreground, lurching into motion as the dramatic and forensic elements of the scene once more begin to blur together: "The judge bangs his gavel, the bailiff springs up, the curtain starts hurriedly and jerkily down as if the judge, the officers, the court itself were jerking frantically at it to hide this disgraceful business. . . . The curtain descends rapidly, hiding the scene, the lights fade rapidly into darkness." The subtext here could not be more clear. Nancy's behavior is responded to as that which is literally obscene, that which must, along with Nancy herself, be removed from view. The public space of the courtroom/stage before us thus reverts to a space of secrecy, and there arises a choral commentary on the spectacle we have just witnessed: "from somewhere among the unseen spectators there comes the sound of a woman's voice—a moan, wail, sob perhaps" (45).

The unsettling detail of the wailing woman alerts us to another side of the "disgraceful business" in the Jefferson courtroom, a palpable gender tension that works to objectify Nancy even further. The judge who sentences her, the ominous "MAN'S VOICE" that orders her to her feet, and the bailiff who shouts for order as the scene ends—every speaking part in the scene but Nancy's is almost indisputably male (though it would be an interesting experiment to stage this scene with women in these roles). The discourse of these characters, tending toward imperatives, redundancies in service of "clarity," and other ostensibly value-neutral pronouncements, is one that objectifies and demeans in precisely the manner described by a leading advocate of feminist jurisprudence:

> Formally the state is male in that objectivity is its norm. . . . If objec-
> tivity is the epistemological stance of which women's sexual objectifi-
> cation is the social process, then the state will appear most relentless
> in imposing the male point of view when it comes closest to achieving
> its highest formal criterion of distanced aperspectivity. When it is most
> ruthlessly neutral, it will be most male; when it is most sex-blind, it will
> be most blind to the sex of the standard being applied. When it most
> closely conforms to precedent, to "facts," to legislative intent, it will most
> closely enforce socially male norms and most thoroughly preclude ques-
> tioning their content as having a point of view at all. (MacKinnon 62,
> 71–72) [10]

This problem is compounded by the presence of another dubious hierarchy. Consider how the four speaking parts are referred to in this
scene: a "Judge," a "Bailiff," and a "Man's Voice," while "Nancy" is
the only speaking part given a personal name rather than a title or
a generic label. A second conflict thus emerges between the abstract,
quasi-allegorical personae officiating at the trial and the specific, flesh-
and-blood individual on trial. *Representative* men as well as representative *men*, all three speak with man(kind)'s voice, which has become
inseparable from the voice of the law. In the end Nancy is at least triply
alienated—as a woman by men, as a concrete, subjective identity by
abstract, objective ones, and as an individual by an institution. There
is also of course the strong possibility that her alienation is racially
inflected, that the objectifying male voices that surround her in the
courtroom are also white voices, ready, as Gowan Stevens will be in the
following scene, to see her as irrevocably, inscrutably *other*.

It is significant that when Temple finds herself in a comparable
predicament, facing two representatives of the state at the governor's
office in the second act, the threatening hierarchies outlined above
are largely alleviated, and the result is a more equitable encounter in
which the woman's voice is allowed full participation. The governor and
the county attorney are flesh-and-blood creatures named Henry (RFN
99) and Gavin, and both men attempt to delegate the responsibility
of speaking to Temple, favoring the subjectivity of her confession over
the alienating objectivity that would impose a story upon her. Given
the much bleaker situation at Nancy's trial, however, it would appear

to be more than a coincidence that the voice we hear sobbing in the background as the curtain lurches down belongs to a woman.

We now begin to understand the full significance of the "Order! Order in the court! Order!" for which the bailiff cries so volubly at the trial's conclusion (45). Nancy is precisely that unruly element which the court is attempting to order—to command, and to contain—but it can do so only by resorting to methods that dehumanize and dominate her.[11] Creating order out of flux is an act that makes life and meaning possible but also one that, in the hands of an institution like the court, entails a sacrifice of human complexity—the story behind the authorized courtroom narrative—complexity that may at times approach the unacceptable, outrageous, obscene. All of this raises the possibility that the disgraceful business effaced by the falling curtain refers not to Nancy's "outlawed voice talking back" but to the court's own insistence on "hear[ing] in that voice only illicit defiance, the court's own binary opposite, to which it can only respond with its own (now more uneasily) sanctioned violence" (Moreland 210). If so, judicial theater has become a source of civic shame and embarrassment rather than civic pride.

The problem of containing Nancy and the threat she poses to the social stability, moral inflexibility, and reductive legality (for every violation a single violator) of Jefferson repeats a dilemma that is as old as the community itself—a dilemma, in fact, already prefigured and explored in *Requiem*'s first prologue, which traces the history of the courthouse, and the law, in Yoknapatawpha. The prologue reveals the courthouse's self-proclaimed status as eternal monument, "centennial and serene" beyond the reach of mutability (41), to be a myth of legitimation for an institution whose local origins are quite humble, contingent, equivocal, and, of course, political. Indeed, the courthouse, Faulkner explains, has "come into existence at all" only "by chance and accident," by the "simple fortuity" of a jailbreak (4), some of the most important implications of which go unnoticed in the frontier settlement not yet named Jefferson.

The jailbreak documents the failure of the same techniques of institutional control over "outlaws" that are deployed more successfully (though still to a degree subverted) at Nancy's trial. The frontier energies of the unnamed town maintain a precarious equilibrium until a "gang" of three or four mysterious strangers stumbles "by chance" upon "an incidental band of civilian more-or-less militia" in a swamp bottom outside Jefferson and is "brought into the Jefferson jail because it was the nearest one" (5). Confronted with the irruption of a socially marginal element that may well represent "underworld" forces, Jefferson responds by attempting to contain that element as rapidly, effectively, and comprehensively as possible. First, the threat must be quarantined, like the social disease it is, so the strangers are locked in the little "log-and-mudchinking jail" (6). Few places, after all, are further "outside" the spaces of legitimate social practice than the inside of a prison. To be an insider there is to be a social outcast, just as to be a social insider is to be positioned outside the jail. Located, suggestively enough, at the geographic center of the community, the jail affords the members of that community their principal means of articulating the boundaries between social legitimacy and social illegitimacy. Locking the strangers in the jail always also means locking themselves out of it, confirming their status as law-abiding citizens.

An additional technique of containment is to articulate the threat—in the sense of cutting it off, holding it apart, as well as the sense of identifying it—by giving it a name and a narrative. *Requiem*, of course, is preoccupied with the act of naming—what to name the town, how to identify the strangers, what label to give Nancy's act, whether "Temple Drake" or "Mrs Gowan Stevens" is to be the subject of storytelling—and here we can begin to see that this preoccupation is never free from political consequences, never entirely innocent. From the moment the strangers are brought into town, rumor and gossip begin circulating in an attempt to fill the literally nameless void they represent. Even the phrase "gang" begins to impose a particular identity on them, one with unsavory connotations. No longer mere strangers, who might be from anywhere—who might be law-abiding citizens, for that matter—they soon become "Natchez Trace bandits," "on the way across country to their hideout from their last exploit" (4–5). Efforts are also made to connect them with the notorious Harpes, with "Mason's ruffians," or with "John Murrel's organization": names that in frontier Mississippi are the very emblems of the exogenous and the outlaw. There is speculation that these "bandits" may even have "rewards on their heads." In this manner the strangers can be even further estranged, rendered more menacingly, but at the same time more reassuringly, other. By imposing a "criminal" personality upon them, the town can put even more social distance between itself and them.

The community's efforts to enclose and neutralize the strangeness in its midst, however, meet with ironies and contradictions from the very start. For one thing, the strangers are never definitively named, and the narratives assigned to them fail to achieve more than apocryphal status. Whatever threat the "bandits" may have posed to the settlement remains unarticulated (unexpressed by the strangers themselves, and unenunciated by the town), and as such difficult to distinguish from the much more overtly threatening posture Jefferson assumes toward them. The precariousness of social distinctions here, however, is nothing compared to the systematic subversion of almost every point of apparent contrast between the socially representative body of the militia and the socially marginal band of strangers. The militia, for instance, is only on hand at Hurricane Bottom to capture the "bandits" because it has been booted out of town for "drunken brawling" during a rather exuberant Independence Day celebration. The thematically relevant irony of the date here should not go unnoticed: for the anarchic "independence" of the militia is no less problematic than that of the alleged bandits. The home guard's own lawlessness and social eccentricity, that is, resemble that of its captives. And this irony is only compounded by the possibility, explicitly raised in the text, that one of the bandits is a former militiaman or—even worse—that the militia commander is himself a former bandit. The delegation that invades Jefferson, in other words, is indeed more of a "confederation" than a rigidly striated group of "captors and prisoners" (5–6).

The jailing of the strangers is also subject to ironic revision. Their confinement is necessary not simply as a strategy of containment and control but also as a means of preservation, not just "to protect the settlement from the bandits" but even more "to protect the bandits from the settlement." For no sooner do the prisoners arrive in Jefferson than they are met by a lynching party, a "small but determined gang" that, it should be noted, contains the most savage characters in the story, the only ones indisputably bent on violence (12). As such its behavior makes a mockery of arbitrarily imposed distinctions between lawful and outlaw elements in Yoknapatawpha, as does the description of the lynching party as a "gang," the same term used earlier to describe its intended victims.

These distinctions collapse altogether when the local "law-and-order party" clears Jefferson's streets of lynchers and militiamen alike, who now join the original prisoners in the lockup. At this point the jail has simply become a microcosm of the community itself: either the jail is a little settlement, or the settlement is one big jail. Either way, however, there is an indisputable connection between the lawless element in the jail and the law-abiding element outside it. As such, the boundaries that seal off the (anti)social space of the jail from the social space of Jefferson have already been ruptured. The breakout, in which an entire wall of the building is removed and dismantled, "leaving the jail open to the world like a stage" (and thus paving the way for the self-reflexive stagecraft of the play-scenes), is only the physical enactment of an already-completed social drama that reveals the jail to be truly central to the community in ways that go beyond mere geography (14). The bandits escape without having been punished or even named. Their stories untold, their connection to the community only imperfectly (and implicitly) articulated, they are an unformulated, unformulable remainder. This is precisely the fate that confronts Nancy when she is brought before the law more than a century later.

The courthouse, construction on which begins almost immediately after the jailbreak is discovered, reasserts and rearticulates the boundaries separating civil(ized) and uncivil(ized) behavior that have just been so unceremoniously dismantled. Before this project can get fully underway, however, the town must deal with another, closely related problem: it has unlawfully removed the padlock on the government mail pouch to use on the jailhouse door, from which the lock disappears during the breakout. This only casts further aspersions on the legitimacy of the town as a political and legal entity, as does its decision to buy the silence of the mail rider, Thomas Jefferson Pettigrew, by naming itself after him. The citizens of Jefferson, that is, are just as complicitous, just as guilty, as the legendary "bandits" who get the drama of communal origins rolling in the first place. Indeed, they and not the "bandits" are the only undisputed thieves in the tale. In retrospect, Jefferson is fortunate to have had the Hurricane Bottom bandits. But for their timely appearance, there would be no one to blame for the misrule that threatens the town but the citizens themselves. Or perhaps Jefferson has literally manufactured the bandits out of mere strangers or even—who knows?—unruly citizens, willfully forgetting, covering up, its own transgressive behavior and projecting that behavior instead onto the "outlaw" element it dredges up out of the swamp.

Once the crisis of the padlock is resolved, however, work on the courthouse can proceed, and the results are at once impressive and disturbing. As it rises higher and higher, "musing, brooding, symbolic and ponderable," its utterly contingent origins are repressed beneath what is all too literally a facade, "tall as cloud, solid as rock, dominating all: protector of the weak, judiciate and curb of the passions and lusts, repository and guardian of the aspirations and the hopes" (35). In this way, the institution of law literally erects a myth of its necessity, permanence, and infallibility, the same myth it legitimates by invoking God at Nancy's trial. As "the center, the focus, the hub; sitting looming in the center of the county's circumference like a single cloud in its ring of horizon," the courthouse defines an ideological as well as a geographical (and, of course, political) dialectic of interior and exterior, center and margin, legitimacy and eccentricity.[12] It authorizes, for instance, the containment and eventual dispossession of the Indians, the lawful banishment to the margins of America of a population deemed alien— a historical event recorded in all three prologues. Nancy is only the latest victim in a series of similar dispossessions traced throughout the novel, all of them under the sign and sanction of law. In this way, the events of "The Courthouse" are indeed a prologue to Nancy's trial. They also provide the proper context in which to interpret Gavin Stevens's decision to divest himself of the office of county attorney and represent Nancy instead. Stevens's willingness to dissociate himself from the oppressive, dehumanizing strategies of the prosecution (the official voice of the state in the courtroom), to defend an individual rather than an institution, to resist rather than represent the symbolic order, reflects his sensitivity to the deep structure of county history, a sensitivity that Faulkner depicts here and elsewhere as one of the lawyer-citizen's most exemplary qualities.[13]

. . . .

If the courtroom scene thus emerges as a contest of rhetoric between unequal parties, then we should also be prepared to interpret the conflict between Temple and Gavin that develops over the next several scenes as a fundamentally rhetorical one.[14] Temple's initial appearance upon the stage in act 1, scene 2 reveals a "brittle and tense, yet controlled" woman torn between the urge to confess her involvement in the events of September ninth and the equally powerful urge to con-

ceal that involvement and wound her adversaries. This sense of vacillation is captured in her recurring habit of lighting a cigarette, then
crushing it out, or asking for a drink, then leaving it untasted (see for
example 51–52, 80–81, 100–105). The stage directions allude specifically to Temple's repression and "controlled hysteria" as she speaks
her first lines, a lacerating parody of Nancy's words from the dock that
demonstrates that their subversive value has been lost on Temple: "Yes,
God. Guilty, God. Thank you, God. If that's your attitude toward being
hung, what else can you expect from a judge and jury except to accommodate you?" (47). Another revealing gesture, however, expresses
Temple's latent penitence. Just after she so bitterly mimics Nancy, she
kneels by the hearth to light a fire (48), a posture that suggests the
kind of confessional impulse that might lead her back toward the cause
and scene of her hysteria.

The same set of contradictory desires is present in Gowan. He too
lashes out hatefully at Nancy, referring to her repeatedly as a "murdering nigger" and a "nigger dope-fiend whore." The racist rhetoric would
seem to indicate that Gowan's only means of making sense out of the
death of his daughter is to make it the result of "murdering" impulses
he projects onto the reified otherness of "niggers." Gowan also reserves
a good deal of vituperation for his uncle, who has outraged him by
representing Nancy at her trial. And while Temple wishes to conceal
her role in the family tragedy, Gowan is tempted to evade his altogether,
seeking an "immunity" from his own past deeds that, as Gavin reminds
him, is never more than hypothetical (61–62). Finally, however, Gowan
too acknowledges his need to purge himself of his anger and shame
(52). And when he admits to Gavin that he has never forgiven his wife
for enjoying her period of captivity in the Memphis whorehouse, he
seems to benefit from the opportunity to confess (62–64).

Clearly, then, the Gowan Stevenses are struggling to find an adequate response to their suffering, and an adequate understanding of
its causes. The death of their child, however, continues to resist meaningful interpretation. Nothing in the experience of this couple has prepared them to grapple with Nancy's act, which is no doubt why they are
tempted to pronounce it mad. As Moreland writes, "Something tragic
has happened, without here any higher realm of order, authority, or
vision either to give that tragedy meaning," and such an "unrepresent-
able, unthinkable" act can only be conceived of by those left outside

its conception and execution as insane (210). The Stevenses' plan to run from their grief, to escape to California (RFN 49), however, is but one more version of that westward journey toward regeneration which has been such a central American myth from the frontier days onward—but a myth whose ironies have been exhaustively mapped by a host of American writers (think of the wanderings of Joe Christmas in *Light in August*, for example, or Jack Burden's agonizing trip to Long Beach in Warren's *All the King's Men*, or the experiences of Tod Hackett in West's *The Day of the Locust*, or even Huck Finn lighting out for the territories). These ironies are only compounded when we recall Temple's similar flight from Jefferson at the end of *Sanctuary*, after another traumatic murder trial (a comparison noted in Vickery, *The Novels of William Faulkner* 120). That time her path lay to the east, toward Europe, where, we learn in *Requiem*, she and Gowan were married. But if Paris and Cap Ferrat "couldn't fumigate [their] American past" (RFN 133), there is little reason to believe that California or Hawaii or Canada will offer them a haven this time around. In fleeing their past, Temple and Gowan only threaten to repeat it.

This is where the forensic figure, and his rhetorical training, come in. The task that devolves upon Gavin Stevens as the play-scenes unfold is not so much to impose an alien rhetoric upon his niece and nephew, as to guide these would-be escapists toward the purgative voice that already exists within them, toward the confrontation of primal scenes and revelations. The most pressing part of this task is to get Temple and Gowan back to Jefferson, which Gavin accomplishes by sending the couple a telegram in California (67). Stung by its frank indictment of their flight, Temple and Gowan return with two days to spare. The telegram, then, the first hint of Stevens's rhetorical savvy,[15] serves as a subpoena, calling Temple home to testify, while for Gowan it is more like a summons, since he is called home mainly to hear his wife's confession.

Temple's return to Jefferson, as she herself admits, is already a tacit acknowledgment of her complicity in Nancy's act. Furthermore, Gavin points out early in the third scene that Temple's unflinching attendance at the murder trial ("Every day. All day, from the time court opened" [70]) would seem to be motivated by something more than the desire for vengeance she professes—something like her own sense of connectedness with the accused. This is enough to arouse Gavin's suspicion that Temple is hiding something.[16] Yet she continues to struggle against telling her secret, and her favorite evasive maneuver in the emotional exchanges of scene 3 is to bring up the issues of Nancy's insanity (the inexplicability of her act, that is) and Gavin's incompetence in order to steer the debate away from herself. Temple's mission, as she interprets it, is to have the death sentence commuted, and the most effective way to do this, she reasons, is to prove that Nancy is crazy, or at least that she was not in full possession of her faculties on the night of September ninth. From Temple's point of view, establishing Nancy's mental impairment would also demonstrate Gavin's unfitness as a defense attorney, since he failed to plead Nancy insane. And it would still beg the question of Temple's own involvement in the tragedy. Temple thus casts herself as an eleventh-hour savior, outlawyering the lawyer. "All we need is an affidavit," she tells Gavin (71), and as she goes on to explain, she herself is that affidavit—her most candid admission thus far that she harbors, indeed embodies, a hidden story. But Temple quickly resumes her reticent pose, informing Gavin that "[a]ll we need now is to decide just how much of what to put in the affidavit" (72). *Putting in* is the operative concept here: Temple as living affidavit is less the organic expression (in the etymological sense) of her own story in her own voice than a site to which a whole collection of artificial "facts, papers, documents" (77)—and outright lies if necessary (80)—may conveniently be appended. When Gavin asks how she will account for the last-minute change of testimony she proposes, Temple says, "Tell them the district attorney bribed me to keep my mouth shut" (73), a most unfortunate answer, coming as it does from *Sanctuary*'s star perjuror for the prosecution. According to her plan, Temple need only recite the trumped-up statement, sign it, and once again dodge the bullet of her conscience.

Stevens, however, isn't buying. It is difficult to imagine what Temple could tell a judge that would constitute proof of Nancy's insanity (75). Furthermore, Stevens insists that it is too late for the plan anyway. "If that could have been done, would have sufficed, I would have thought of that, attended to that, four months ago" (78). What Gavin means by this statement is not that the idea of an insanity defense never occurred to him, but that he opted against it, then as now, because Nancy is not insane. It could have been done, that is, but it would not have sufficed. Legally, after all, an insane act is a meaningless act, an act that cannot be given legal meaning, that stubbornly evades, resists, or exhausts all other modes of legal description. Stevens, however, is convinced that Nancy's act has meaning, meaning that deserves to be brought to light. This is precisely what the legal system has denied Nancy and what Temple is denying her now. "In the eyes of the law," Gavin explains, Nancy "is already dead. In the eyes of the law, Nancy Mannigoe doesn't even exist" (72). Remember, however, that Stevens has for this trial dissociated himself from his official connections with "the law"—its eyes are not his eyes. (Nor, we might add, are its ears his ears.) It is not that Nancy's dying is ultimately "nothing" to Gavin, as Temple suggests (77), but that her life and death are doomed to remain inscrutable as long as Temple refuses to speak. Justice for Nancy is less a matter of "saving a condemned client whose trained lawyer has already admitted that he has failed," to quote Temple's mocking assessment (74)—less a matter of absolving Nancy from a punishment that she accepts, believes that she deserves, and to some degree does deserve—than a matter of understanding her, discovering the moral and legal meaning of her act. And to be understood, this act demands a context that only Temple's buried narrative can provide. By breaking her long silence, Temple can begin to bridge the gap between Nancy and the community that has so ruthlessly alienated her, and there is the further promise that the act of confession—itself, like all forms of storytelling, a binding force—might afford Temple a way out of her self-imposed isolation, a way to sleep again at night (79).[17]

There is one final relapse into evasion, however, before the first act ends. Stevens senses that the story Temple is repressing reaches far beyond September ninth, into the depths of her past. That is, the story may involve not only "Mrs Gowan Stevens," the bereaved mother, but also "Temple Drake," "the all-Mississippi debutante whose finishing school was the Memphis sporting house" (101). Gavin warns Temple that if her confession is to be meaningful, she must be prepared to tell everything, even the story of Temple Drake. Temple, on the other hand, stubbornly insists that her past life is dead and buried. Stevens, whose experiences in *Intruder in the Dust* have taught him that what is dead and buried can also be—and sometimes must be—exhumed, responds to Temple with *Requiem*'s most quoted line: "The past is never dead. It's not even past" (80)—a sentiment he has already voiced in an earlier scene (62).[18] The brute fact of September ninth is enough to drive this lesson home: the past isn't dead, the *future* is, smothered in its crib by a woman whose presence in the Stevens household is itself an index of Temple Drake's (the past's) stubborn survival. It is only when Temple confronts what remains of that future, her surviving child, asleep on the sofa—living emblem not only of the child she has already lost, the future she has already squandered, but also of the responsibility she still habitually seeks to evade—that she agrees to go with Stevens to see the governor.

. . . .

Forensic, religious, and psychoanalytic motifs converge in the opening scene of act 2, which takes place in the governor's office. The set occupies the same, upper-left-hand quadrant of the stage as the courtroom set in act 1, which hints that we may be about to witness a replay of the trial scene, with Temple rather than Nancy as the center of attention. Above the governor's thronelike seat—"the last, the ultimate seat of judgment," according to the stage directions—rests "the emblem, official badge, of the State," complete with an icon of the scales of justice and "a device in Latin perhaps" (98). These symbols are all too evocative of the menacing abstraction that characterized the anonymous officials of state at Nancy's trial, and there are elements of the governor's portrait that contribute further to this effect. "He is symbolic too: no known person, neither old nor young; he might be someone's idea not of God but of Gabriel perhaps, the Gabriel not before the Crucifixion but after it"—that is, the voice that calls souls to judgment on the Last Day (98–99). Yet the very next sentence begins to humanize this imposing figure. The dressing gown that he wears over his collar and tie, for instance, resembles a judge's robes, but in an informal, unpretentious way. Further, "his hair is neatly combed," a minor detail that, at two in the morning, reveals just the slightest, endearing touch of personal vanity. And as if to place the governor firmly on a human level, Gavin greets him by name (99).

In front of the governor's desk are a pair of chairs "turned slightly to face each other, the length of the desk between them" (98), an arrangement that reminds more than one reader of a confessional.[19] The references to Gabriel and to the governor's robelike dressing gown therefore acquire new, ecclesiastical overtones. But if the governor, in beckoning Temple to be seated, suggests a priest inviting her to enter the confessional, he is also a judge directing her to the witness stand,

as he overtly acknowledges (101). And when Temple requests a blind-
fold (99), alluding ironically to herself as a firing squad victim, the
reader attuned to the forensic elements of this scene will immediately
think of the blind icon on the governor's wall: is Temple unconsciously
indicating her readiness to become, at last, an agent of justice? Appropriately enough, a Freudian slip brings the therapeutic dimension of
the scene firmly into the foreground. Temple once again is seeking to
goad Gavin, but her words are revealing: "Dont lawyers always tell their
patients—I mean clients—never to say anything at all, to let them do
all the talking?" (101). These intersecting lines of imagery suggest that
in the governor's office, at least—if not in the Jefferson courtroom—
judgment can go hand in hand with analysis, atonement, and healing.

As the scene progresses, Temple returns over and over to the issue
of confession, voicing more and more explicitly her deep need to share
her story. She also begins to shed the pretense that the desire to save
Nancy's life is what motivates this need. "I've got to say it all," she realizes, whether or not the governor will pardon Nancy, "or I wouldn't be
here" (112). This need to tell, we discover, dates from long before the
recent tragedy. It was, in fact, already present during Temple's Memphis days, expressed most fully in her letters to her lover Alabama Red.
Since Popeye, her captor, inevitably watched while the couple made
love, the letters were in a very real sense Temple's only moments alone
with Red, her sole opportunity to lend a semblance of dignity to their
relationship. For this beleaguered couple, written intercourse was more
intimate than sexual intercourse.

The purgative impulse is also at the heart of Temple's marriage to
Gowan, which is in many ways a substitute for the earlier bond with
Red. At their wedding, Temple reports, she and Gowan were seized
by an urge "to kneel down, the two of us, and say 'We have sinned,
forgive us'" (133–34). Even after the couple has settled comfortably in
with the "right" crowd in Jefferson, the memory of the Memphis days
and the desire "to have someone to talk to" about them, someone who
"could speak her [Temple's] language" (105), still haunt Temple, leading her to hire Nancy Mannigoe. In one of the novel's central passages,
Temple attempts to evoke the sense of tranquility she experienced in
the company of Nancy, who was less a nursemaid, really, than

[s]omebody to talk to, as we all seem to need, want, have to have, not to
converse with you nor even agree with you, but just keep quiet and lis-

ten. Which is all that people really want, really need; I mean, to behave themselves, keep out of one another's hair; the maladjustments which they tell us breed the arsonists and rapists and murderers and thieves and the rest of the anti-social enemies, are not really maladjustments but simply because the embryonic murderers and thieves didn't have anybody to listen to them: which is an idea the Catholic Church discovered two thousand years ago only it just didn't carry it far enough . . . and maybe if the world was just populated with a kind of creature half of which were dumb, couldn't do anything but listen, couldn't even escape from having to listen to the other half, there wouldn't even be any war. Which was what Temple had: somebody paid by the week just to listen. (137–38)

The references to the Church and to psychopathology are in accord with the scene's dominant motifs of confession and repression.

Whenever Temple threatens to lapse into her old habits of stalling and denial, her listeners intervene: the governor by gently coaxing her to continue, Stevens less patiently, by prompting her or by filling in missing details himself (after the trip to Jackson, he seems to know a good deal more now about Temple's past). These contrasting styles— fatherly and adversarial—combine effectively to keep Temple talking.[20] Interestingly, Gavin's interruptions and revelations quite often mitigate the harshness of Temple's self-portraiture. Especially near the end of the scene (139–49), when Stevens basically takes over the narration, he depicts Temple more sympathetically than she depicts herself, which leaves me unable to concur with Noel Polk's opinion that Stevens's primary goal here and elsewhere in *Requiem* is to humiliate or "crucify" Temple (*Faulkner's* Requiem xiii; see also 124–25).[21] Indeed, Gavin seems intent on making *Gowan*, the Virginia gentleman, a prominent character in the narrative of corruption and complicity (see especially RFN 110–19, 134–40). Perhaps this is even a way for Gavin to acknowledge his own involvement in the Stevens family tragedy, since the gaps in Gowan's gentility arguably indict Gavin's own genteel background.

The story that begins to emerge during this scene is in best Faulknerian fashion a collaborative effort, out of whose fits and starts we gradually reconstruct Temple's secret. From the very beginning Mr. and Mrs. Gowan Stevens labor under the strain of their ritualized enactments of forgiveness and gratitude, and neither parenthood nor the presence of Nancy can really ease this strain. Then Red's younger brother appears in Jefferson, seeking to blackmail Temple with her Memphis letters to Red—letters of which Gowan is still unaware. It is here that Mrs. Gowan Stevens reverts to her identity as Temple Drake. Infatuated with her blackmailer, who perhaps reminds her of Red, she agrees not only to meet his demands but to run away with him, leaving at least one of her children motherless. Hearing of these plans, Nancy hides Temple's money and jewelry in order to prevent her from leaving and to keep the Stevens family intact. When this effort fails, however, Nancy turns to more drastic measures.

. . . .

The long scene that opens act 2 should be read as a crash course in the art of telling. Late in the scene, as Stevens pushes the story of Temple Drake Stevens onward toward its heart of darkness, the stage lights, as if in sympathy with the onstage narration, begin to flicker and dim, lowering steadily until they "go completely out" (148). All that we see or hear from the darkened set is Gavin's voice, which closes out the scene with an entreaty to Temple that is also an invocation: "Now tell him" (149). Gavin's words, which cede narrative control and authority to Temple, are in stark contrast to the unseen "MAN'S VOICE" of the opening scene, a voice that silences Nancy, intimidates her, and orders her around. Moreover, we may hear in Gavin's encouraging words an echo of another Faulkner text, the *Knight's Gambit* tale "Tomorrow," in which Stevens is able to elicit stories from his constituents among the Yoknapatawpha plain folk with a simple injunction to "tell it." Here, however, his rhetoric is even more effective. For as Temple assumes the full burden of narration for the first time in the novel, the result is one of the most striking examples of the incantatory power of storytelling in all of Faulkner, one that contrasts sharply with *Sanctuary*'s dark brothel scene, where Temple tells Horace Benbow essentially nothing.

Act 2, scene 2 (150–67), which depicts Temple's climactic encounter with Nancy in the final moments before the baby's death, is the ethical and epistemological center of the novel, *Requiem*'s primal scene, as it were. Like all primal scenes, it is accessible only through narrative reconstruction, through memory and story. This story, however, is no longer merely recounted from the governor's office. Rather, it is enacted directly onstage, a play-within-a-play whose dramatic immediacy signals the psychological impact of Temple's "offstage" narrative on teller and listener alike. The teller and the scene of telling disappear into the tale itself, and what we behold is literally what Temple's story looks like, the *fabula* of which her narrative is the *sjuzet*. In calling forth light out of darkness and summoning the past directly to the stage, this tour de force of storytelling confirms Temple's emergence as a raconteur and thereby constitutes a resounding endorsement of Gavin Stevens as the teacher and maieutic figure who leads her to confront this scene in language rather than continue to repress it and thus to "speak" it only hysterically.

With the very first word of the stage directions, "Interior," we enter a poststructuralist's no-man's-land, a psychological space where past events are immediately accessible and motives that have been unfathomable elsewhere in the play become suddenly comprehensible. The setting, "Temple's private sitting- or dressing-room" (150), is particularly appropriate, given the intensely personal nature of the events that are to take place there. Further details of scene 2 reiterate the privileged status of its content. Here, for instance, the blackmailer, about whom Gavin Stevens could supply only sketchy details, comes fully to life, and his name—Pete—is mentioned for the first time in the novel (150). The real significance of the scene, however, lies in its unflinching acknowledgment of Temple's complicity in her daughter's fate. Pete, we learn, gives Temple the opportunity to burn the letters and preserve her family. She cannot decide at first, much as she has vacillated about whether to smoke at several earlier points in the text, but she eventually decides against burning the letters and in favor of running away with Pete. With this decision it becomes clear that Temple has put her own desires ahead of the welfare of her children, who will apparently be separated when the marriage breaks up. In an attempt to weaken Temple's resolve, Nancy forces her to voice her intentions explicitly:

NANCY: Maybe I am ignorant. You got to say it out in words yourself, so I can hear them. Say, I'm going to do it.

TEMPLE: You heard me. I'm going to do it.

NANCY: Money or no money.

TEMPLE: Money or no money.

NANCY: Children or no children.

(*Temple doesn't answer*)

To leave one with a man that's willing to believe the child aint got no father, willing to take the other one to a man that dont even want no children—

> (*They stare at one another*)

If you can do it, you can say it.

TEMPLE: Yes! Children or no children. Now get out of here. (164)

Neither Nancy nor Pete, it seems, can successfully coerce Temple. "It wasn't even the letters," she admits to Nancy. "It was me" (166).

Nancy's determination to keep Temple from destroying her family is the other crucial feature of this scene. She tries reasoning with Temple, appealing to her conscience, even hiding her money and jewelry—all to no avail. Then, and only then, she turns to violence. As she herself tells Temple, "I tried everything I knowed. You can see that" (165). That Nancy first exhausts all of her other options, however, seems to me a measure of her essential sanity. In order to avoid any potential misunderstandings, I should make it clear that I do not mean by this statement to condone infanticide. I do think, however, that Nancy's act should be recognized as a product of careful deliberation, an act of will that, though tragically misguided, is neither deranged nor even ultimately malicious. Indeed, this scene suggests that love and not malice is what motivated Nancy's deed, what she had aforethought, as it were. Hindsight thus reveals the basic soundness of Gavin Stevens's legal judgment after all—since his client was indeed responsible for her actions, he honors her dignity and autonomy by foregoing an insanity defense. He is also right to insist that Temple's confession be directed toward easing her own suffering rather than Nancy's. Finally, and most important, if Nancy is not insane, then the death of Temple's baby girl is not meaningless. The story that is presented in scene 2 affirms that meaning and Temple's part in it.

. . . .

This story, however, is not an end but a beginning.[22] For Temple, remembering the past and repeating or reliving it must be supplemented by a third process. We can call this process by the name Freud gave it, *working through,* or by the older name of atonement, but either way it is still an interpersonal phenomenon, primarily verbal and peculiarly open-ended in nature. As Freud learned to his frustration, and as any Catholic confessor would no doubt agree, the talking cure is a perversely interminable affair. Yet as we return to the governor's office for the beginning of scene 3 Temple is ready to declare her story over and done with. "And that's all," she announces (167), as though she plans to rise from her knees, walk away from the governor's office a new woman, and leave the messy business of penitence behind her. A moment later, she refers to her confession in the past tense: "all of this was not for the sake of [Nancy's] soul because her soul doesn't need it, but for mine" (169).

Is Temple about to fall back into the silence, secrecy, and denial that have characterized the last eight years of her life? It is to insure against just such an eventuality that Gavin Stevens has arranged for Gowan to come to Jackson and to change places with the governor during Temple's flashback. With the governor's exit, the Stevenses are left alone onstage, and Temple's confession becomes a family matter rather than an official one. This personal context works against the possibility of evasion, for the moment Temple looks up to find herself speaking to her husband (173), any hope of leaving her skeletons behind her in some closet of the capitol becomes moot. The past is not dead. It's not even past. There is an important lesson here for Gowan also. The revelations of the last two scenes leave him unable to deny the fact that his own weakness and self-absorption have contributed significantly to the anguish of his family. All of this, of course, should inspire his empathy and forgiveness, but he greets Temple with only a simulacrum of these feelings. His clipped phrases fairly bristle with repressed hostility, a sign that he, like Temple, harbors a lingering aversion to the prospect of working through his problems.

> GOWAN: [T]his may be the time for me to start saying sorry for the next eight-year term. Just give me a little time. Eight years of gratitude might be a habit a little hard to break. So here goes.
>
> (*to Temple*)
>
> I'm sorry. Forget it.
>
> TEMPLE: I would have told you.

GOWAN: You did. Forget it. You see how easy it is? You could have been
doing that yourself for eight years. . . . I guess that's all, isn't it? We can
go home now. (174–75)

He then petulantly stalks offstage (176), leaving Temple to return to
Jefferson with Gavin. As his wife was earlier, however, Gowan is clearly
mistaken in declaring "That's all." It is far too late for the immunity
he alludes to so wistfully in the first act. He and Temple can no longer
avoid each other and the terrible knowledge they now share. Sooner or
later their dialogue will begin.

This private dialogue, however, is only half the battle. For Temple
and Gowan there remains the further task of overcoming the inertial
pull of their mutual grief and anger, expiation and love, and reenter-
ing Jefferson life. This outward movement toward the wider horizons of
community and one's role in it under the symbolic covenant is a central
feature of the novel's final act, set appropriately enough in the "common room" of the Yoknapatawpha County lockup. As the prologues
reveal, the very existence of the jail, along with its prominent role in
local history, attests to the inconceivability of community—in Faulkner
at least—apart from guilt, travail and expiation, and, by implication,
the inconceivability of expiation in the absence of community. Yet while
Temple is no stranger to the outside of the jail (see 169–70), there is
no evidence in either *Sanctuary* or *Requiem* to suggest that she has
ever entered this building or visited its inmates. Before now, that is.
For her long-overdue trip to the jail in act 3, a trip she makes with
Gavin Stevens, is a tacit acknowledgment of her bond with the other
sinners and sufferers housed there and elsewhere in the community.
This rekindled sense of social awareness is the final stage in the education of Temple Drake Stevens, an education—in the root sense of a
"drawing out" into group life—which is in great part the work of her
uncle Gavin.[23]

The strong emphasis here on collective, communal approaches to
guilt, grief, and suffering leaves me uneasy with the contention of critics such as Joseph Urgo that Temple's regeneration is a strictly personal, individualistic affair, that only when Temple "ceases to rely on
the authority of others" will she "begin to save her soul" (Urgo 137).
Temple must discover her own voice in *Requiem*, it is true, but other
voices such as Nancy's, Gavin's, and the other inmates', play a large

role in leading her to that discovery. It is not the result of her intuition, or her will, alone. Indeed, Temple's stubbornly individualistic insistence that she was in no way connected to Nancy's act other than as a victim of it was her way of repressing both her involvement in the death of her daughter, and the voice in which she might have confessed and confronted that involvement. All along, her independence has been one of the primary obstacles to her regeneration.

Temple's visit to the jail, however, gives her an opportunity to observe that grief and anguish can be shared rather than borne alone. Among the black inmates of the jail, this sharing is expressed in a particularly striking, choral format. It may not be entirely shocking to discover that Nancy Mannigoe leads this chorus, but her first recruit, as Temple learns from the jailor, is something of a surprise.

> Every Sunday night, and every night since last Sunday except last night—come to think of it, Lawyer, where was you last night? We missed you—Lawyer here and Na—the prisoner have been singing hymns in her cell. The first time, he just stood out there on the sidewalk while she stood in that window yonder. Which was all right, not doing no harm, just singing church hymns. . . . [I]t happened that me and Mrs Tubbs hadn't went to prayer meeting that night, so we invited him to come in; and to tell the truth, we come to enjoy it too. Because as soon as they found out there wasn't going to be no objection to it, the other nigger prisoners . . . joined in too, and by the second or third Sunday night, folks was stopping along the street to listen to them instead of going to regular church. (227–28)

The conjoined voices of the inmates hark back to the collective and complicitous origins of their community, in the "one conjoined breathing" of Jefferson's pioneer founders (28). These voices are choral in the Greek sense, as we have already seen the jail itself to be. The hymns offer a sober but nonetheless stubbornly affirmative commentary upon the inescapable presence of suffering and atonement in collective life. And Gavin's participation in this chorus—which, as one critic has perceptively noted, redeems his earlier inability to participate in a similar chorus of grief in "Go Down, Moses" (Moreland 234)—suggests that his role in Temple's personal drama verges at times upon choral commentary.

When suffering is shared among many, forgiveness is likely to fol-

low, and the jail scene proves no exception. Jailor Tubbs, for instance,
who is in his own rude way a representative of community sentiments
and values, confesses that while he finds Nancy's act "about as horrible
a crime as this county ever seen," he bears "[n]o hard feelings" for
her (RFN 242). Similarly, Tubbs implies that the "home folks here in
Jefferson and Yoknapatawpha County both" are ready to forgive Lawyer Stevens and to accept him back into their fold, "even if some of
us might have thought he got a little out of line" in taking Nancy's
case (227). Nor does his willingness to forgive these two threaten his
sympathy for Temple, whom he treats with gentleness and respect. The
jail thus emerges as a central site of forgiveness and human kindness,
where people are treated as subjects rather than objects. It was there, we
recall from the first prologue, that the boundaries separating legitimate
and illegitimate elements of society were temporarily, and productively,
dismantled. They are dismantled again when Temple is literally locked
in the bull-pen for her final encounter with Nancy (231). This episode
directly invokes the earlier scene at the jail in which the militiamen
and the bandits are locked up together. Once again, that is, citizen and
outlaw share the same social space, and once again this positioning
signals a deeper connectedness between them.

Nancy's final appearance (232–43) bears witness to the inherent
value and necessity of the act of telling while confirming that this act
can offer only a palliative, not a panacea, for suffering. Jailor Tubbs
reveals that Nancy, who has seemed so silent and self-assured throughout the play, has arranged to spend the eve of her execution in the
company of a preacher (242). Nancy, that is, is going out of this world
in dialogue. The particular genre of storytelling that we call confession can for her end only when life itself does. Her example is thus a
lesson to Temple, who even now yearns for final answers. "This time
tomorrow," she tells Nancy, "you wont be anything at all. But not me.
Because there's tomorrow, and tomorrow, and tomorrow. All you've got
to do is, just to die. But let [God] tell me what to do. No: that's wrong:
I know what to do, what I'm going to do; I found that out that same
night in the nursery too. But let Him tell me how. How? Tomorrow,
and tomorrow, and still tomorrow. How?" (236). She also questions the
ultimate morality of *Requiem*'s ethic of connectedness: "Why cant you
buy back your own sins with your own agony? Why do you and my little
baby both have to suffer just because I decided to go to a baseball game

eight years ago?" (237). Nancy, however, offers no final answers. "Is there a heaven, Nancy?" Temple asks. "I dont know," Nancy replies. "I believes." "Believe what?" "I dont know. But I believes" (241). And again, in her closing lines, just before she is locked away from Temple forever:

NANCY (*moving on after the Jailor*): Believe.

TEMPLE: Believe what, Nancy? Tell me.

NANCY: Believe. (243)

Nancy refuses to impose a belief, whether orthodox or subversive, upon Temple. Instead, Nancy insists that Temple create, define, and personalize her own belief. With no guarantee of either salvation or peace, the survivors are left to fend for themselves, and one of *Requiem*'s most salient points is that the best way they can do so is by continuing to ask their questions, to tell their stories, to argue over their beliefs, to correct their misstatements, to share their moments of happiness and pain—in short, to keep alive the dialogue that Gavin Stevens has helped open.

Requiem's third prologue paves the way for this discovery by demonstrating the dire necessity of collaboration and dialogue in twentieth-century life. The prologue traces the intertwined histories of the jail and the county from the frontier days to Faulkner's present day of 1951 and even beyond, to the centennial of Appomattox (217). The "progress" of Yoknapatawpha County through these one hundred and thirty years is revealed as a series of dispossessions and displacements, but the most insidious chapter in this history is the advent—or onslaught—of modernity and urbanization. This onslaught is depicted as an all-out invasion of noise that threatens to overwhelm individual and regional distinctions and to drown out all meaningful forms of expression and communication.[24] The final dispossession is that of silence itself:

[A]nd, now and at last, the last of silence too: the county's hollow inverted air one resonant boom and ululance of radio: and thus no more Yoknapatawpha's air nor even Mason and Dixon's air, but America's: the patter of comedians, the baritone screams of female vocalists, the babbling pressure to buy and buy and still buy arriving more instantaneous than light, two thousand miles from New York and Los Angeles . . . one swirling rocket-roar filling the glittering zenith as with golden feathers, until the vast hollow sphere of [the] air . . . is murmurous with [man's]

fears and terrors and disclaimers and repudiations and his aspirations
and dreams and his baseless hopes, bouncing back at him in radar waves
from the constellations. (210, 213)

Against this background buzz and its homogenizing tendencies, story
and dialogue become the most viable means of self-defense, a way to
assert individual dignity without falling prey to the solipsisms of monologue and private language.

In "The Jail," Faulkner not only preaches but practices this gospel
of collaboration. Late in the prologue, as if in response to the assault
of modernity and "progress" he describes, Faulkner's narrator directly
solicits the narratee, addressing this figure in the second person and
describing her/him in revealing detail. Here, that is, for the first and
only time in his fiction, Faulkner explicitly incarnates the storytelling
bond at the outermost level of narrative structure:

> [S]uddenly you, a stranger, an outlander say from the East or the North
> or the Far West, passing through the little town by simple accident, or
> perhaps relation or acquaintance or friend of one of the outland fami-
> lies which had moved into one of the pristine and recent subdivisions,
> yourself turning out of your way to fumble among road signs and filling
> stations out of frank curiosity, to try to learn, comprehend, understand
> what had brought your cousin or friend or acquaintance to elect to live
> here—not specifically here, of course, not specifically Jefferson, but such
> as here, such as Jefferson—suddenly you would realise that something
> curious was happening or had happened here. (217)

The narrator and narratee gather around a kind of kernel text, a young
girl's dated signature, scratched into the glass of a jailhouse window
ninety years ago: "*Cecelia Farmer April 16th 1861*" (197; Faulkner's emphasis). Working conjecturally, they tease a story out of this historical
artifact, a collaborative creation that is itself something of a talking
cure, conquering time and distance, actively constituting community,
and healing the breaches wrought by the dispersive forces of contemporary culture.[25] The collaborators read Cecelia's signature as precisely
the kind of linguistic self-assertion demanded by their own precarious situation within modernity: " '*Listen, stranger; this was myself: this
was I* '" (225; Faulkner's emphasis). The signature, that is, represents
Cecelia's refusal to be objectified, her insistence on speaking as a sub-

ject, on naming and thereby asserting herself, an insistence that has led Moreland to read Cecelia's autograph as a harbinger of *écriture feminine* (196). In its own small way, then, the signature counters the march of alienation and lawful dispossession in Yoknapatawpha, much as Nancy has tried to do in the courtroom and Temple must now and henceforth try to do.

The novel's conclusion implies that Temple has at long last reconciled herself to an ethic of connectedness and collaboration. From offstage Gowan calls her name, an apparently innocuous act that turns out to be frustratingly difficult to interpret. On the one hand, it may signal Gowan's sincere desire to make amends for his immature behavior in the previous scene. On the other hand, "Gowan's Voice," as it is labeled here, may simply represent a new version of that dehumanizing "MAN'S VOICE" that addresses Nancy at the outset of the trial scene. Gowan's real aim, in other words, may be further objectification, alienation, intimidation, recrimination, or outright domination. Despite this ambiguity, however, Temple is willing to take her chances with him. Her response to his call, "Coming," is the last spoken line in the play, and it expresses her commitment to reunion and also to that most precious commodity in Faulkner, motion. *Requiem*, in other words, is ending where it began, with an escape from jail and a reentry into society. Here, however, Temple emerges from the jail with a better understanding of, sympathy for, and solidarity with the outlaw she leaves behind there. This is the legacy of Gavin Stevens and his maieutic forensics: in the aftermath of the prison door's apocalyptic "clash and clang" (245), the puny inexhaustible voice of Temple Drake Stevens will still be talking. Her story, and Nancy's, will go on.

. . . .

CHAPTER SIX

Reappraising the Forensic Figure:
Gavin Stevens and His Discontents
in *The Town* and *The Mansion*

Picture a small southern town in the early decades of the twentieth century, an agrarian community with a modest business sector and a decent, god-fearing citizenry. This community is held together first of all by talk—by rumor, anecdote, conversation, pleasantry, sermon, conjecture, query, even humor—but also in large part by a fundamental respect for the law and the law-abiding. Wealth and power tend to accumulate in the hands of the already wealthy and powerful, a small group of respectable, genteel town fathers, but for the other citizens there at least remains the comforting, if seldom realized, promise of economic opportunity and social mobility, a lingering hint of the American Way. Suddenly, however, the town finds itself besieged by grasping exogenous forces, which mount a series of incursions against the socioeconomic stability of community life. Conspicuous as they may seem, the invaders themselves prove to be silent, inscrutable presences, making their threat to the community all the more difficult to pinpoint and contain. One of them, in fact, has married his way into a prominent landowning family from the southern part of the county.

If this narrative of encroachment seems lifted straight from the pages of *Knight's Gambit*, it is also a rudimentary plot summary of *The Town* and *The Mansion*, the latter volumes of the Snopes trilogy, in which Flem Snopes, after conquering Frenchman's Bend in *The Hamlet*, moves onward and upward to the greener pastures of Jefferson. The creeping threat of the Snopeses is depicted by one Jeffersonite as both a pestilence and a military invasion (T 106), while at other times Jefferson seems to conceive of it as an epidemic, not unlike the outbreak of polio traced to a nameless family of "new people" that has just moved to town (T 301). By turns social vermin, social interlopers, and social disease, the Snopeses become for Jefferson the very image of alterity, the incarnation of the alien.

Knight's Gambit has already taught us how insular, homogeneous communities such as Jefferson protect themselves against the encroachment of outsiders, a lesson reinforced by the first prologue of *Requiem for a Nun*. The principal (and most dependable) policing force in Jefferson, for instance, is narrative itself. The rich colloquial life of the natives, particularly their gossip and storytelling, provides them with a pervasive surveillance network, a means of detecting, isolating, and neutralizing difference. And if colloquial detection proves insufficient, Jefferson's legal codes offer a more formal set of institutional responses to alien designs against the community and its members, as the interminable series of lawsuits, contractual disputes, and criminal complaints filed against the Snopeses (all in the vain hope of keeping them "in their place") will attest.

Both of these strategies of containment are in place in Jefferson from the opening pages of *The Town*. In the "Centaur in Brass" episode (T 9–29), for example, what foils Flem's plan to filch every brass part and fitting from the town power plant is the colloquial exchange of information and conjecture among three of the plant's employees, Tom Tom, Turl, and Mr. Harker. The crucial moment in this episode occurs when Tom Tom learns that Turl has been cuckolding him. Instead of violence, however, what breaks out between the two men is a conversation, in which Tom Tom and Turl figure out Snopes's scheme and vow to prevent it. They do this by dumping the embezzled brass into the town water tank, where the contraband, along with Flem's dream of getting rich quick, is for the time being safely contained.

Moreover, no sooner does Snopes resign from the power plant than a second level of colloquial containment emerges in the story of the brass plot, which quickly begins to circulate among concerned citizens such as V. K. Ratliff and Gavin Stevens. Narratives like this one, no matter how homely or insignificant they may seem, are part of Jefferson's perpetual struggle to understand the Snopeses, take their measure, and assay their menace, so it is probably no coincidence that the textual account of the power plant incident is framed by a conversation in which

Stevens and Ratliff speculate about just that menace—or that this conversation is in turn framed by the first-person narrative structure of chapter 1, a story told by Chick Mallison, who is himself in easygoing dialogue with the novel's other chapter-narrators, Stevens and Ratliff. At the outermost level of narrative structure, then, *The Town* is an extended act of colloquial surveillance, an ongoing conversation among citizen-storytellers about the nature and scope of "Snopesishness" (T 136).

Another early episode in *The Town* provides a suggestive glimpse of legal techniques of containment at work in the community.[1] When the city electrician, Mr. Buffaloe, takes Jefferson's first automobile out for its inaugural run in 1904, he reaches the town square just as Colonel Sartoris pulls away from his bank in a horse-drawn carriage. The horses, of course, are spooked by the noisy machine, so enraging the colonel that at the next meeting of the local board of aldermen he personally rams through "an edict that no gasoline-propelled vehicle should ever operate on the streets of Jefferson" (T 11). This anachronistic measure reveals the fundamental conservatism of the law in Jefferson, for what it seeks to neutralize is change itself, any progressive element that might undermine the monopoly of "the old dug-in city fathers" on status and power (T 12). The same anxiety, suspicion, and rejection will greet the Snopeses upon their arrival in Jefferson. It is no doubt a harbinger of things to come, then, that the automobile law immediately backfires, as it were. The city fathers are voted out of office in a landslide election, and the new mayor, Manfred de Spain, is a champion of progress who puts Mr. Buffaloe on the city payroll and mockingly hangs a copy of the automobile edict in the courthouse, "where pretty soon people were coming in automobiles from as far away as Chicago to laugh at it" (T 13). De Spain also buys himself a flashy sports car, sells his horses, and converts his livery stable into "the first garage and automobile agency in Jefferson" (T 14). De Spain's career in Jefferson, and his ability to circumvent legal containment there, directly foreshadow the rise of that other local upstart, Flem Snopes, who, as it happens, gets his first big break in Jefferson, the power plant job, from the new mayor. Indeed, de Spain, upon whose coattails Flem rides to power in the community, is the transitional figure in Faulkner's thick description of the class struggle and the rise of the poor-white in the turn-of-the-century South: as an iconoclast and a center of controversy, he is overtly linked to Flem and his ilk, but he is also the scion of an established Jefferson family with links to the Sartorises, McCaslins, Compsons, and Stevenses. This is why Faulkner can cast de Spain as one of Gavin Stevens's principal antagonists but also, paradoxically, as one of Flem's.

Given the centrality of colloquial surveillance and legal policy in the effort to check subversive threats against the Jefferson status quo, it is not exactly a surprise to find Stevens, an important character in *The Town* and *The Mansion*, enlisted in Jefferson's crusade against Flem Snopes and his brethren. Indeed, the storytelling lawyer-sleuth and exemplary citizen of *Knight's Gambit* would seem to be a natural choice to lead this crusade. Late in *The Mansion*, for instance, in an embedded tale published separately as "Hog Pawn," Stevens proves true to his *Knight's Gambit* form by interceding in the "guerilla feud" that breaks out between Orestes Snopes and an old man named Meadowfill, spoiling Snopes's plan to coerce the old man out of a valuable piece of real estate. Thanks to Stevens's intervention, property remains in its rightful hands, and Chick Mallison supplies an additional point of convergence with *Knight's Gambit* by serving as Gavin's sidekick and conversation partner throughout the episode (see M 328–49).

It is one of the great ironies of *The Town* and *The Mansion*, however, an irony that marks the distance between these novels and *Knight's Gambit*, that the "Hog Pawn" incident is only the exception that proves the general rule of Stevens's lack of success in combating what he calls "Snopesism" (M 137). Though he daydreams about turning in Flem to the FBI as a communist (M 241–43), this fantasy of legal containment is as close as Gavin ever comes to thwarting Jefferson's arch-capitalist. A figure much given to resignation and renunciation throughout the Snopes novels, Gavin all but relinquishes the roles of colloquial detective and local Cincinnatus in these works, and the characters who inherit these roles make rather unlikely allies, to say the least.

The character who most closely approximates Stevens as colloquial detective in the trilogy actually precedes him in this role. At the very beginning of *The Hamlet*, a novel in which Stevens does not even appear, V. K. Ratliff emerges as an affable raconteur and veteran watcher of Snopeses, blessed with a steel-trap mind and the social instincts of the canny salesman he in fact is. Throughout the trilogy, Ratliff is a leading figure in the war on Snopesism, a much more effectual figure, by and large, than his friend the county attorney. It is Ratliff, after all, who lends Wallstreet Panic Snopes enough money to keep his grocery business out of the clutches of his cousin Flem (T 147–49). As a result, Wall, a decent fellow and therefore, like his father Eck before him, reckoned a "non-Snopes" by local opinion, goes on to build a nationwide empire of self-service groceries. (One is tempted to call them Wall-Marts.) It is also Ratliff who more or less single-handedly derails Clarence Snopes's bid for a seat in the United States Congress, in the "By the People" episode of *The Mansion* (M 295–321). While Gavin Stevens bemoans Clarence's victory as inevitable (M 310), Ratliff unflappably sets about preventing it. At the traditional election-year picnic, where Snopes is scheduled officially to enter the congressional race, Ratliff directs a pair of young practical jokers to whisk the candidate's pants legs with a few dampened switches from a nearby thicket that doubles as "a dog way station," "[a] kind of dog post office you might say" (M 316)—thus plugging poor Clarence into a rather pungent network of canine exchange. The humiliated Snopes is forced to withdraw from the race, and for eliminating him, Ratliff is christened "Cincinnatus" by Gavin Stevens (M 320)—the irony, of course, being that this title was once, but is apparently no longer, Gavin's own (see RFN 43, 184). It is perhaps in tribute to Ratliff's active role in the trilogy as protector of the polis that Faulkner at one point outfits him in a policeman's slicker: a homely but fitting image of *homo politicus* in Yoknapatawpha (T 257).

Ratliff also tends to be a more reliable source of information than Stevens. He is first, for example, to recognize that what makes Flem Snopes tick is not simply greed so much as a powerful (and quite ordinary) desire for respectability (T 259). Stevens, on the other hand, repeatedly misses this point. Likewise, when Flem's daughter, Linda, is prohibited from going away to college, Stevens blames the girl's mother, Eula, for keeping her at home, while Ratliff correctly perceives that Flem, who stands to lose control over Linda's inheritance in the event that she marries, is responsible (T 227). When Mink Snopes is finally released from prison, it is Ratliff, with his "terrifying capacity for knowledge or local information or acquaintanceship" (M 381), who personally travels to Parchman farm and verifies that Mink, who has jealously nursed his hatred for his cousin Flem for forty-three years, is bound for Jefferson and bent on murder. By contrast, Gavin's elaborate intelligence-gathering operation, which stretches to Memphis as well as Parchman, turns up nothing whatsoever about Mink until well after he has reached Jefferson and his archaic pistol has functioned (M 395). And at the very end of *The Mansion*, it is, predictably, Ratliff who unerringly locates Mink and leads Stevens to a quiet but cathartic confrontation with him (M 429–34).

Time and time again in the trilogy, Ratliff's understanding of Snopes behavior, Snopes motives, and even Snopes whereabouts is prior and superior to Gavin's. "Ratliff," Chick Mallison admits, "was how we first began to learn about Snopes. Or rather, Snopeses" (T 4). He is the colloquial source for much of what we learn about Flem's brass-stealing plot, as well as I. O. Snopes's richly deserved misadventures with Mrs. Hait in the "Mule in the Yard" episode of *The Town* (T 231–44). In both cases, telling about the Snopeses is a way for Ratliff to keep an eye on them, as it were, and on occasion to hold them in check. So incomparable is Ratliff's command of Snopes lore in general that "Ratliff told me" becomes a minor refrain in *The Town* and *The Mansion*. Indeed, the radio and television franchises with which Ratliff supplements his sewing machine business suggest the scope of his oral reconnaissance network. Like the electromagnetic signals that fill the airwaves, that is, Ratliff is capable of reaching every household in the county, and like the electronic equipment he sells, he proves a most sensitive receiver.[2]

Ratliff is joined in his counterattack on Snopesism by none other than Flem Snopes himself. As he mounts Jefferson's economic pyramid en route to the presidency of Colonel Sartoris's bank, Flem realizes that if he is to gain the civic esteem he so desperately covets, he must do something about his more rough-hewn, disreputable relatives. The taciturn Flem hardly qualifies as a colloquial detective, but whether he invokes the law or simply relies upon his own considerable bargaining skills, he proves more adept at ridding Jefferson of his country cousins than does any other single citizen, including Ratliff. Mink Snopes, whom Flem allows to be sent away to Parchman for the murder of Jack Houston, is only the first in a long line of such dispossessed kinsmen.[3] When Montgomery Ward Snopes is arrested and jailed for running an illicit French postcard operation out of a town square alley, Flem has several gallons of corn whiskey planted on the premises so that Monty will be charged with bootlegging rather than distributing pornography (see

T 161–76). This strategy, in which Gavin Stevens and Sheriff Hampton are unwittingly enlisted, allows Flem to protect Jefferson's good name, and his own, by having Monty prosecuted for a "decent" offense (one the community can acknowledge and perhaps even grudgingly admire) rather than an indecent one (which threatens to taint other, more upstanding Snopeses—Flem, in other words—by association). It also insures that Monty will be sentenced to Parchman (rather than the federal penitentiary in Atlanta), where he can talk the brooding Mink into an abortive escape attempt that will add years to Mink's sentence and thereby to Flem's life (see M 52–87).

Monty's father, I. O. Snopes, a bigamist and confidence man, is another casualty of Flem's campaign for respectability. I. O. has for years been getting away with an illicit insurance scam, filing claims against the railroad for compensation against the loss of mules that have been roped to a blind section of the track, but when he accidentally sets a woman's house on fire after chasing a runaway mule into her yard, a genuine scandal threatens to erupt. Flem quickly intervenes, however, buying I. O. out of his mule business and sending him home to Frenchman's Bend, after extracting from him a promise never to do business in Jefferson again (T 253). Flem also presides over the ceremonial expulsion of four half-breed Snopes children whom Byron Snopes, an embezzler on the lam in Texas (see *Flags in the Dust*), has mailed him from El Paso. When the children prove so barbaric and inscrutable that neither Jefferson nor even Frenchman's Bend can contain them, Flem simply returns them to sender, collect, to the immense relief of the crowd that gathers at the depot to see them off (T 370–71). The county attorney, it should be noted, is involved in each of these incidents, but only marginally. Flem is really the one who engineers them, becoming something of a minor local hero in the process. In this context, one may be reminded of the homely speech Mink Snopes delivers in the wake of his murder trial. "You done the best you knowed," Mink tells his inexperienced attorney. "You jest wasn't the man for the job. You're young and eager, but that wasn't what I needed. I needed a trader, a smart trader, that knowed how to swap" (M 45). More aptly than he can possibly know, Mink sums up a general pattern in the Snopes novels, where lawyers like Gavin Stevens yield to expert traders like Flem and Ratliff in the business of swapping Snopeses out of Jefferson.

The most unmanageable of these Snopeses are to be found under

Flem's own roof. Eula, for instance, is an adulteress, whose relationship with Manfred de Spain has been common knowledge in Jefferson for years. At first the affair works to Flem's advantage, since he receives a series of jobs from de Spain—culminating in the vice-presidency of the bank—in exchange for his willingness to look the other way. The higher Flem rises in the community, however, the more Eula's indiscretions come to jeopardize his standing there, so he eventually threatens her with public exposure and censure, driving her to suicide and her grief-stricken lover away from Jefferson permanently. Thus two more impediments in Flem's path to power fall by the wayside, leaving him not only a respectable widower but a bank president as well.

Linda, however, turns out to be the fly in Flem's ointment, the most difficult and ultimately uncontainable Snopes of all. She has, of course, been Flem's principal source of leverage over his wealthy and powerful in-laws, the Varners, ever since he gave Eula Varner and her unborn illegitimate daughter his name.[4] Flem is only too aware, however, that as Linda matures, she will begin to grow away from the man she believes to be her father, and as his authority over her dwindles, so will Will Varner's interest in him. He thus searches for ways to keep Linda under his thumb. When it comes time to select a college, for example, Flem vetoes Linda's out-of-state choices in favor of, first, the local academy and, second, the university at Oxford. As it turns out, however, probate law offers Flem a more effective means of securing himself against Linda's inevitable departure from the nest. He somehow plants the idea in her mind to draw up a will naming him as her sole legal heir, a move that guarantees him continuing influence among the Varners. He is then only too happy to pack Linda off to Greenwich Village (much as he has packed Mink off to Parchman), for even in that mecca of eccentricity, she no longer poses a threat to him.

Linda's exit leaves Jefferson temporarily free of unruly Snopeses (M 152), but two decades later she returns as a widowed and deafened veteran of the Spanish civil war who is the incarnation of unconventionality: not only a Jew by marriage and an unregenerate, card-carrying communist, but a hard drinker to boot, whose father, at considerable risk to his carefully cultivated reputation, must chauffeur her on liquor runs. This time around, Flem is basically powerless to stop Linda's subversive activities, and if he fears guilt by association, the racist slurs that begin to appear on the sidewalk in front of his home must be especially

unsettling to him (M 228).[5] By this point Linda has become to Flem
what Charles Bon was to Thomas Sutpen, the willful, illegitimate child
he would prefer to forget, the repressed who returns to systematically
dismantle the grand design that Flem has so laboriously built up over
the years. The master stroke in Linda's counterdesign is obtaining, with
Gavin's help, the early release of Mink Snopes from Parchman. While
her father has utilized the law as a method of containment, Linda turns
it into an explosive force, an instrument of liberation she uses in engi-
neering the return of another repressed Snopes to Jefferson, knowing
full well the murderous intentions he harbors—or perhaps we should
say that Linda utilizes the raging, uncontainable force that is Mink
Snopes in her scheme to contain the man who has sought throughout her entire life to contain her. Once released, Mink turns out to be
something of a colloquial detective, patiently gathering the information he needs in order to track down and kill Flem. It is nothing less
than poetic justice, then, that Flem is finally eliminated by a pair of
his former victims, and by the very techniques he has used against so
many of his own unruly kin.

. . . .

If Snopeses themselves thus struggle to contain and control other
Snopeses, if, conversely, "to save a Snopes from a Snopes" proves the
order of the day on other occasions (T 182), and if Flem Snopes can
emerge as a model citizen precisely by virtue of the one-man resistance movement he leads against the Snopes invasion, then the boundaries that ostensibly separate Snopes values and interests from the
values and interests of the community threaten to become hopelessly
blurred. Compared to the villains of the *Knight's Gambit* stories, for
instance, the Snopeses make rather equivocal interlopers, no doubt because the values they represent aren't really alien at all. Far from it:
their craving for wealth, power, and status is eminently conventional.
And where have the Snopeses learned these values, if not from Jefferson
and Frenchman's Bend—from the very communities, in other words,
whose values the Snopeses are supposedly out to destroy? Destroying
communal values is the last thing the Snopeses have in mind. They
simply want to redistribute them, appropriate them for themselves.
Their peculiar genius and their peculiar horror lies in their ability to
assimilate communal values and to live out even the wildest contradic-

tions and darkest implications of these values in raw form, without the veneer of class or respectability to legitimate this enterprise, to soften its impact, or to distract one from pursuing it to the fullest. Straddling the line between insider and outsider, the lawful and the outlaw, "gentility" and "trash" (as de Spain straddled it before them, though less outrageously), the Snopeses actively unsettle these distinctions, so crucial to small-town social organization, revealing them to be arbitrary, ideological, neurotic categories deployed by a moribund elite desperate to maintain its tenuous grip on power against a rising poor-white element characterized by seemingly limitless energy and initiative.

The Town and *The Mansion* drive this point home by methodically collapsing putative semantic distinctions between "Snopes" and "Jefferson." It should be noted first of all that "Snopes" itself is anything but a monolithic category in these novels, that meaningful distinctions appear within this category, making abstraction about it risky. What, for example, is Jefferson to do with basically pleasant, unoffending characters such as Eck, Wall, and Dewey Snopes, other than simply to pronounce them "non-Snopeses," a makeshift and unconvincing policy at best? ("When is a Snopes not a Snopes?" the local riddle might go.) Even Montgomery Ward Snopes, who borders on sheer amorality in *The Town*, takes on a more human face in *The Mansion*, where he not only proves capable of genuine compassion for his cousin Mink, but develops something very like a tragic vision of the world's suffering and misfortune, a vision Ratliff and Stevens will also come to share by novel's end.

Meanwhile, Flem has gradually shed his marginal status and become a true Jefferson insider, working his way up the social ladder in a series of discrete stages, including an invitation to the prestigious Cotillion Club Christmas ball (T 56); the bank presidency; the purchase, renovation, and occupation of the de Spain mansion, to which Flem admits no visitors, turning the tables on his fellow Jeffersonites and literally, pointedly making outsiders out of them (M 155); and a deacon's seat in the Baptist church, perhaps the culmination of Flem's quest for respectability (M 222). Snopes has thus become the very figure he used to terrorize, an old dug-in Jefferson city father. Indeed, the county itself ultimately becomes "his domain, his barony" (M 219), and he its leading genius loci. It should come as no surprise, then, that practically every element of local society is represented in the crowd that attends

Flem's funeral (M 420): by the end of the trilogy, Snopes simply is Jefferson (compare T 217). The terms have become indistinguishable.

This is the same subversive logic that produces Clarence Snopes as a contender for Congress. Who, after all, could be a more appropriate choice to represent Jefferson in Washington than a Snopes, if "Jefferson" and "Snopes" have in fact become synonymous? Nowhere is this logic more explicit, however, than in the case of a local boarding-house that comes under Snopes ownership and management. At first the establishment goes by the name of the Snopes Hotel, but by the end of *The Town* it has been quietly rechristened the *Jefferson* Hotel, as if to stress the utter interchangeability of the terms (T 360).

Distinctions between "Snopes" and "Stevens" fare no better in *The Town* and *The Mansion* than those between "Snopes" and "Jefferson," despite Gavin Stevens's active posturing to the contrary. The friendships between Eula Snopes and Maggie Stevens in *The Town*, and between Linda Snopes Kohl and Melisandre Stevens (Gavin's wife) in *The Mansion*, seem to arise in the absence of such distinctions. Furthermore, in chapter 2 of *The Town*, Gavin experiences a vision of his own dispossession in Jefferson's legal economy at the hands of a Snopes. "[G]ive them time," he tells Ratliff, meaning by "they," of course, "Snopeses." "[M]aybe they have got one taking a correspondence-school law course somewhere. Then I wont have to be acting city attorney any more either" (T 44). As it happens, this premonition is only half fanciful, since Flem Snopes will largely supplant Stevens as defender of the commonweal and as representative citizen. On other occasions, in fact, Stevens finds himself treated as an object of derision or contempt, or as an outright interloper—as a "Snopes," in other words. During his affair with Eula, for instance, Manfred de Spain makes an even bigger laughingstock out of Gavin than out of Flem, roaring past the Stevens home with his cut-out wide open, in a none-too-subtle display of male one-upmanship. The sound of de Spain's cut-out, a raucous "HAhaHAhaHAha" (T 66), is a mocking echo of the laughter with which Stevens and Ratliff have sought, unsuccessfully, to contain and dismiss the Snopes threat.

Or consider the relationship between Gavin and the adolescent Linda Snopes, which in its awkward twists and turns invokes *Knight's Gambit* plot elements and character types, only to subvert them. For if Stevens at first, and in best *Knight's Gambit* fashion, neutralizes the threat of a brash young Ohioan named Matt Levitt, an outlander with designs on Linda, Gavin himself then becomes a similar threat, a "meddling white-headed outsider" (T 287) who is Flem Snopes's worst nightmare, out to seduce Flem's daughter not sexually but intellectually, with books of poetry whose outland-ish ideas promise to awaken her to the existence of a larger world beyond Jefferson.

> You see? The middle-aged (whiteheaded too even) small-town lawyer you would have thought incapable and therefore safe, who had actually served as his, Flem's champion in the ejection of that first, the Ohio gorilla, threat, had now himself become even more of a danger, since he was persuading the girl herself to escape beyond the range of his control, not only making her dissatisfied with where she was and should be, but even showing her where she could go to seek images and shapes she didn't know she had until he put them in her mind. (T 285–86)

Insofar as Gavin now plays the interloper, he has assumed a "Snopes" role. Indeed, his proprietary interest in Linda mirrors Flem's previous interest in Eula Varner, another daughter of a prominent Yoknapatawpha squire. Moreover, by becoming a kind of Snopes, Gavin effectively forces Flem to assume the very role that he so intently covets, the "Stevens" role of protecting community and family against the incursion of menacing alien values. The two men have thus exchanged their "official" Jefferson identities.

Small wonder, then, that Gavin and Flem, each of whom proves capable of subversive ("Snopes") or conventional ("Stevens") behavior in his attempts to foil the other, also find their interests coinciding on a significant number of occasions in *The Town* and *The Mansion*. Note how often they find themselves in league against a common antagonist: Manfred de Spain, Matt Levitt, Montgomery Ward Snopes, I. O. Snopes, Orestes Snopes, even Jason Compson, whom Flem outwits and Gavin refuses to represent during the "Hog Pawn" incident (see M 322–28).[6] The two men work together to design and install a suitably reverent and imposing monument over Eula's grave (T 348–55). In *The Mansion*, both men are troubled by Linda's communist sympathies, though for different reasons (Gavin for her sake, Flem for his own), and at one time or another in the trilogy both encourage her to leave Jefferson. Finally, when he learns of Mink's pardon, Stevens takes active steps to protect Flem's life, though his efforts are ultimately to no avail. Thus a man who is by vocation a guardian of the community emerges, ironically, as a guardian of the very figure whom he has long regarded as the principal nemesis of that community. Indeed, as Joseph Urgo has noted, Gavin here "delivers to Flem . . . what he had been after all along. How much more 'respectable' can a man be than to have the county prosecutor put up two hundred fifty dollars of his own money to save his life? . . . Gavin has welcomed Flem as a legitimate member of the community" (201). Seen in this light, Gavin's earlier fears of becoming "family friend to Flem Snopes, who had no more friends than Blackbeard or Pistol" (T 205), would appear to have been quite justified, even prophetic.

. . . .

If *The Town* and *The Mansion*, as forensic fictions, wreak havoc with familiar *Knight's Gambit* paradigms, these novels also thoroughly subvert or even *unwrite* important parts of the other two volumes of Faulkner's forensic trilogy. The relationship between Gavin Stevens and Chick Mallison, for instance, is once again characterized by storytelling and instruction, but ultimately to little effect, since Chick remains for the most part morally and politically inert in the Snopes novels, a witness to and wry commentator on the action but only rarely a direct participant in it. Though he is apparently destined for a career as a lawyer (he is enrolled in law school during much of *The Mansion*), Chick never emerges as an agent of reform, as in *Intruder in the Dust*, or as a colloquial detective, as in "Knight's Gambit." Moreover, the comfortably avuncular relationship we remember from *Intruder* and *Knight's Gambit* seems to grow more libidinal in the Snopes volumes, where there is a distinctly competitive edge to the verbal jockeying, not all of it entirely good-natured, that goes on between Chick and his uncle over Linda Snopes Kohl.[7]

It should also be noted that the forensic figure's stance vis-à-vis the law in the Snopes novels is almost diametrically opposed to the position he occupies in *Requiem for a Nun*. Nowhere in Faulkner do communal efforts to identify, isolate, and neutralize the alien by instituting legal boundaries between "lawful" and "outlaw" elements of society come under more devastating and systematic critique than in the first prologue and the opening scene of *Requiem*. By renouncing his role as county attorney in order to defend Nancy Mannigoe, Stevens establishes his vehement rejection of such dehumanizing tactics and principles. In *The Town* and *The Mansion*, however, Stevens does his best to employ these very tactics, to enforce—indeed to represent—these principles. He is never more the public prosecutor than in these volumes, where, incidentally, he is not above using his office to pursue purely personal vendettas.

Moreover, the strategies of containment Gavin invokes against upstarts like Flem and de Spain are not that far removed in form or intent from the structures of legal(ized) and institutional(ized) discrimination associated with southern racism. As such, they are symptomatic of a dangerously abstract habit of mind that plagues Stevens throughout *The Town* and *The Mansion*. It is Gavin, after all, who coins the term "Snopesism," reifying it as an abstract and monolithic force. Elsewhere he speaks of "Snopesishness" as a patrilineal trait, passed on from fathers to sons, while remaining unexpressed in wives like Eula and daughters like Linda (T 136). He habitually employs a "we"/"they" vocabulary to distinguish himself (and "Jefferson") from all Snopeses, a dichotomy that again suggests the rhetoric of racism (and, one might add, remembering here that *The Town* and *The Mansion* are products of the fifties, the rhetoric of McCarthyism). He reduces Snopeses to the status of animals and vegetables, taking "Mink" rather literally, for instance, as "a little kinless tieless frail alien animal that never really belonged to the human race to start with" (M 392–93), and dismissing other members of the clan as "crops" harvested by their cousin Flem (T 31).[8]

Stevens saves his most objectionable display of abstraction, however, for chapter 17 of *The Town*, where he indulges in a tour de force of conjectural narration that in its wanton ascription of personality, perspective, and motive to Flem recalls nothing so much as the very suspect account of Joe Christmas's final flight into oblivion that Gavin provides in chapter 19 of *Light in August*. Compare, for instance, the opening sentences of the two accounts: "At last we knew why he had moved his money" (T 262) versus "I think I know why it was, why he ran into Hightower's house for refuge at the last" (LIA 491). Almost any passage lifted at random from Gavin's lengthy portrait of Flem will serve to illustrate the excessive degree of interpretive latitude Stevens grants himself as narrator.

> Perhaps he would never, could never, have fallen in love himself and knew it: himself constitutionally and generically unfated ever to match his own innocence and capacity for virginity against the innocence and virginity of who would be his first love. But, since he was a man, to do

that was his inalienable right and hope. Instead, his was to father another man's bastard on the wife who would not even repay him with the passion of gratitude, let alone the passion of passion since he was obviously incapable of that passion, but merely with her dowry. (T 263)

He had no friends. I mean, he knew he didn't have any friends because he had never (and never would) intended to have them, be cluttered with them, be constantly vulnerable or anyway liable to the creeping sentimental parasitic importunity which his observation had shown him friendship meant. I mean, this was probably when he discovered, for the first time in his life, that you needed friends for the simple reason that at any time a situation could—and in time would, no matter who you were—arise when you could use them; could not only use them but would have to, since nothing else save friendship, someone to whom you could say "Dont ask why; just take this mortgage or lien or warrant or distrainer or pistol and point it where I tell you, and pull the trigger," would do. (T 279)

This is precisely the sort of poisonous verbal tactic that Roland Barthes attributed to the prosecution at the Dominici and Dupriez murder trials in France: the imposition, by sheer rhetorical muscle, of an odious, reductive, indeed pathological personality upon a silent and thereby defenseless victim. It is also essentially the same strategy that turns a few unspecified strangers wandering through Hurricane Bottom into "Natchez Trace bandits" in the opening pages of "The Courthouse."

Finally, Gavin's equivocal relationship with Linda in *The Mansion* parodies the socratic principles underlying his rapport with earlier characters such as Chick Mallison in *Intruder* and Temple Drake Stevens in *Requiem*. In those texts, we recall, Stevens leads his young charges toward the condition of storytelling, an important precondition of maturity in Chick's case, and expiation in Temple's. He teaches them to speak for themselves, an endeavor that proves educative in the root sense of the word. Stevens has something analogous in mind for Linda, who, as a result of her war injury, talks in the "dry harsh quacking duck voice that deaf people learn to use" (M 199), a voice that literally bespeaks her isolation. Stevens, however, plans to help her "restore . . . the lost bridehead of her mellifluity" (M 200) by giving her voice lessons. As he envisions it, Linda will flourish under his guidance and overcome her deafness, just as Temple overcame her guilt and shame. She will once again be able to tell her own story in her own voice.

As it turns out, however, Linda's "duck voice" never gets any better, and there is ample evidence to suggest that Gavin's intervention aggravates rather than ameliorates her situation, leading her deeper and deeper into silence and solitude. Chick makes it clear that, despite her handicap, Linda is capable from the start of holding up her end of a spoken conversation, as she does with Maggie Stevens (M 216–17). Gavin, on the other hand, is more patronizing. He insists on displacing his communications with Linda into the mediatory space of writing, supplying her with "a little pad of ivory leaves just about big enough to hold three words at a time" (M 216) and later with a foolscap pad on which "she could read the words as [his] hand formed them, like speech, almost like hearing" (M 237). This little ritual of writing, however, lacks the immediacy and the reciprocality of the spoken exchanges between Linda and Maggie. In fact, as one critic has noted, it is a "totally dependent process," a game heavily stacked in Gavin's favor, which puts him in "a position of almost total control over the creation of meaning. Stevens knows immediately whether [his] words are having the desired effect, and, if they are not, he revises them, rewrites them, making them larger and more insistent, until at last Linda accedes to their power" (Zender, "Faulkner and the Power of Sound" 105), as in the following passage:

> "No," she said.
> He wrote *Yes*
> "No," she said.
> He printed *YES* this time in letters large enough to cover the rest of the face of the tablet and erased it clean with the heel of his palm and wrote *Take someone with you to hear you   Will be killed*
> She barely glanced at it, nowhere near long enough, anyone would have thought, to have read it, then stood looking at him again. . . . "I love you," she said. "I have never loved anybody but you."
> He wrote *No*
> "Yes," she said.
> He wrote *No* again and even while she said "Yes" again he wrote *No No No No* until he had completely filled the tablet and erased it and wrote *Deed* (M 425–26)

If obliterating Linda's attempts at self-assertion beneath a barrage of printed words fails to convert her to his way of thinking, Stevens simply changes the subject. As Zender notes, Gavin's "direct, almost brutal form of artistic control" threatens to overwhelm Linda's individuality, serving "assiduously to protect Linda from all knowledge of what is happening" around her, reducing her to the role of "a helpless southern maiden." While she returns from Spain an ardent communist, for example, "the system of beliefs that she represents recedes . . . into the background" under Gavin's tutelage ("Faulkner and the Power of Sound" 105).[9] All in all, scribbling on pads and knocking on hotel room walls in the night (M 249–50) are less a recovery of communication for Linda and Gavin than an attenuated mockery of it. We are a long way here from the maieutic forensics and narrative "Interiors" of *Requiem*.

. . . .

The portrait of the forensic figure in *The Town* and *The Mansion* is further complicated by yet another point of contact with *Knight's Gambit*. As I argue in chapter 4, the title story of Faulkner's 1949 volume is an unusual hybrid of detective story and sentimental romance, in which the characterization of the forensic figure is similarly divided, into an active, glib, public, and pragmatic man at law, and an effete, taciturn, retiring, and idealistic man in love. This fault in the persona of the county attorney (and I mean "fault" here in the sense of a failing as well as a fracture) resurfaces in the latter volumes of the Snopes trilogy, where the lover at times subsumes the lawyer.[10] In his never-to-be-consummated relationships with Eula and Linda, Stevens emerges as an attenuated romantic hero, a parodic latter-day Gawain who obstinately, even perversely, champions a pair of damsels who are more than capable of fending for themselves.[11] Gavin's forensic skills seem to suffer as a result of his obsession with these women. Equivocal at best in the trilogy as a guardian of civic values, he retreats into private fantasies that he continues to cultivate at the public's expense, placing the resources of his office in service of his own personal agenda. And in particularly unflattering moments, he resembles his escapist precursor-at-law in Yoknapatawpha, Horace Benbow.

We must turn to *The Hamlet*, however, in order to find the character who most clearly anticipates the ineffectual lawyer in love of *The Town* and *The Mansion*. The Frenchman's Bend schoolteacher Labove (H 102–26) is in many ways a working sketch for the portrait of Gavin Stevens that emerges in the later Snopes novels.[12] Labove is an untutored farmer's son who puts himself through law school, where his "invincible conviction in the power of words as a principle worth dying for if necessary" is written on his "forensic face." Labove appears to be destined for greatness as a lawyer or even a politician until he catches a glimpse of his preadolescent pupil Eula Varner—the same Eula whose gravitational pull will entrap Stevens a decade or so later. From this moment forward Labove is utterly lost. He cannot leave Frenchman's Bend without assuaging his desire for Eula, nor can he allow himself to indulge this desire. So he lingers on, for three long years, by which time "the bleak schoolhouse, the little barren village" has become "his Gethsemane and, he knew it, his Golgotha too. He was the virile anchorite of old time" (H 118). And before long he is practicing a degrading ritual of obsession, "waiting until the final class was dismissed and the room was empty so that he could rise and walk with his calm damned face to the bench and lay his hand on the wooden plank still warm from the impact of her sitting or even kneel and lay his face to the plank, wallowing his face against it, embracing the hard unsentient wood, until the heat was gone. He was mad. He knew it" (H 119). If this is Labove's idea of proper behavior before the Bench, he may not amount to much as a lawyer after all. When Eula catches him in his worshipful pose before her seat, he tries unsuccessfully to rape her. Her subsequent failure even to mention the incident to anyone becomes the last straw for the thoroughly humiliated Labove, who locks up the schoolhouse and beats a hasty retreat from Frenchman's Bend in a final gesture of renunciation that once again anticipates Stevens, who quits Jefferson for Heidelberg after his unsuccessful lawsuit against Manfred de Spain (T 101–2).[13]

This lawsuit (T 82–87, 97–99), the only act of litigation in *The Town* or *The Mansion* in which Stevens is directly involved, demonstrates just how much his forensic ability and his legal judgment have been impaired as a result of his infatuation with Eula. In the wake of Flem Snopes's failed brass-stealing scheme, Stevens, the acting city attorney, sues de Spain's bonding company, "charging malfeasance in office and criminal connivance" (T 83). What prompts him to press the suit, however, is not the public servant's disinterested desire to protect the welfare of his constituents. Rather, the suit, which begins before the board of aldermen and winds up in court, is an extension of Gavin's childish rivalry with de Spain for Eula's affections, a rivalry Stevens has already lost and is destined to go on losing. The action against de Spain is likewise a no-win situation for Gavin, for until the water tank is drained, there can be no evidence of theft, but once the tank is drained and the brass discovered inside it, no crime has occurred at all, since the brass has never left the lawful possession of the city.

Blinded, however, by his sexual jealousy [14] and his desire to one-up de Spain, Stevens blunders ahead with the suit, which is at one point sardonically compared to a duel (T 87). As he paints himself further and further into a corner, he turns to rhetoric to try to extricate himself, but this rhetoric only grows strained and ridiculous:

> "If there is brass in that tank—valuable property of the city unlawfully constrained into that tank by the connivance and condonance of a employee of the city, a crime has been committed. If we find brass in that tank—valuable property belonging to the city unlawfully constrained into that tank with the connivance or condonance of a employee of the city, even if it is recovered, a attempt at a crime has been condoned by a employee of the city. But that tank *per se* and what brass may or may not *per se* be in it, is beside the point. What we have engaged the attention of this honorable bonding company about is, jest which malfeasance did our honorable mayor commit? Jest which crime, by who, did our chief servant of our city condone?" (T 86)

This is the first and only time in Faulkner's fiction that Gavin Stevens lapses into lawyer talk. His great strengths as an attorney have always been his colloquial vigor and his willingness to adapt his rhetoric to the idiom of his audience. Here, however, he sounds like something out of Dickens, who elevated this circular, obfuscating style of discourse to a kind of forensic idiolect in novels such as *Bleak House*, *Great Expectations*, and *The Pickwick Papers*. Perhaps sensing his ridiculousness, Stevens withdraws the charges against de Spain the next morning. He then withdraws himself from Jefferson, to pursue a doctoral degree at Heidelberg, leaving Snopes and de Spain to pursue their separate interests more or less unchecked.

No less complex or problematic is Gavin's romance with Eula's daughter. Chick understands, even if his uncle does not, that Stevens romanticizes, fetishizes, even apotheosizes Linda's deafness. Uncomfortable with Linda as a living, moving, changing woman, Gavin immobilizes her in his own private mythology. "She was free," Chick comments, ridiculing his uncle's point of view, "absolved of mundanity;

who knows, who is not likewise castrate of sound, circumcised from having to hear, of need too. She had the silence: that thunderclap instant to fix her forever inviolate and private in solitude; let the rest of the world blunder in all the loud directions over its own feet trying to find first base at the edge of the abyss like one of the old Chaplin films" (M 211). This language evokes Quentin Compson's similarly foredoomed efforts in *The Sound and the Fury* to hold his sister Caddy inviolate in silence above a loud world of motion and change, but Gavin's image of Linda as a "bride of silence, inviolable in maidenhead, fixed, forever safe from change or alteration" (M 203) more nearly resembles Horace Benbow, who makes a Keatsian bride of quietness out of his sister Narcissa.[15] Willfully contributing to the silencing of an individual in this way is a particularly egregious sin for a lawyer, trained to help the silent and inarticulate find a voice in society— that is, to advocate—rather than to compound their problems. We have already seen this kind of tyranny over socially marginal elements associated with the legal institution in "Monk" and *Requiem for a Nun*, but in those texts Stevens was part of the solution, not part of the problem.

. . . .

Despite the many ironies that attend the forensic figure in the Snopes novels, however, there are redeeming moments reserved for the embattled county attorney. By trilogy's end, Gavin Stevens has finally begun to see past his bigotry against the Snopeses, abandoning the ideological attempt to render them abstractly other and admitting them to the ranks of all "[t]he poor sons of bitches," himself included, "who have to cause all the grief and anguish they have to cause" (M 430). If there have been times in *The Town* and *The Mansion* when Stevens reverts to the provincial cast of mind he once exhibited in *Light in August*, he ultimately, as in "Go Down, Moses" and *Intruder in the Dust*, proves educable, capable of learning from his mistakes.

One of the crucial stages in Gavin's education is his awakening to the political consequences of his bigotry and to himself as a thoroughgoing political man. No single episode proves more instrumental in catalyzing this awakening than the brief meeting that takes place in *The Mansion* between the county attorney and an FBI agent sent to Jefferson to investigate Linda (M 233–36). The year is 1940, a time of great national anxiety, and the agent is attempting to contain Linda's

critical difference by turning her into a government informant against
her fellow communists, a venture in which he hopes to enlist Stevens.
This meeting proves revelatory for Gavin. In the agent, who more than
once likens communism to prostitution (once a communist always a
communist, he likes to point out), Stevens sees a form of institutional
bigotry and suspicion that also supplies him, if he can only recognize it,
with an image of his own attitude toward the Snopeses. Hasn't he, after
all, conceived of Flem and his brethren from the very beginning as
the local equivalent of a red scare, a creeping alien menace out to disrupt the American Way in Yoknapatawpha? If so, Gavin's rejection of
the agent's proposition may be his first important step out of this crippling mentality. The rejection is itself a political act, by means of which
Stevens may be acknowledging the political inflection of every thought,
word, and gesture he has brought to bear against the Snopeses.

Stevens must also himself learn the lesson of complicity he helped
teach Temple Drake Stevens in *Requiem for a Nun*, a lesson that brings
new insight and wider, if more painful, vision. In *The Town*, for instance, he must face the fact that he is to a very real degree responsible
for Eula's suicide. Eula pleads with Stevens to marry Linda and thus
to free the girl from Flem's manipulative hold on her, but Gavin's response is equivocal (see T 319–35). His reticence is undoubtedly what
drives Eula to more desperate measures, for that very night she takes
her life. The final encounter between Eula and Gavin, in which so
much is at stake, is immediately preceded in the text by a moving and
starkly beautiful passage whose forlorn, crepuscular accents portend
the tragic events to come. Stevens narrates this passage (which I quote
at length here, in order to convey both its elegiac tone and its rich content) in a mode of self-address that conveniently doubles as readerly
address:

> There is a ridge; you drive on beyond Seminary Hill and in time you
> come upon it: a mild unhurried farm road presently mounting to cross
> the ridge and on to join the main highway leading from Jefferson to the
> world. And now, looking back and down, you see all Yoknapatawpha in
> the dying last of day beneath you. There are stars now, just pricking out
> as you watch them among the others already coldly and softly burning;
> the end of day is one vast green soundless murmur up the northwest
> toward the zenith. Yet it is as though light were not being subtracted

from earth, drained from earth backward and upward into that cooling
green, but rather had gathered, pooling for an unmoving moment yet,
among the low places of the ground so that ground, earth itself is lumi-
nous and only the dense clumps of trees are dark, standing darkly and
immobile out of it.

Then, as though at a signal, the fireflies—lightning-bugs of the Mississippi child's vernacular—myriad and frenetic, random and frantic,
pulsing; not questing, not quiring, but choiring as if they were tiny incessant appeaseless voices, cries, words. And you stand suzerain and solitary
above the whole sum of your life beneath that incessant ephemeral span-
gling. First is Jefferson, the center, radiating weakly its puny glow into
space; beyond it, enclosing it, spreads the County, tied by the diverging
roads to that center as is the rim to the hub by its spokes, yourself de-
tached as God Himself for this moment above the cradle of your nativity
and of the men and women who made you, the record and chronicle of
your native land proffered for your perusal in ring by concentric ring
like the ripples on living water above the dreamless slumber of your
past; you to preside unanguished and immune above this miniature of
man's passions and hopes and disasters—ambition and fear and lust
and courage and abnegation and pity and honor and sin and pride—
all bound, precarious and ramshackle, held together by the web, the
iron-thin warp and woof of his rapacity but withal yet dedicated to his
dreams. (T 315–16)

Here more than anywhere else in Faulkner we sense the resonance
of Stevens's title: despite Flem's emergence as a rival genius loci, the
county is indeed Gavin's special jurisdiction. Behind his sweeping survey of his native land—panoramic in both space and time—we catch
a glimpse of the author himself, surveying with a creator's eye his vast
fictional design and holding it up against the greatest achievements of
his predecessors: the Spirit's brooding over the waters and the Lord's
satisfaction with His *lux fiat* in Genesis; Moses's Pisgah view of the
promised land in Deuteronomy; Adam's mountaintop survey of human
history in books 11 and 12 of *Paradise Lost*; even the valedictory accents
of Prospero in *The Tempest*. Further, in the broad sweep of its world's
wheel-rim, the passage evokes the concentric cosmos of Dante, and its
spring evening carries an autumnal sadness, complete with mournfully
choiring insects, learned from Keats. It also harks backward almost

forty years, to one of Faulkner's earliest fictional sketches, "The Hill" (1922), in which a "tieless casual" gazes over a sleepy southern landscape from a neighboring hilltop (see Faulkner, *Early Prose and Poetry* 90–92). All things considered, it is hard to imagine a single passage in Faulkner that bears more personal significance for the author than the Seminary Hill episode. Why, then, given his many lapses, is Gavin Stevens chosen above all the other men and women in Yoknapatawpha County to receive this view?[16] Why but as a kind of compensation for these very lapses, a compensation that is in fact unthinkable in Faulkner's world without the hard-won knowledge failure inevitably brings?[17]

In the concluding chapter of *The Mansion*, Stevens must similarly come to grips with his complicity in the death of Flem Snopes. The county attorney, after all, has been an active and willing partner in Linda's campaign to free Mink Snopes, a campaign that seals Flem's doom. Gavin even discovers a kind of resignation and decency in Flem upon informing him, in what proves to be their last encounter, of Mink's release and prompt disappearance (M 379–81). So when Mink inexorably returns to Jefferson and murders his cousin, Stevens, after participating in yet another funeral (recall *Light in August*, "Go Down, Moses," "Hand upon the Waters," and *The Town*), must face the fact that he, Ratliff, and Linda are all, whether consciously or unconsciously, conspirators in the crime. To Gavin's credit, however, he faces this terrible knowledge unflinchingly, without a trace of the denial and escapism that sent him packing for Heidelberg after the de Spain lawsuit. Even the translation, the lure of the ivory tower, can no longer tempt him (M 392, 427). He is involved and he knows it. This candid self-scrutiny and gritty self-acceptance are signs of a maturity that comes better late than never in the Snopes trilogy. And with this maturity comes a rekindled sympathy for others, as evidenced by Gavin's final conversation with Ratliff, in which, ever the advocate, he voices his sympathy for all the poor sons of bitches of the world. Stevens thus leaves the Yoknapatawpha saga exactly as he entered it in "Hair" —in dialogue with a friend and constituent, and in touch with deeper human sympathies.[18]

In this context, it is certainly significant that the Snopes trilogy concludes with the descent of the autumn sun into the house of Libra, the scales of justice (M 417, 433). More than simply an ironic reference to the final, fatal containment of the last remaining Snopeses of any account in Yoknapatawpha, the Libra allusion also signals the moral regeneration of Gavin Stevens: a de-*liber*-ate authorial affirmation of the reemergence of a responsible citizen, the rebirth of a credible arbiter and agent of justice. If not quite the indefatigable Cincinnatus-at-law he has proven on other occasions, Faulkner's favorite forensic figure is still, as Chick likes to call him, "a good man" (M 230) and a good citizen, for whom the closing image of the scales proves a fitting valediction, and benediction.

NOTES

. . . .

INTRODUCTION. The Faulknerian Forensic Figure

1. On the Farleys, see FAB 142, 356–58. On Lee Russell, see FAB 81–82, 243–45, 528. On James and Jack Stone, see FAB 133, 158–61, 191. On Ben Wasson, see FAB 182–83, 283–84, 306, 366–67, 546, 563; and Wasson's own *Count No 'Count*. On Jim Kyle Hudson, see Snell, "Phil Stone and William Faulkner" 175–76. On Lucy Somerville Howorth, see FAB 1348.

2. On John Wesley Thompson, see FAB 10–13. On William Clark Falkner, see FAB 42–49. André Bleikasten reminds us that "identification with the [Old Colonel] was perhaps one of the very germs of Faulkner's literary vocation" ("Fathers in Faulkner" 144). On J. W. T. Falkner, see FAB 36–190 passim. On J. W. T. Falkner, Jr., see FAB 117, 278, and 340. On J. W. T. Falkner IV, see FAB 768. On Jack Falkner, see FAB 339–40, 345, 365, 427, 488, and 536; and Jack's own *The Falkners of Mississippi*.

3. The psychological development of the human subject, according to Lacan, is grounded in "the fundamental conflict which, through the mediation of rivalry with the father, binds the subject to an essential, symbolic value" finding its principal representative in the Name-of-the-Father ("The Neurotic's Individual Myth" 407). It is thus from the Name-of-the-Father that all actual fathers derive their authority as lawgivers (*Écrits* 67). For useful elucidations of this concept, see Gallop and Jameson.

4. On Lemuel E. Oldham, see FAB 194, 238. On Cornell Franklin, see FAB 176, 192–93, 204–5, 315. On Phil Stone, see FAB 161–64, 168–72, 234, 313; Minter, *William Faulkner* 14, 25–27, 113; and Snell, "Phil Stone and William Faulkner" and *Phil Stone of Oxford*. On Guy Lyman, see Blotner, "Author-at-Law" 16.

5. On *The Sound and the Fury* as both instrument and allegory of the breakup, Faulkner's truest declaration of independence from Stone, see Kartiganer's insightful analysis in "A Marriage of Speaking and Hearing."

6. The turbulent history of this relationship is documented movingly by Brodsky, whose volume contains ninety-nine letters written by Phil Stone, many of them addressed to Faulkner scholars doing research on the novelist. The letters run the gamut from an admiration bordering on awe, through a

testy indifference, to utter condescension. It must, therefore, have given Faulkner a bittersweet satisfaction when Stone encountered severe financial hard-
ships in the wake of his father's death in the thirties. In 1939, Faulkner, at
great personal cost, assumed Stone's debts to the tune of six thousand dollars,
a sum that was never repaid. As far as we know, Faulkner never pressured
Stone for the money, though he needed it badly and though his letters reveal
that the matter irritated him to no end. It must have taken a supreme effort of
will for Faulkner to resist turning the tables on the man who had attempted to
exercise such a degree of control over him in the past, but perhaps the comfort
for Faulkner of knowing that he, a writer, was more solvent than his forensic
friend outweighed any dollar figure.

  7. "By defeating Redmond, Bayard seems to have avenged his father's death,
but another interpretation is even more likely: by defeating the man who killed
his father, Bayard has proved himself a better man than his father; he has supplanted that overpowering, debilitating image of the father in the life of the son
by psychically doing away with the threatening father-surrogate. In defeating
his father's killer, Bayard is symbolically killing his father, and when Bayard
confronts Redmond, the man who actually did what Bayard had unconsciously
desired to do as an implicit part of his incestuous desire for his stepmother, i.e.,
kill his father, Bayard confronts a double of himself. It is a theme that Faulkner
never tires of reiterating: by courageously facing the fear of death, the fear of
castration, the fear of one's own worst instincts, one slays the fear" (Irwin 58).

  8. A brief taxonomy of such possible stances, each of which gives us a significantly different Faulkner, might run as follows: (1) *Privilege resistance.* From
this stance emerges a romantic, rebellious Faulkner, a champion of individual
autonomy and a master of language and form. Narratives of resistance and
characters in rebellion provide this Faulkner with critical spaces from which
to interrogate the symbolic order and the ideology through which it articulates
itself. This stance will of course tend to deprivilege narratives of accession, in
which individual sovereignty is often compromised. (2) *Privilege accession.* This
stance produces a Faulkner who sees the desire for autonomy and mastery as
infantile, destructive, and often self-subverting. Characters who are too individual, too rebellious against cultural strictures and codes, may come under
deep suspicion or outright censure here (think of the Agrarian interpretation
of Faulkner, for instance). Emphasis tends to fall instead on the gathering of
individuals into the symbolic fold, on narratives of initiation and rightful accession to symbolic power. It is also possible to focus on accession at the level
of style and technique, to fashion a Faulkner who gives himself over to the play
of language instead of attempting to manhandle it. (3) *Search for a dialectical
synthesis* between what appear to be two antithetical possibilities. (4) *Com-
pose a developmental narrative* for Faulkner's career, charting a course from

one position to the other, from resistance to accession or from accession to resistance.

As I continue to read and reread Faulkner's forensic fictions, however, I find the possibilities of resistance and accession simultaneously present—in dialogue if not vociferous debate—at every moment of Faulkner's career, in a way that none of the models above ultimately allows for. This is why I suggest that we (5) *suspend the terms*, let the dynamic of resistance and accession remain unresolved, opening ourselves to the critical spaces in Faulkner from which the symbolic order and the drive toward mastery and autonomy are foregrounded and problematized.

9. As James Boyd White, a leading figure in the law and humanities movement, writes, "The basic premise of the hearing is that two stories will be told in opposition or competition and a choice made between them" (*Heracles' Bow* 42). Milner S. Ball agrees that the law operates "through the telling and connecting of stories" (23), and Bruce A. Ackerman suggests that "we look upon lawyers as if they were storytellers, and 'statements of the facts' as their effort to tell convincing stories" (52).

With his analysis of the law as a "culture of argument" (*When Words Lose Their Meaning* 231–74), White raises the issue of the agonistic dimension of legal procedure, a dimension that the pervasive orality of litigation works to reinforce. On the links between orality and agonistic behavior, see Ong, *Fighting for Life*, especially 122–25.

10. White states categorically, "The legal case is always a narrative" (*When Words Lose Their Meaning* 265). On the lawyer's "narrative imagination," see White, *The Legal Imagination* 242–96. For more on the narrativity of legal procedure, see Weisberg and Barricelli 152, 161–62, 164; and Turner 153, 164.

11. On writing's susceptibility to erasure, see Ong, *Orality and Literacy* 104, and Barthes, *The Grain of the Voice* 3–4.

12. Thus the unintentional but revealing pun in Peter Brooks's comment that "the power of conviction" is "the ultimate goal of storytelling" (284).

13. Austin describes speech acts involving judgment and punishment as *verdictives* (42). It seems to me, incidentally, that legal discourse, more than any other kind, is constructed to account for the peculiar characteristics and liabilities of performative language. Verdictives, and the unproblematic ease with which we typically heed them, are a case in point.

14. As Barthes explains, speech wages this battle for power in the name of a mythical precision and clarity. "Silence and vacillation are equally forbidden. . . . The spoken word is 'clear'; the banishment of polysemy (such banishment being the definition of 'clarity') serves the Law—*all speech is on the side of the law*" ("Writers, Intellectuals, Teachers" 192).

15. While Mink suffers dearly for his silence before the Bench, his cousin's

parsimony with words ironically works in his favor in the wake of the spotted horses incident. Flem does not even appear at the lawsuit brought against him, winning his case *in absentia et in silentia,* since no witness can conclusively link him to the wild ponies. On the other hand, Mrs. Tull loses her suit against Eck Snopes because the law ironically refuses to acknowledge the oral transmission of property: the justice of the peace rules that Eck's pony, given to him on the spot in a word-of-mouth agreement, was never legally his, so he cannot be considered liable for its actions, as he would have been had the transaction been drawn up and recorded in writing (H 329–31).

16. For more on this concept, see Genette 3–6; Hawkes 51; and Hayden White, *Tropics of Discourse* 277.

17. On reading Faulkner as a performative as well as interpretive activity, see Wadlington.

18. Geertz explores law as a cultural system in *Local Knowledge* (167–234), as does Roeber in his discussion of the colonial Virginia law court as an "arena in which authority, law, and custom mingled in ritual exchanges." Interestingly, Hayden White suggests that narrative is grounded in "topics of law, legality, legitimacy, or, more generally, *authority,*" rather than the other way around, as Cover argues (see White, "The Value of Narrativity" 13). The issue of priority here is really moot and can be avoided by simply acknowledging that law, narrative, and rhetoric have been inseparably entwined as long as Western discourse has been aware of itself.

19. Much of the discussion that follows has been corroborated or otherwise influenced by Simonett, Posner (78), James Boyd White (*Heracles' Bow* 190–91), and especially Ball's work on judicial theater (42–63).

20. Our pleasure in indeterminacy creates a "potential prostitution of the dramatic" that is, however, "curtailed in the courtroom play because action in the form of a judgment is always its end" (Ball 68). Paul Brest, on the other hand, argues that no court "is obliged to find certainty where none exists (though there are strong institutional pressures to do so)," that "[e]ven a finding of indeterminacy" serves as a "final judgment delineating the bounds of what is and is not (legally) known" (770).

21. Ball claims that judges are responsible for the "[o]verall direction" of legal proceedings, but, in my view, judges are better off leaving the heavily interpretive burden of direction to lawyers—at least in jury trials. The ideal judge is a conscientious moderator of courtroom action rather than a director (or producer) of it.

22. Though they lack his approving tone, Gabel and Harris agree with Ball that "courtroom ritual serve[s] to reinculcate the political authority of the State, and through it the legitimacy of the socioeconomic order as a whole" (317).

23. The absent Charlotte, by the way, seems cast as her lover's tragic victim

(rather than, say, her husband's predatory victimizer), and the community's unwillingness to allow her a frankly transgressive role reveals its own deep anxiety about female sexuality, especially when expressed in other than conventional ways.

24. The story of Cincinnatus can be found in Livy (III.xxvi–xxix). On the depiction of Washington as Cincinnatus in our national mythology, see not only Wills but also B. Schwartz 107–48; Bryan 77, 123, 167; and Longmore 172–73. Parson Weems's infamous *Life of Washington* (1808) contains several implicit as well as explicit references to Washington as Cincinnatus (see 37, 55–58, 120, 128–29). Weems has been credited with initiating a shift in the portrayal of Washington's character from biblical to secular terms (Wills 25–36).

25. A number of these points are discussed in Ferguson 199–202; Horwitz 109–60, 253–66; and Bloomfield 136–90.

26. Sutpen's "design is safest when he remains silent, for . . . he possesses no instinct for saying the right thing" (Ross 230).

27. A phenomenon I would ascribe, however, to nodding on Faulkner's part rather than deliberate citation on Stevens's.

CHAPTER ONE. The Failure of the Forensic Storyteller:
     Horace Benbow

1. Sundquist describes this situation as "the shock produced by the intrusion of the modern into the domain of southern puritanism and the southern cult of memory" (21), while Kinney claims that *Flags* "is first a testament to, then finally an indictment of" outdated antebellum values (74). I wonder, however, whether Kinney would list storytelling itself among those obsolescent values. On the ambivalent status of memory, myth, and tradition in the novel—as sources of order but also of stasis, illusion, and ennui—see Bleikasten, *The Ink of Melancholy* 34–35; Vickery, *The Novels of William Faulkner* 15–27; Ross 31–33; and Corrington.

2. Kinney cogently argues that here as so often in Faulkner the opening scene "sets up a dialectic with the middle of the book" that the reader is left to resolve (74).

3. Bassett notes that Jenny "is not so much a character in the novel as a voice" ("Faulkner, Sartoris, Benbow" 41), yet this voice has its moments. And while King finds fault with the "monumentalizing, mythopoeic power of memory" that Jenny and the other members of the old guard exhibit (82), both Watson (63) and Bleikasten (*The Ink of Melancholy* 36–37) link this power to Faulkner's own creative genius. Morris calls Jenny a strong misreader of her tradition, in Harold Bloom's sense of the term (120; and see 112–21 generally on "nostalgic narration" in Faulkner).

4. Eventually, however, Narcissa's reading strategies ensnare her. She decides against her better judgment to keep a series of unsigned obscene letters, which are subsequently stolen back by their author, Byron Snopes—only to resurface several years later, as readers of "There Was a Queen" will recall. In that story Narcissa prostitutes herself in order to regain the letters. In the end, her reticent habits have led her toward an economy of extortion rather than exchange. For further remarks on the letters, see Watson 64–71, 74–75, 100–103.

5. Among the many critics who have examined the novel from the perspective of psychoanalysis, see Kubie (the earliest example I know of and a frequently cited one as well); Massey; Rossky; Langford; Adamowski; Wittenberg 89–102; Polk, "Law in Faulkner's *Sanctuary*"; and Mellard 208–14. Oddly enough, the most important psychoanalytic reading of Faulkner in the history of Faulkner scholarship, Irwin's *Doubling and Incest*, fails to mention *Sanctuary* even once (though Irwin does discuss Horace Benbow as a character).

6. For the bibliographical history of the novel, see Collins; Massey; Millgate, *The Achievement* 113–18; Langford 3–33; and Polk, "Afterword."

7. In fact it is the nonreciprocity of the relationship between Horace and Popeye throughout this scene, the power that the latter wields over the former, that strikes me as even more suggestive than the conventional notion of Horace and Popeye as doubles that has become something of a critical commonplace (see for example Bleikasten, *The Ink of Melancholy* 257–58, and Polk, "Afterword" 303–4). Even if we grant that Popeye functions as Horace's dark doppelganger here, a hypothesis the rest of the novel can certainly be invoked to substantiate, it is Horace's inability to master the other through language that stands out in my reading of the scene.

8. He does, however, give a single, cryptic indication of a potentially stable source of value in *Sanctuary*'s relativistic fictional cosmos. For a splendidly ironic moment, Pap becomes a heliotrope—literally an indexical sign—and the sunlight he seeks (and signifies) stands in elemental contrast to the novel's relentless night world: "The azure shadow of the cedars had reached the old man's feet. It was almost up to his knees. His hand came out and fumbled about his knees, dabbling into the shadow, and became still, wrist-deep in shadow. Then he rose and grasped the chair and, tapping ahead with the stick, he bore directly down upon them in a shuffling rush, so that they had to step quickly aside. He dragged the chair into the full sunlight and sat down again, his face lifted into the sun, his hands crossed on the head of the stick" (48). Pap is the only character in *Sanctuary* to seek the light with this degree of tenacity or success—though he seeks it, of course, for purely hedonistic reasons. Later, the chilling antithesis of this episode will occur in a Memphis bordello, where

Horace is forced to interview Temple Drake in total darkness because, as the madam explains, "She wont have no light" (222).

9. The complex symbolic correspondences that link paternity, judgment, punishment, and interdiction at the deepest levels of culture and psyche are manifest throughout this text, as throughout Faulkner generally. Bleikasten ("Fathers in Faulkner") notes that paternity in Faulkner is just as much a socio-cultural construction as power itself is. The role of father in a Faulkner text is a kind of open structural slot that can be filled by a number of social actors, and one's "father" is as likely to be a surrogate as he is one's progenitor. Surrogate fathers, of course, appear everywhere in *Sanctuary*, and the fact that they are depicted without fail as actual or parodic figures of judgment is only further confirmation of Bleikasten's Lacanian argument.

10. The absence, indifference, or outright blindness of the scene's many judges contradicts Polk's vivid notion of law in the novel as "an all-encompassing pair of eyes" ("Law in Faulkner's *Sanctuary*" 243), and Gresset's similar argument that Faulkner's characters are "doomed to poses and postures under the intolerably immobile and everlastingly open eye of the beholder" (56). What strikes me about scenes of horror such as Temple's rape, however, is the degree to which "the Law" or "the beholder"—in the form of ineffectual avatars such as Pap—simply looks away from the most blatant acts of cruelty or miscarriages of justice, as though Polk's formula should be amended to read: "[t]he Law in *Sanctuary* is an *always averted* pair of eyes." The novel's figures of surveillance are precisely those characters who run rampant over the law, who stand above or beyond its reach.

11. See generally Foucault 170–77, 195–231, 293–308. For Foucault, panoptical social control—an eighteenth- and nineteenth-century concept out of whose shadow we have not yet fully emerged—culminates in what he calls "the disciplinary society" (209), a giant "carceral network" that has "no outside" (301). And by the time the nineteenth century is through perfecting and institutionalizing carceral techniques, Foucault implies, the Panopticon simply *is* society itself (as Popeye's Memphis and Frenchman's Bend domains might seem to confirm).

12. Could one say, conversely, that Popeye has stared Horace down at the spring so as *not* to have to shoot him, to keep him from running (since only if he runs can what he has seen incriminate Popeye)?

13. The subject of voyeurism in the novel is one that has been addressed by several critics, with uneven results. On voyeurism and the Oedipus myth, see Polk, "Law in Faulkner's *Sanctuary*" 235. On voyeurism and the family romance of fathers and daughters, see Duvall 62–63. On storytelling itself as a response to watching and the reader as a "voyeur of telling," see Parker 73.

On voyeurism as one manifestation of the general motifs of transgression and intrusion in the novel, see Bleikasten, *The Ink of Melancholy* 231–36. And on voyeurism and *Sanctuary*'s generic links with pornography, see Fiedler 90–92.

Sundquist, whose treatment of the subject is the most convincing I have yet encountered, examines voyeurism as one aspect of *Sanctuary*'s generic debt to hard-boiled detective fiction, "where the technique of observation, the moral skill *par excellence*, is concomitantly a method of survival and method of administering justice." Detective fiction itself, Sundquist adds, "grow[s] out of the nineteenth century novel's own incorporation of administrative techniques of surveillance." In *Sanctuary*, however, the possibility of "administering justice" by means of observation is compromised by the radical instability of the observer, since "[t]he assumed objectivity of the aesthetic of observation is . . . exactly what is at stake in the novel." Hence the gaps between what Horace sees and what he knows, and the inseparability of surveillance and voyeurism, in a logic that implicates the reader of *Sanctuary* as well (50–51). Since the generic rise of detective fiction, the first real literature of surveillance, mimics the broader pattern of cultural development that Foucault surveys, Foucault and Sundquist, in effect, are describing the same phenomenon on different levels of cultural expression.

14. It should be apparent how strongly I disagree with characterizations of the trial scene as "obligatory" (Hurd 426), or mere melodrama. Faulkner spent much time composing and revising this scene, and the spartan quality of its prose only amplifies its peculiar intensity.

15. On the courtroom in Faulkner as "a male space," and on courtroom discourse in *Sanctuary* as a force that simultaneously idealizes Temple, objectifies her, and thus violates her all over again, see Duvall 70–80. As the master of this patriarchal forensic rhetoric, Eustace Graham once again plays the role of pathological lawyer-citizen, a representative of and spokesman for the provincial ideology of his community.

16. For a particularly unconvincing guess, see Powers 85. Parker believes that Faulkner intended to leave the object of Temple's gaze ambiguous (82). All well and good, but any critic who rests on a judgment of "ambiguous" should consider how dissatisfying a similar verdict would be if it were rendered in a legal context: by a jury in a criminal trial, for instance, or a judge in an appellate court. As meaning-making beings, we tend to desire the resolution of ambivalent matters rather than the appreciation of their ambivalence, and this desire becomes particularly acute in legal interpretation.

Cleanth Brooks writes that the story Benbow hears from Temple at Miss Reba's brothel is "mixed up with posturing and histrionics" (*The Yoknapatawpha Country* 132), but he doesn't really extend this observation to the trial scene (where Temple's histrionics seem especially calculated and crucial). No one else, to my knowledge, has attached the dramaturgical significance to Temple's rearward stare that I do here.

17. What I here call vorticular John T. Matthews might describe as elliptical. He argues that the "figure of ellipsis as silence, repression, and narrative elision," dominates *Sanctuary* both syntactically and thematically (248). Matthews, however, emphasizes psychoanalytic motifs at the expense of legal ones, neglecting, for instance, the Goodwin trial (itself riddled with gaps) in favor of exploring the intricacies of Benbow's incestuous "complex." Perhaps as a result of these priorities, Matthews quotes the unrevised *Sanctuary* galleys more often than he does the published text. While Matthews, the premier poststructuralist student of Faulkner, sees ellipsis, aporia, and displacement as inevitable results of textuality itself, after a Derridean model, my view is that "the elliptical nature" of the text is a more contingent, social symptom of breakdowns in communication which are potentially correctable, that the text's silences iterate the *need* for communication among its characters rather than the impossibility of it.

18. Watson, the foremost student of epistolarity in Faulkner, has analyzed Horace's letters to Narcissa in *Flags* and the *Sanctuary* galleys (66–72, 103–4), and I am indebted to him for some of my insights here.

CHAPTER TWO. The Emergence of the Lawyer-Citizen:
Gavin Stevens

1. The "workaday legal Latin" here was at one point a working title for *Knight's Gambit* (see SL 287).

2. Nor perhaps is Gavin meant to replace Benbow alone. Consider the rather obvious homonymy between Gavin and his nephew *Gowan*, another of *Sanctuary*'s notable moral failures who disappears from the Faulkner canon until the publication of *Requiem for a Nun* in 1951: is Gavin, at least in his earliest appearances, the heroic-chivalric *Gawain* figure his nephew cannot be?

3. Why of all people does a probate lawyer like Benbow, who makes a living, as it were, off of death—whose professional existence depends utterly upon it, in fact—attempt to intervene in the courtroom between an innocent man and wrongful death? And why, at the moment Horace realizes how far he has ventured into (for him) untested legal waters, does he simply give up, wilt into silence, with fatal consequences for his client?

4. "Hair," *American Mercury* 23 (May 1931): 53–61; slightly revised for publication in Faulkner, *These Thirteen* 208–31. The revised version was later reprinted in *Collected Stories* (131–48), from which I quote here. "Smoke,"

Harper's 164 (April 1932): 562–78; slightly revised for publication in Faulkner, *Dr. Martino* 120–58. The revised version was reprinted in *Knight's Gambit* (3–36), from which I quote here.

5. Some critics have groundlessly assumed that the narrator is V. K. Ratliff—see for example Reed 26.

6. On this subject in Faulkner generally, see Swink, and C. Brown, "Faulkner's Use of the Oral Tradition."

7. It is probably significant that the epistolary version of the events is somehow insufficient or unsatisfying, and indeed, in his paraphrase of what he tells Stevens (CS 145–47), the narrator supplies new and extra details, as though the oral encounter brings out the best of his narrating abilities.

8. "A Rose for Emily" and the Chick Mallison sections of *The Town* also feature this narrative voice.

9. "[A] moment's thought will show that a lawyer's professional experience and even his professional uses of language are not confined to the use of words. He talks in nonverbal ways as well, all the time—think of the shifts of demeanor the skillful attorney displays in arguing to a jury, negotiating a contract, or cross-examining an expert witness; and behind all his languages, verbal and nonverbal, is a world of feeling, thought, and judgment that is never expressed at all" (J. White, *The Legal Imagination* 1).

10. I do not mean to defend these wild improbabilities of plot on aesthetic grounds. The plot of "Smoke" at more than one point makes the reader feel manipulated. This is not to obviate, however, the aesthetic interest of these very improbabilities themselves.

11. "Evil enters the community, usually from the outside, whenever the hereditary transmission of property is interrupted. A society linked to the land requires a clear order of possession, and efforts to transgress that order disrupt the social fabric" (Grimwood, *Heart in Conflict* 198; and see 186–221 passim). Klinkowitz addressed the theme of community in *Knight's Gambit* several years before Grimwood, but while Klinkowitz insists that the detective plot and the community plot are mutually exclusive and thus that Gavin Stevens is an unnecessary distraction who must be set to one side in order to get to the real meaning of the stories, Grimwood rightly understands that the two dimensions of the novel mutually support each other, that Stevens as detective serves as the agent by which the community isolates and deals with transgressors and thereby affirms its solidarity.

12. Ong notes that inculcating cultural values by "speaking for everyone to everyone about what every adult already knows" is one of the hallmarks and primary responsibilities of the rhetor in an oral society (*Interfaces* 278). And while Ong is actually speaking here about preliterate cultures such as Homer's Greece, recycling common knowledge in the way Ong describes is exactly what

Stevens, member of a southern culture Ong has described elsewhere as "highly oral" (*Fighting for Life* 128), is doing before the grand jury. See also Weaver, 169, 172–73, 182.

13. The room where nothing ever moves: a favorite motif in Faulkner (think of Miss Rosa's parlor in *Absalom, Absalom!*, or the bedrooms of Emily Grierson or Caroline Compson) no doubt inspired by Miss Havisham's house in Dickens's *Great Expectations*.

14. "As Gavin knows, a trial provides an occasion when one can probe publicly through language a mystery that affects the community" (Samway, "Gavin Stevens" 153). Samway, echoing Milner Ball on judicial theater, also explains that a trial "serves as a means of instructing the community in the nature of the community," a performance society puts on for its own benefit and instruction in the courtroom. In this case the reviews are generally affirmative.

15. In fact, old Anselm himself initially qualifies as one of these interlopers. As Grimwood notes, "The victims [throughout *Knight's Gambit*] . . . include proprietors whose lands are usurped and inheritors dispossessed of their patrimonies. The criminals are men either foreign to or alienated from the traditions of the community. Their modus operandi frequently involves marrying into the closed society, to which they nevertheless remain strangers" (*Heart in Conflict* 201). Recall the opening of "Smoke": "Anselm Holland came to Jefferson many years ago. Where from, no one knew. But he was young then and a man of parts, or of presence at least, because within three years he had married the only daughter of a man who owned two thousand acres of the best land in the county, and he went to live in his father-in-law's house, where two years later his wife bore him twin sons and where a few years later still the father-in-law died and left Holland in full possession of the property, which was now in his wife's name" (KG 3). Grimwood further explains that "rightful owners jeopardize the legitimacy of their tenure when they neglect or abuse their land or when they threaten its future stewardship" (198), and we know not only that old Holland feuded bitterly with both of his sons, but also that, near the end of his life, he had committed "the unpardonable outrage" against land and kin by "digging up the graves in the family cemetery where his wife's people rested, among them the grave in which his wife had lain for thirty years" (KG 4). Old Holland's death comes hard upon this offense. It seems undeniable that his demise subscribes to the logic for which Grimwood argues.

16. Quoted in Blotner, "Author-at-Law" 277.

17. "Go Down, Moses," *Collier's* 107 (25 January 1941), 19ff.; revised for publication in *Go Down, Moses* (369–83), from which I quote here. Between 1932 and 1941, three other stories appeared featuring Gavin Stevens, all detective tales: "Monk," *Scribner's* 101 (May 1937), 16–24; "Hand upon the Waters," *Saturday Evening Post* 212 (4 November 1939), 14ff.; and "Tomorrow," *Satur-*

day Evening Post 213 (23 November 1940), 22 ff. These three were later collected
in *Knight's Gambit*, so I defer my discussion of them until I examine the an-
thology as a whole in chapter 4. "Lawyer Gavin Stevens" appears but is confined to a single sentence in another story, "The Tall Men," *Saturday Evening
Post* 213 (31 May 1941), 14ff.; later included in *Collected Stories* (45–61).

18. The community additionally believes both killers are black, though
Faulkner, of course, leaves the referential status of Joe Christmas's "nigger
blood" open to question.

19. "[T]he test in reading 'Go Down, Moses' will be to appreciate within
the momentarily nauseated fright and more habitual, willful irony of a man
like Stevens (or Stevens' friend the newspaper editor, or a white woman like
Miss Worsham) those revisionary, 'signifying' possibilities in Butch and Mollie
Beauchamp's stories that Stevens both resists and listens for with a profound
ambivalence of fear and love" (Moreland 187).

20. Likewise, Selzer calls the translation a "useless, pedantic task" (91) and
Grimwood pronounces it "quixotic and doomed to failure" ("Faulkner and the
Vocational Liabilities of Black Characterization" 269).

21. That is, does it suggest "moral sensitivity," as Early argues rather uncon-
vincingly (98), or is it precisely Gavin's morality that may be "unstable"?

22. Moreland concurs that Stevens's efforts to collect money around the
square "should be appreciated not as a meager attempt to ransom the town's
white conscience but as a symbolic exchange, its awkwardness and overt inadequacy making it more valuable than it might seem at first" (190).

23. Wilmoth perhaps more than partially so: the editor appears ready and
willing to continue to the cemetery. It is Gavin, after all, who reaches over to
cut the switch.

24. Gavin uses very similar words to analyze Mrs. Hines of *Light in August*,
who, like Molly, loses her grandson. "I believe," Stevens says, "that all she
wanted was that he die 'decent,' as she put it. Decently hung by a Force,
a principle; not burned or hacked or dragged dead by a Thing" (LIA 491).
This hypothesis is just as subject to readerly reservations as the one in "Go
Down, Moses."

25. In Moreland's words, Stevens may be "still trying, though feebly and also
fearfully, to waive [Mollie's] grief away as a melancholic affinity for the cere-
monialized shock of grief 'itself' (as if the funeral had completed the process
of mourning), and not as a continuing love for the particular boy she raised
and lost, for whom she is apparently more ready to begin the arduous process
of mourning than Stevens is" (191).

26. Zender cites a related ambiguity when he suggests that Stevens is a character through whom Faulkner "could explore and perhaps affirm the shared
values of his culture," yet at the same time a most ironic authorial surrogate

whose attempts to create meaning and value are repeatedly "evaded, resisted, and denied" (*The Crossing of the Ways* 83–84).

CHAPTER THREE. "We're After Just a Murderer, Not a Lawyer": Gavin Stevens in *Intruder in the Dust*

1. This approach has indeed been taken, for instance, by Fowler (*Faulkner's Changing Vision*), Gold, Kartiganer (*The Fragile Thread*, especially 144–46), Moreland, Morris (234–35), and Snead (especially 213–26). With the exception of Moreland, these critics locate the point of transition from the "early" to the "late" phase in the forties. At about this time, another reader has suggested, Faulkner's fictional treatment of the law shifts from a preoccupation with injustice and punishment toward a new interest in "reward, hope, salvation" (Guerard, "Justice in Yoknapatawpha" 55). Stonum, by contrast, sees Faulkner's career in four evolutionary stages rather than an early/late dichotomy.

Lawrence Schwartz's interesting book historicizes "the development of Faulkner's literary fame in order to understand why, in the special context of the postwar period, this novelist emerged as a celebrated writer" (1). Schwartz argues that a postwar coalition among New Critics, New York intellectuals, and the publishing industry, in search of a single great author to extend America's newfound world leadership to the aesthetic front, lighted on Faulkner. Schwartz sees Faulkner's rejuvenated reputation as the conscious contrivance of this coalition rather than the "natural" or "innocent" rediscovery of a great author still toiling away in obscurity. "In short, the ideological shift prompted by the war converted Faulkner into the postwar moralist and symbol of solitary literary genius, a shift in ideology that achieved public consciousness by 1948, just as Faulkner returned to the mainstream with *Intruder in the Dust*" (28).

2. This oxymoronic quality is what allows Cleanth Brooks to argue—quite rightly, I think—that Stevens's "notions . . . represent for the boy at once a resource and an impediment" (*The Yoknapatawpha Country* 288).

3. Urgo insightfully argues that individual acts of resistance and rebellion (such as Lucas Beauchamp's refusal to "be a nigger" or Chick's willingness to violate a grave) are the key catalysts of social change in the novel (85–89), but Urgo fails to consider the extent to which Stevens's individual acts of storytelling and anecdote simultaneously ground and catalyze his nephew's emergence as a reformer. Urgo sees in Stevens only a talky obstacle to reform, and while this describes one side of the county attorney, he has other sides as well.

4. As Harvey Breit ("Faulkner After Eight Years") and Eudora Welty ("In Yoknapatawpha") recognized in their early reviews.

5. Polk argues that the courthouse/jail dialectic is characteristic of Faulk-

ner's entire oeuvre, but he later revised this view. "Indeed, one is struck with the relative *absence* of the courthouse from the Yoknapatawpha of the twenties, thirties, and even forties. . . . [I]t is a constant factor in the geographical landscape, but not much of one in the psychological, moral, or even, finally, legal landscape" ("Law in Faulkner's *Sanctuary*" 227). This is also true to a degree of *Intruder*, as I argue in this chapter.

6. It did not have to be this way. Indeed, just before he launches into this speech, Gavin draws on his specific knowledge of the region's social history in order to evoke the differences between the families and clans who settle along Yoknapatawpha's pine ridges, "people named Gowrie and McCallum and Fraser and Ingrum that used to be Ingraham and Workitt that used to be Urquhart only the one that brought it to America and then Mississippi couldn't spell it either" (ID 148), and those who farm the river valleys, "the people named Littlejohn and Greenleaf and Armstead and Millingham and Bookwright" (149). But Stevens turns from Gowries and Greenleafs to *the* Negro, and the trouble begins.

7. What exactly Gavin means by "homogeneity"—or what he means to prove by it—has puzzled critics over the years. Most readers have been generous enough not to suggest that the term refers to biological or racial purity. The mere presence of Lucas Beauchamp would immediately controvert any such allegation, since Lucas "not only descends from a mixed racial background but seems in *Go Down, Moses* and *Intruder in the Dust* to derive him his [sic] strength, pride, and dignity by combining things out of both racial pasts" (Bassett, "Gradual Progress" 211). Cleanth Brooks suggests that "[i]n calling a people homogeneous Gavin can only mean that they have a community of values that is rooted in some kind of lived experience" (*The Yoknapatawpha Country* 421), but then Bassett is surely right to counter that, on this definition, "the most homogeneous people in the novel are the Gowries and their ilk from Beat Four, who provide the murderer and the lynch mob both" (211). Is Stevens willing to accept murder and xenophobia along with "the literature, the art, the science, that minimum of government and police which is the meaning of freedom and liberty, and perhaps most valuable of all a national character worth anything in a crisis," as the legacy of a homogeneous people? Samway is troubled by the fact that "the premise of homogeneity is not a legal premise but a sociological one," one that thus draws Stevens out of his intellectual element, to his ultimate detriment (*Faulkner's* Intruder 107). And Snead, whose reading of Faulkner's rhetoric is organized throughout around aggressively heterophobic "figures of division," finds Gavin's "yearning for an unmixed or uncomplicated racial, cultural, or even linguistic essence" to run counter to "all the premises of Faulkner's plots here and elsewhere" (219). Perhaps Faulkner intends Gavin's fuzzy terminology to confirm Chick's suspicion

that regional friction between the North and the South stems ultimately from linguistic difficulties, that between northerners and southerners "there was no longer any real kinship and soon there would not even be any contact since the very mutual words they used would no longer have the same significance and soon after that even this would be gone because they would be too far asunder even to hear one another" (152–53).

8. For an interesting explanation of interruptibility and its implications for cybernetic systems, see Brand (46–47).

9. Nor perhaps only Mallison's uneasiness. One of the questions a skeptic may pose here is whether Faulkner did indeed intend for the set speeches to be read ironically or whether, as many critics have insisted, he simply used Gavin Stevens as a spokesman for his own views. Indeed, one critic has even praised Faulkner for the probity of Gavin's speeches, finding them prophetic of the crisis to come in Mississippi's "closed society" of the fifties and sixties (see Lewis). But I'm not sure whether the question of Faulkner's intention in writing these speeches for Gavin really obviates their irony. Anyone who believes that Gavin's statements are the sincere expression of Faulkner's beliefs about race and politics must still reckon with the conspicuous textual devices that make it impossible for us to pass over these statements with an uncritical eye. If Gavin is a mouthpiece for Faulkner he is thus a mouthpiece whom Faulkner himself, whether consciously or unconsciously, undermines. For a generally convincing response to "mouthpiece" theories about Gavin Stevens, see Monaghan.

10. "There are many ways to tell the same story, to make very different points, or to make no point at all. Pointless stories are met (in English) with the withering rejoinder, 'So what?' Every good narrator is continually warding off this question; when his narrative is over, it should be unthinkable for a bystander to say 'So what?'" (Labov 366; see also 370, and Prince 528–30, 532–35). Pointless stories tend to be forgotten more quickly than pointed ones, so were the material Gavin shares with Chick merely irrelevant, it is doubtful it would have embedded itself so deeply in the youth's consciousness.

11. Zender, who has noted the habitual presence of "scenes of instruction" in Faulkner, downplays their impact in *Intruder*, where, like Urgo, he argues that "Chick Mallison's most significant breakthroughs" should be attributed to "private moments of intuition" rather than to "institutional education" ("[O]nly by staying out of school can Mallison learn a lesson about society that school, by its nature, must fail to teach him") or to the kind of individual instruction Gavin Stevens offers him (*The Crossing of the Ways* 123–24). Zender finds Stevens's efforts at instruction to be compromised by a desire to bring his nephew back into the Yoknapatawpha fold, to rechannel Chick's "transgressive" discoveries (and self-discoveries) along socially acceptable lines, and thus

to neutralize the political effectiveness of these discoveries (127–30). I can't agree, however, that Gavin's role as instructor is this minimal or that his motives are this explicitly inimical. What Stevens knows, apparently better than Zender, is that nothing is to be gained by letting Chick's disgust with southern racism lead to total repudiation of the region or, worse, outright exile from it. The South has always resisted attempts at reform that it perceives as forcibly imposed upon it from outside. Thus Gavin does not necessarily seek to subvert Chick's subversive potential in counseling tolerance to the boy. (Isn't it southern intolerance, after all, that Chick finds so intolerable?) As I argue in more detail later in this chapter, bringing Chick back into the fold stands to enhance rather than to inhibit his effectiveness as a reformer.

12. Indeed, as Gwin notes, it would be uncharacteristic of Lucas to cancel such an obligation, since his office in the novel is to show Chick "the invalidity of his desire for mastery" and to endorse in place of this desire "a new narrative of human interaction and moral responsibility" (95).

13. Hoffman has noted how often material objects, as well as people or places, serve as nuclei for stories in the oral economy of Yoknapatawpha, and how these objects are in turn defined and informed by the stories they inspire (16).

14. Millgate has the set speeches in mind when he writes that "Charles's actions . . . become the practical text for his uncle's sermons on the South" (*The Achievement* 215). What I wish to emphasize here, however, is the prior degree to which these actions themselves depend upon Gavin's language.

15. As Vickery herself seems to acknowledge in her perceptive book chapter on *Intruder*, where she outlines a process of mutual dependence and interaction between Gavin and Chick that strongly suggests dialectic (*The Novels of William Faulkner* 142–44). Bassett has also characterized the Gavin-Chick relationship in *Intruder* as dialectical ("Gradual Progress" 208, 212), as has Fadiman (*Faulkner's* Intruder 12).

16. As Urgo points out, the "respect for the dead and for the sacred idea of the grave" that characterizes Yoknapatawpha (and especially Beat Four) functions as a form of ideological masking, insuring that the secret of fratricide will remain safely buried away—until Chick's untimely and outrageous intervention, that is (85–86).

17. *Intruder*'s master-trope of exhumation extends beyond the unearthing of bodies or even of murder. In the largest (or deepest?) sense, what is "exhumed" in the novel is ideology itself, the "structures by which Mallison," and indeed every citizen of Yoknapatawpha, "has been taught, or fed, his racism" (Urgo 88).

18. Dunlap reads Chick's assumption of a judgmental role as a sign of his maturity, all the more so when he comes to judge Stevens as well ("The Achievement of Gavin Stevens" 59).

19. This is precisely the point Zender misses in suggesting that "transgressive" or subversive social values are somehow utterly incompatible with citizenship in Yoknapatawpha County, that "reenter[ing] Yoknapatawpha" would require Chick to conform utterly to its racist politics (*The Crossing of the Ways* 127).

20. Posner calls this tolerance a legal "craft value," arguing that "[t]here is no better advice to a legal advocate than to empathize—with the client (what would the client say on his own behalf if he knew the content and methods of law?), with the client's adversary (what can he say in reply to my points?), and with the judge (what will appeal to him in my position, what will trouble him, and how can I limit my submission so that its acceptance would not require an unsettling change in doctrine or have untoward practical consequences?)" (304–5).

21. Or as Vickery more forcefully puts it: "Chick's repudiation of Jefferson and its ledgers, of the South and its history . . . is dangerously close to being moral and spiritual withdrawal. . . . It is Gavin Stevens who leads Chick back into the society he so bitterly denounces" (*The Novels of William Faulkner* 142).

CHAPTER FOUR. Colloquial Detection; or, "Discovering
It by Accident" in *Knight's Gambit*

1. See for instance Klinkowitz, Skei, and Grimwood, *Heart in Conflict* 187–222.

2. The term is Grimwood's (*Heart in Conflict* xiv–xv).

3. Profitable comparisons have been made between the *Knight's Gambit* stories and the fiction of a number of detective writers who were Faulkner's contemporaries or near-contemporaries. For links with the "Philo Vance" stories of S. S. Van Dine (Willard Hundingdon Wright), see Gidley 104–5, 114–15, and O'Brien 101–7. On Faulkner's possible knowledge of G. K. Chesterton's "Father Brown" stories, see Gidley 99, 103. On the Gavin Stevens stories and Irvin S. Cobb's "Judge Priest" tales, see Cleanth Brooks, *Toward Yoknapatawpha and Beyond* 375–76. And for links between *Knight's Gambit* and the "Uncle Abner" stories of Melville Davisson Post, see Grimwood, *Heart in Conflict* 195–200.

4. See for example Watkins 3–10, 169–276. The title of Watkins's work reveals a rather Manichaean interpretive stance: to Watkins, the verbal and the corporeal in Faulkner are rigidly separate realms. Watkins is quite right to note Faulkner's distaste for "the user of empty words" (5), but Broughton offers a more balanced appraisal of this issue (and a direct response to Watkins) in her cogent study of Faulkner, where she writes, "The abstraction which is language in fact is a fulfillment, not an evasion, of existence. Properly used language

affirms being" (192). Vickery provides one of the earliest comprehensive treatments of "Narrative as Theme and Technique" in Faulkner, but still one of the most judicious (*The Novels of William Faulkner* 266–81). Vickery suggests that of all Faulkner's "verbal" characters, Gavin Stevens "alone has the ability to move from the logical and the abstract to the simple and concrete," and she cites (interestingly) *Knight's Gambit* to prove her point (278).

5. As Samway points out in "Gavin Stevens as Uncle-Creator in *Knight's Gambit.*"

6. Broughton argues that the phrase "It's the law" excuses "any number of injustices . . . in Faulkner's world" and that "the fiction indicates that legal knowledge plays little or no part in justice" (88–89). This claim seems overstated to me. I agree with Broughton (and with Jean-François Lyotard, who makes a similar point in *Just Gaming*, his short, socratic treatise on the act of judgment as a Wittgensteinian language game, more art than science), that no amount of legal knowledge can insure or codify justice. But mature legal wisdom includes an awareness of law's limitations. When lawyers candidly admit, as they inevitably must, that the law is an imperfect institution rather than some kind of discovery procedure which leads us unfailingly to moral certitudes (which, in other words, is directed toward the true rather than the just), they take an important step forward in the pursuit of justice. Thus Judge Dukinfield, who is held up as a model of judicial probity in the story "Smoke," and who never "bec[a]me confused and self-doubting with too much learning in the law," is reputed to allow that fully "fifty per cent" of justice is "legal knowledge," provided this knowledge allows for the "confidence in [one]self and in God" that makes up the other fifty percent (KG 11). Gavin Stevens, as I read him, has the same healthy respect for the enabling as well as the blinding qualities of legal wisdom.

7. While I agree with Volpe's claim that detectives and literary artists alike rely on supposition and inference, his further assertion that invention "is the special tool of the artist" ("Faulkner's 'Monk'" 88) betrays a rather reductive, positivistic conception of how detectives (and lawyers) go about their search for "the facts." Especially Faulkner's detectives: the example of Quentin and Shreve in *Absalom, Absalom!* is enough to prove beyond doubt that detective work can be rich in invention.

8. That Faulkner once designated Chick as the "nephew-protagonist" of "Monk" indicates that he intended the boy's role in the story to be more than an incidental one (see SL 287).

9. On the state penitentiary at Parchman, see C. Brown, *A Glossary* 145.

10. Here compare Roland Barthes's analysis of the Dominici murder trial in France, where the state employed literary tropes and genres and the "essentialist psychology" of the nineteenth-century bourgeois novel to build an air-

tight case around an inarticulate (indeed illiterate) shepherd, by literally (and literarily) constructing a criminal personality for him (*Mythologies* 43–46).

11. Gidley observes that there are moments in "Error" where "speculating virtually takes the place of narration" (111; italics removed). On conjectural narration as a general strategy in Faulkner, see Guerard, *The Triumph of the Novel* 332–39.

12. That chess and language are analogous in significant ways is hardly a novel observation. See the well-known structural analyses of the two systems in Saussure 22–23, 88–89, 110. On the many chess metaphors and allusions in the novella, see Dunlap, "William Faulkner's 'Knight's Gambit' " 231–32, 234–35.

13. The same tension permeates the climactic scene between Stevens and Captain Gualdres, only the lexical polarities, if you will, are reversed.

> 'Wait,' his uncle said in Spanish. . . . 'We have come to do you a
> favor.' . . . Captain Gualdres *hadn't moved*. There had never been doubt,
> disbelief in his voice; now there wasn't even astonishment, surprise
> in it. . . .
> 'A wager then,' his uncle said.
> Captain Gualdres *didn't move*.
> 'A request then,' his uncle said.
> Captain Gualdres *didn't move*.
> 'A favor to me then,' his uncle said.
> 'Ah,' Captain Gualdres said. *Nor did he move* even then. (KG 214–15;
> my emphasis)

This time the primary sense is that Gualdres is literally motionless, but he is also, at this moment anyway, refusing to take his turn in the game of etiquette with Gavin. Who will save face in this encounter? Who will back down first? For now Gualdres simply suspends play.

14. For more optimistic readings of the translation than I can muster, see Grimwood, *Heart in Conflict* 220–22, and Samway, "Gavin Stevens" 150–51.

15. Moreover, Stevens is a master of the telegram, using it effectively as a mode of communication and detection (KG 198, 204)—in direct contrast to Horace Benbow, whose own exercise in the genre is so ridiculously effusive and expensive (FD 32).

16. Volpe later tempers this assessment, arguing that "Gavin's feeling for an Edenic past does not eradicate, as it does for so many of Faulkner's other characters, a desire and willingness to live in the present." By citing the detective plot as evidence that Gavin is capable of "participat[ing] in the real world" (238), Volpe observes the very same detective/lover dichotomy I have been describing.

17. Perhaps this is why Stevens initially attributes the breakup to translation difficulties, in a tall tale to Chick that nonetheless makes a certain ironic sense (see KG 235–37).

18. Faulkner himself wrote Saxe Commins that the novella "mark[s] the end of a phase of Stevens' life" (SL 287).

19. Weisberg argues that in *The Town* Gavin's personal life is profoundly influenced by his professional standards of conduct, that he embarks on a "quest for silence" which the practice of law has taught him to value (see "Quest for Silence"). While I have my doubts whether this quest is really motivated by legal experience, and whether it is even ultimately successful or strategically wise, I would point out that the silence Weisberg finds characteristic of the later Stevens is already present in "Knight's Gambit," as we have seen.

CHAPTER FIVE. Maieutic Forensics; or, *Requiem for a Nun*
             and the Talking Cure

1. On the many affinities between the early *Requiem* fragments and *Sanctuary*, see Polk, *Faulkner's* Requiem 238–40; Millgate, *The Achievement* 221; and Millgate, "Faulkner's First Trilogy" 90–109.

2. The two abandoned openings are reproduced in their entirety in Polk, *Faulkner's* Requiem 238–41. In the appendix to his book, Polk offers a succinct history of the novel's composition (237–45). For a more extended account, see FAB 1309–95 passim.

3. "How can characters in business suits be made to speak a language ordinary enough to be spoken in an apartment and unusual enough to sustain the high level of tragic destinies? Faulkner's style, with its stacatto breathing, its interrupted sentences, its repeats and prolongations in repetitions, its incidences, its parentheses and its cascades of subordinate clauses, gives us a modern, and in no way artificial, equivalent of the tragic soliloquy. It is a style that gasps with the very breathlessness of suffering. An interminably unwinding style of words and sentences that conducts the speaker to the abyss of sufferings buried in the past" (Camus 313–14).

4. The term is Reed's (42).

5. On the fundamental role of language in the psychoanalytic situation, see Benveniste 65–75, and Lacan, *Écrits* 30–113. And for a detailed examination of the entire drama as Temple's "extended analysis and transference onstage," see Moreland 214–33.

6. On the self-conscious, self-critical dramaturgy of this scene, see also Moreland 199–200.

7. Polk offers a reading of this character sketch that is diametrically opposed

to my own at almost every point (*Faulkner's* Requiem 56–61). Polk's Stevens represents a present-day degeneration from the Yoknapatawpha past: abstract, proprietary, irresponsible, fixated upon nostalgia, and "poetic" only in the most ironic, escapist sense.

8. As Ruppersburg has demonstrated, even the "dramatic" play-scenes of *Requiem for a Nun* are the work of a figure who selects and arranges material, identifies speakers, transmits dialogue, and provides the copious stage directions, which include not only blocking instructions but subjective commentary and outright conjecture (133–34). I am happy to go along with Ruppersburg's choice of the term "narrator" for this particular figure, but insofar as something like this overarching "narrator" could be posited for every dramatic work and not just for narratives (like *Requiem*) that incorporate dramatic materials, the term is potentially misleading and should be used with caution. Perhaps an old chestnut like Wayne Booth's "implied author" is preferable, since it could be used neutrally, to delineate this function in all modes of literary representation.

9. Though considerations like these may appear to be semantic quibbles, they take on real ethical weight in certain cases. Think of so-called "mercy killings," for instance, in which an individual suffering the last debilitating stages of a terminal disease is killed by a loved one (or, less frequently, a doctor) in order to be spared further pain. Acts such as these are willful and often premeditated, but are they really malicious? How much distance should properly obtain between the semantic content of "kill" and that of "murder" in such cases? The answer to these questions could have a bearing on a judge's ruling or a jury's deliberations.

10. See also Heinzelman 16.

11. Or as Moreland puts it, "Th[e] exemplary institution of this society's . . . decorous silencing and banishment of the anomalous is here strategically confronted and disturbed by one such anomaly in Nancy Mannigoe" (209).

12. Ruppersburg sees an analogy between the function of the courthouse here and the function of the jar in the Wallace Stevens poem "Anecdote of the Jar" (173, n. 6).

13. The second prologue will posit an egregious bond between "men with mouths full of law" (RFN 90) and the interests of wealth, an alliance cemented early in Mississippi history (92). If shallow legalism goes hand in hand with the equivocal march of progress—if the law boils down to so many words, a verbal smoke screen underwriting ruthless economic and political exploitation—then Gavin's readiness to act contrary to his office seems all the more justified.

14. This observation is not entirely original. Long ago Vickery noted the tension between Temple's "rhetoric of evasion" and Gavin's contrasting "rhetoric of persuasion" (*The Novels of William Faulkner* 123). Likewise, Zender in-

terprets the conflict between the two characters in terms of their antithetical "views of the function of the imagination," views that, of course, are ultimately given discursive form. "Very nearly the whole objective of Gavin Stevens's long struggle with Temple Drake is to have her tell the story of her life in a new way, one that will not renew her illicit memories but will instead purge her of them" (*"Requiem for a Nun"* 274, 277).

15. Once again compare Stevens's effective use of the telegram here and in "Knight's Gambit" with Horace Benbow's gross mismanagement of the medium in *Flags in the Dust*.

16. He need not necessarily know what she is hiding, however, though at first she seems to think he does. In fact, all that Gavin knows, and all that the text gives any indication that he knows before he drives to Jackson with Temple, is that there was a man at Temple's apartment on the night of the killing, and that Gowan was not that man (RFN 55–56). One can imagine any number of sources—neighbors, the landlady, passers-by, officers on the scene—for this revelation. It need not have been coaxed or bribed or frightened out of Nancy. Even Temple seems to intuit this at one point: "Oh, God, oh, God, she hasn't told you anything" (55). For the contrary view that Nancy has told Stevens everything, see Polk, *Faulkner's* Requiem 77–79, and Singleton 108.

17. Cf. Urgo, who sees in Temple's "ability to narrate her past, the 'history' of her soul," a source of affirmation, regeneration, catharsis, salvation, reconstruction, liberation, individuation, self-confrontation, and self-examination (132–37). Telling her story is a way for Temple to confirm that her life (as well as Nancy's) has not been meaningless.

18. Some readers, however, have taken Gavin to task for these statements. Millgate, for instance, sees the novel as "not an affirmation but a rejection of Stevens's conception of the past" ("'The Firmament of Man's History'" 33). According to Polk, Stevens's assertion expresses "his belief that the past simply overwhelms the present" (*Faulkner's* Requiem 94). It seems to me, however, that Gavin's primary aim is merely to point out the undeniable relevance of the past in any attempt at understanding the present, a relevance demonstrated simply and incontrovertibly by the act of narrating itself, since at any given point in a story meaning is contingent in important ways upon our understanding of those parts of the narrative that have gone before.

19. See for instance Giermanski 121 and Camus 312.

20. Moreland has also noted these contrasting styles, though with some reservations about Gavin's attempts not only "to translate, or to interrupt and correct" Temple's narrative but also "to preempt and commandeer her story in its hysterical tendency to stray from the way he expects and wants it told" (222). Stevens, in other words, is uncomfortable with Temple's story unless he

can rechannel it into conventional narrative patterns. This may be true to a degree, but it appears to be a largely necessary evil: scene 2 of act 1 has already demonstrated that, without Stevens's intervention, Temple's hysterical discourse fails to lead her toward either insight or purgation.

21. Zender, on the other hand, defends Gavin's "emergence as a speaker," suggesting that "[h]is voice replaces Temple's because she has developed to the point where her outlook is ready to merge with his" (*"Requiem for a Nun"* 279).

22. Or as Zender more equivocally puts it, "the supposed cathartic function of the flashback scene has at best been incompletely realized" (*"Requiem for a Nun"* 281).

23. That Stevens is Temple's uncle creates an implicit analogy between their relationship in *Requiem* and the Gavin-Chick relationship in *Intruder*, an analogy that emphasizes the central role of storytelling and instruction in each novel.

24. For a more extensive treatment of this subject than I can offer here, see Zender, "Faulkner and the Power of Sound," especially 92–93, 97–100.

25. An interesting footnote to this discussion is that when Faulkner first resumed work on the *Requiem* project in 1951, he envisioned it as a play to be written jointly with his young protégée, Joan Williams. When Williams had second thoughts about the collaboration, Faulkner wrote her, "[T]he play is yours too. If you refuse to accept it, I will throw it away too. I would not have thought of writing one if I hadn't known you" (SL 300). Obviously, however, he went ahead on his own, and the novel is by all indications the work of his hand alone. Even so, he continued to think of the dramatic sections as collaborative efforts. "I still think of it as our play," he wrote Williams as the novel neared publication, "even though you have repudiated it" (SL 317).

CHAPTER SIX. Reappraising the Forensic Figure: Gavin Stevens
and His Discontents in *The Town* and *The Mansion*

1. Similarly, the opening section of *The Mansion* documents the process of legal containment at work, in the (not unjustified) incarceration and prosecution of Mink Snopes. The state, in fact, has more than one mode of legal containment at its disposal: it can seek either to prosecute Mink as a murderer or to commit him as a madman (M 45–46).

2. Stevens pays explicit tribute to these receiving skills: "[W]hat Yoknapatawphian had not seen at some time during the past ten or fifteen years the tin box shaped and painted to resemble a house and containing the demonstrator machine, in the old days attached to the back of a horse-drawn buckboard and since then to the rear of a converted automobile, hitched or parked beside the

gate to a thousand yards on a hundred back-country roads, while, surrounded by a group of four or five or six ladies come in sunbonnets or straw hats from anywhere up to a mile along the road, Ratliff himself with his smooth brown bland inscrutable face and his neat faded tieless blue shirt, sitting in a kitchen chair in the shady yard or on the gallery, listening" (T 229).

3. Mink's trial is recounted in all three novels: H 332–33, T 81–82, and M 40–47.

4. In other words, Flem begins his long climb to power in Yoknapatawpha as a mercenary version of the Name-of-the-Father: not as Linda's biological sire but as the symbolic representative of the paternal function, imported by Will Varner to serve precisely this role, at a cost Varner cannot even begin to anticipate. Once we realize this, we can see Flem's entire career, and the ambition that drives it, in Lacanian terms, as an all-out campaign to co-opt symbolic power for himself, to consolidate the tenuous hold upon phallic authority that the trumped-up marriage has given him. Every other end is subjugated to this campaign.

No one is more willing to honor the dictates of the order of law and culture than Flem Snopes. He covets the material luxuries with which he surrounds himself and his family not for their own sake but as signifiers of respectability— which in turn signifies his arrival as a true city *father*, his accession to symbolic authority and legitimacy. That is to say, Flem only covets what the symbolic order itself covets and has taught him to covet. His understanding and mastery of this logic is in large part what makes him, despite his sexual impotence, the most phallic figure in Jefferson since Thomas Sutpen, whose career in many ways anticipates Flem's own.

That this entire scheme, however, demands Linda's ignorance, or acquiescence, proves Snopes's undoing. For Flem can maintain his precarious grip on Varner power and influence (which underwrites his assault on the symbolic in the first place) only as long as Linda calls him "father"—or, to be more precise, only as long as he can call her "daughter." It is not so much, after all, that Linda needs Flem's name (to keep from being a bastard) as that Flem needs Linda's (to keep from being a nobody, an utter nonentity in Yoknapatawpha's economy and society). This, of course, is why he is so desperate to become the sole beneficiary of her will: more than mere riches, it is her acknowledgment, her sanction, and thus (by contiguity) something of her legitimacy, which he imagines the will conferring upon him. What Flem's obsession with the will thus makes clear is that his legitimacy, his identity as Name-of-the-Father, actually rests, as it has rested all along, on the Name-of-the-*Daughter*. And that name, "Varner," is not even a patrilineal title but a matrilineal one, Eula's maiden name—which, in a final twist, is itself absent from Linda's name, not even named there!

5. For an excellent discussion of the analogies between "anti-Snopesism" and anti-Semitism, see Moreland 144–45.

6. Indeed, distinctions between "Snopes" and "Compson" also fall by the wayside during the "Hog Pawn" incident, where it emerges that, long before the Snopeses try to bilk old man Meadowfill out of his orchard, the Compsons themselves have swindled him out of thirteen feet of valuable frontage that rightfully belongs to him (M 334–35).

7. Cf. Zender, *The Crossing of the Ways* 125.

8. Mink is similarly patronized, and sorely underestimated, at his murder trial, where he is compared to "a dirty child," "small and frail and harmless" (M 41).

9. Zender attributes this desire for artistic control to Faulkner himself, who late in his career turned to representations of silence as a means of defense against the noisy, unruly forces of modernity. On this view, Stevens becomes a direct embodiment of his creator's conservative values. I prefer, however, to leave room for authorial detachment and irony. As I read *The Mansion*, the impulse to silence Linda belongs first of all to Stevens, and the author is well aware of its potential hazards. In his analysis of this epistolary relationship, Watson also seems reluctant to equate Gavin's writing strategies with Faulkner's (178–79).

10. Or as Beck puts it, the "disinterested interventionist" of the earlier fiction begins to face "acutely personal" crises in *The Town* and *The Mansion* (*Man in Motion* 50). Weisberg agrees that "in *The Town* we are forced, perhaps for the first time, to look closely at the *personal* dimension of this complex, highly verbal and reasonably sensitive protagonist" (206). See also Singleton 116.

11. See Harley; C. Brooks, "Gavin Stevens and the Chivalric Tradition" (*On the Prejudices* 92–106); and C. Brooks, *The Yoknapatawpha Country* 192–218 passim.

12. Vickery agrees that Stevens is "but the polished version" of Labove (*The Novels of William Faulkner* 190).

13. For a comparison of Labove and Stevens as bachelors and priest figures, see Mumbach 232–34, 240–50. Mumbach also discusses Ratliff in this context.

14. Beck maintains that Gavin's interest in Eula and later in Linda is primarily custodial rather than sexual, but it seems to me that to deny the strong sexual content of Gavin's feelings for these women is to limit the resonance and dramatic effectiveness of his scenes with them, especially the scenes in which Eula (T 91–92) and Linda (M 238–39) offer themselves to him sexually.

15. Nor does Stevens confine this monumentalizing aesthetic to Linda alone. In "Knight's Gambit," as I note in chapter 4, he treats Melisandre Harriss in much the same way, as a timeless evocation of time past in whom Gavin seeks tranquility and retreat. And of course Stevens sees to it that Eula Snopes is

literally monumentalized in *The Town*, by means of the marble medallion that, in the wake of her suicide, he orders carved in her likeness and affixed to a monument over her grave (T 348–55).

16. Stevens does, it should be noted, pass on something very like this view to Chick Mallison in *Intruder in the Dust* (ID 151–52).

17. Faulkner himself claimed to rate works of art according to the magnitude of their aspiration rather than the scope of their actual achievement, and his career has in turn been analyzed in terms of an ongoing "quest for failure" (I refer, of course, to Slatoff's title).

18. Stevens's exit from the Yoknapatawpha stage is thus in direct contrast to the silent, solitary departure of Horace Benbow depicted in the penultimate chapter of *Sanctuary*.

WORKS CITED

Ackerman, Bruce A. *Reconstructing American Law*. Cambridge: Harvard
  University Press, 1984.
Adamowski, T. H. "Faulkner's Popeye: The 'Other' as Self." *Canadian Review
  of American Studies* 8 (1977): 36–51.
Austin, J. L. *How to Do Things with Words*. 1962. Ed. J. O. Urmson and
  Marina Sbisà. Cambridge: Harvard University Press, 1975.
Ball, Milner S. *The Promise of American Law: A Theological, Humanistic View
  of Legal Process*. Athens: University of Georgia Press, 1981.
Barthes, Roland. *The Eiffel Tower and Other Mythologies*. Trans. Richard
  Howard. New York: Hill and Wang, 1979.
———. *The Grain of the Voice: Interviews, 1962–1980*. Trans. Linda Cover-
  dale. New York: Hill and Wang, 1985.
———. *Mythologies*. Trans. Annette Lavers. New York: Hill and Wang, 1972.
———. "Writers, Intellectuals, Teachers." 1971. *Image—Music—Text*. Trans.
  Stephen Heath. New York: Hill and Wang, 1977. 190–215.
Bassett, John Earl. "Faulkner, Sartoris, Benbow: Shifting Conflict in *Flags in
  the Dust*." *Southern Studies* 20 (1981): 39–54.
———. "Gradual Progress in *Intruder in the Dust*." *College Literature* 13,
  no. 3 (1986): 207–16.
Beck, Warren. *Faulkner: Essays*. Madison: University of Wisconsin Press,
  1976.
———. *Man in Motion: Faulkner's Trilogy*. Madison: University of Wisconsin
  Press, 1961.
Benveniste, Émile. *Problems in General Linguistics*. 1966. Trans. Mary Eliza-
  beth Meek. Coral Gables: University of Miami Press, 1971.
Bleikasten, André. "Fathers in Faulkner." *The Fictional Father: Lacanian
  Readings of the Text*. Ed. Robert Con Davis. Amherst: University of Massa-
  chusetts Press, 1981. 115–46.
———. "For/Against an Ideological Reading of Faulkner's Novels." *Faulkner
  and Idealism: Perspectives from Paris*. Ed. Michel Gresset and Patrick
  Samway, S. J. Jackson: University Press of Mississippi, 1983. 27–50.
———. *The Ink of Melancholy: Faulkner's Novels from* The Sound and the

Fury to *Light in August.* Bloomington: Indiana University Press, 1990.

Bloomfield, Maxwell. *American Lawyers in a Changing Society, 1776–1876.* Cambridge: Harvard University Press, 1977.

Blotner, Joseph. *Faulkner: A Biography.* 2 vols. New York: Random House, 1974.

———. "William Faulkner, Author-at-Law." *Mississippi College Law Review* 4, no. 2 (1984): 275–86.

Boorstin, Daniel J. *The Americans: The Colonial Experience.* New York: Vintage Books, 1958.

Braden, Waldo W. *The Oral Tradition in the South.* Baton Rouge: Louisiana State University Press, 1983.

Brand, Stewart. *The Media Lab: Inventing the Future at M.I.T.* New York: Penguin Books, 1987.

Breit, Harvey. "Faulkner After Eight Years: A Novel of Murder and Morality." *New York Times Book Review* (26 September 1948): 4.

Brest, Paul. "Interpretation and Interest." *Stanford Law Review* 34, no. 4 (1982): 765–73.

Brodsky, Louis Daniel, and Robert W. Hamblin, eds. *Faulkner: A Comprehensive Guide to the Brodsky Collection.* Volume 2, *The Letters.* Jackson: University Press of Mississippi, 1984.

Brooks, Aubrey Lee. *A Southern Lawyer: Fifty Years at the Bar.* Chapel Hill: University of North Carolina Press, 1950.

Brooks, Cleanth. *On the Predilections, Prejudices, and Firm Beliefs of William Faulkner.* Baton Rouge: Louisiana State University Press, 1987.

———. *Toward Yoknapatawpha and Beyond.* New Haven: Yale University Press, 1978.

———. *William Faulkner: The Yoknapatawpha Country.* 1963. New Haven: Yale University Press, 1966.

Brooks, Peter. *Reading for the Plot: Design and Intention in Narrative.* New York: Vintage Books, 1985.

Broughton, Panthea Reid. *William Faulkner: The Abstract and the Actual.* Baton Rouge: Louisiana State University Press, 1974.

Brown, Calvin S. "Faulkner's Use of the Oral Tradition." *Georgia Review* 22 (1968): 160–69.

———. *A Glossary of Faulkner's South.* New Haven: Yale University Press, 1976.

Brown, Peter Megargee. *The Art of Questioning: Thirty Maxims of Cross-Examination.* New York: Collier Books, 1987.

Bryan, William Alfred. *George Washington in American Literature, 1775–1865.* New York: Columbia University Press, 1952.

Camus, Albert. *Lyrical and Critical Essays.* 1967. Ed. Philip Thody. Trans. Ellen Conroy Kennedy. New York: Vintage Books, 1970.

Cash, W. J. *The Mind of the South.* 1941. New York: Vintage Books, 1960.

Casson, Lionel. "Imagine, if you will, a time without any lawyers at all." *Smithsonian* 18, no. 7 (1987): 122–31.

Chapin, Ruth. "The World of Faulkner." *Christian Science Monitor* (8 December 1949): 20.

Collins, Carvel. "A Note on *Sanctuary.*" *Harvard Advocate* (November 1951): 16.

Corrington, John W. "Escape into Myth: The Long Dying of Bayard Sartoris." *Récherches Anglaises et Américaines* 4 (1971): 31–47.

Cover, Robert M. "*Nomos* and Narrative." *Harvard Law Review* 97, no. 1 (1983): 4–68.

Creighton, Joanne. *William Faulkner's Craft of Revision: The Snopes Trilogy, "The Unvanquished," and "Go Down, Moses."* Detroit: Wayne State University Press, 1977.

Davis, Richard Beale. *Intellectual Life in Jefferson's Virginia, 1790–1830.* Chapel Hill: University of North Carolina Press, 1964.

Davis, Thadious M. *Faulkner's "Negro": Art and the Southern Context.* Baton Rouge: Louisiana State University Press, 1983.

Dennis, Stephen Neal. "The Making of *Sartoris*: A Description and Discussion of the Manuscript and Complete Typescript of William Faulkner's Third Novel." Ph.D. dissertation, Cornell University, 1969.

Dennison, D. C. Interview with Errol Morris. *Boston Globe Magazine* (12 February 1989): 8, 10.

Doster, William C. "The Several Faces of Gavin Stevens." *Mississippi Quarterly* 11 (1958): 191–95.

Dunlap, Mary Montgomery. "The Achievement of Gavin Stevens." Ph.D. dissertation, University of South Carolina, 1970.

———. "William Faulkner's 'Knight's Gambit' and Gavin Stevens." *Mississippi Quarterly* 23 (1970): 223–39.

Duvall, John. *Faulkner's Marginal Couple: Invisible, Outlaw, and Unspeakable Communities.* Austin: University of Texas Press, 1990.

Early, James. *The Making of* Go Down, Moses. Dallas: Southern Methodist University Press, 1972.

Fadiman, Regina K. *Faulkner's* Intruder in the Dust: *Novel into Film.* Knoxville: University of Tennessee Press, 1978.

Falkner, Murray C. *The Falkners of Mississippi: A Memoir.* Baton Rouge: Louisiana State University Press, 1967.

Faulkner, Jim. *Across the Creek: Faulkner Family Stories.* Jackson: University Press of Mississippi, 1986.

Faulkner, William. *Absalom, Absalom!* 1936. New York: Vintage Books, 1987.

———. *Collected Stories.* 1950. New York: Vintage Books. 1977.

———. *Early Prose and Poetry.* Ed. Carvel Collins. Boston: Little Brown and Company, 1962.

———. *Flags in the Dust.* New York: Vintage Books, 1974.

———. *Go Down, Moses.* 1942. New York: Vintage Books, 1973.

———. *The Hamlet.* 1940. New York: Vintage Books, 1956.

———. *Intruder in the Dust.* 1948. New York: Vintage Books, 1972.

———. *Knight's Gambit.* 1949. New York: Vintage Books, 1978.

———. *Light in August.* 1932. New York: Vintage Books, 1987.

———. *The Mansion.* 1959. New York: Vintage Books, 1965.

———. *The Reivers.* New York: Vintage Books, 1962.

———. *Requiem for a Nun.* 1951. New York: Vintage Books, 1975.

———. *Sanctuary.* 1931. New York: Vintage Books, 1987.

———. *Sanctuary: The Original Text.* Ed. Noel Polk. New York: Random House, 1981.

———. *Selected Letters of William Faulkner.* Ed. Joseph Blotner. New York: Random House, 1977.

———. *The Sound and the Fury.* 1929. New York: Vintage Books, 1987.

———. *The Town.* 1957. New York: Vintage Books, 1961.

———. *The Unvanquished.* 1938. New York: Vintage Books, 1966.

———. *The Wild Palms.* 1939. New York: Vintage Books, 1966.

Ferguson, Robert A. *Law and Letters in American Culture.* Cambridge: Harvard University Press, 1984.

Fiedler, Leslie. "Pop Goes the Faulkner: In Quest of *Sanctuary.*" *Faulkner and Popular Culture: Faulkner and Yoknapatawpha, 1988.* Ed. Doreen Fowler and Ann J. Abadie. Jackson: University Press of Mississippi, 1990. 75–92.

Foucault, Michel. *Discipline and Punish: The Birth of the Prison.* 1975. Trans. Alan Sheridan. New York: Vintage Books, 1979.

Fowler, Doreen. *Faulkner's Changing Vision: From Outrage to Affirmation.* Ann Arbor: UMI Research Press, 1983.

———. "Time and Punishment in Faulkner's *Requiem for a Nun.*" *Renascence* 38, no. 4 (1986): 245–55.

Gabel, Peter, and Paul Harris. "Building Power and Breaking Images: Critical Legal Theory and the Practice of Law." *Critical Legal Studies.* Ed. Allan C. Hutchinson. Totowa, New Jersey: Rowman and Littlefield, 1989. 303–22.

Gallop, Jane. *Reading Lacan.* Ithaca: Cornell University Press, 1985.

Geertz, Clifford. "Local Knowledge: Fact and Law in Comparative Perspective." *Local Knowledge: Further Essays in Interpretive Anthropology.* New York: Basic Books, 1983. 167–234.

Genette, Gérard. "Structuralism and Literary Criticism." 1966. *Figures of Literary Discourse.* Trans. Alan Sheridan. New York: Columbia University Press, 1982. 3–25.

Gidley, Mark. "Elements of the Detective Story in William Faulkner's Fiction." *Journal of Popular Culture* 7 (1973): 97–123.

Giermanski, James R. "Faulkner's Use of the Confessional." *Renascence* 21, no. 3 (1969): 119–23, 166.

Gold, Joseph. *William Faulkner: A Study in Humanism from Metaphor to Discourse.* Norman: University of Oklahoma Press, 1966.

Graff, Gerald. " 'Keep Off the Grass,' 'Drop Dead,' and Other Indeterminacies: A Response to Sanford Levinson." *Texas Law Review* 60, no. 3 (1982): 405–13.

Gresset, Michel. "The 'God' of Faulkner's Fiction." *Faulkner and Idealism: Perspectives from Paris.* Ed. Gresset and Patrick Samway, S.J. Jackson: University of Mississippi Press, 1983. 51–70.

Grimwood, Michael. "Faulkner and the Vocational Liabilities of Black Characterization." *Faulkner and Race: Faulkner and Yoknapatawpha, 1986.* Ed. Doreen Fowler and Ann J. Abadie. Jackson: University Press of Mississippi, 1987. 255–71.

———. *Heart in Conflict: Faulkner's Struggles with Vocation.* Athens: University of Georgia Press, 1987.

Guerard, Albert J. "Justice in Yoknapatawpha: Some Symbolic Motifs." *Faulkner Studies* 2 (1954): 49–57.

———. *The Triumph of the Novel: Dickens, Dostoevsky, Faulkner.* Chicago: University of Chicago Press, 1976.

Gwin, Minrose C. *The Feminine and Faulkner: Reading (Beyond) Sexual Difference.* Knoxville: University of Tennessee Press, 1990.

Gwynn, Frederick L., and Joseph Blotner, eds. *Faulkner in the University: Class Conferences at the University of Virginia, 1957–1958.* Charlottesville: University Press of Virginia, 1959.

Hall, Kermit L. *The Magic Mirror: Law in American History.* New York: Oxford University Press, 1989.

Hardwick, Elizabeth. "Faulkner and the South Today." 1948. *Faulkner: A Collection of Critical Essays.* Ed. Robert Penn Warren. Englewood Cliffs, New Jersey: Prentice-Hall, 1966. 226–30.

Harley, Marta Powell. "Faulkner's Medievalism and *Sir Gawain and the Green Knight.*" *American Notes and Queries* 21, nos. 7–8 (1983): 111–14.

Hart, John. "That Not Impossible He: Faulkner's Third-Person Narrator."

Studies in Faulkner: Carnegie Series in English 6. Pittsburgh: Carnegie Institute of Technology English Department, 1961. 29–41.

Hawkes, Terence. *Structuralism and Semiotics.* Los Angeles: University of California Press, 1977.

Heinzelman, Susan Sage. "Two Turns of the Screw: Feminism and the Humanities." *Association of Departments of English Bulletin* 91 (1988): 14–20.

Hicks, Granville. "Faulkner's Sequel to 'Sanctuary.'" *New Leader* (22 October 1951): 21–23.

Hodgin, Katherine C. "Horace Benbow and Bayard Sartoris: Two Romantic Figures in Faulkner's *Flags in the Dust.*" *American Literature* 50, no. 4 (1979): 647–52.

Hoffman, Daniel. *Faulkner's Country Matters: Folklore and Fable in Yoknapatawpha.* Baton Rouge: Louisiana State University Press, 1989.

Horwitz, Morton J. *The Transformation of American Law, 1780–1860.* Cambridge: Harvard University Press, 1977.

Howe, Irving. "Minor Faulkner." *Nation* (12 November 1949): 473–74.

——. "The South and Current Literature." *American Mercury* 67 (1948): 495–98.

——. *William Faulkner: A Critical Study.* Chicago: University of Chicago Press, 1975.

Hurd, Myles. "Faulkner's Horace Benbow: The Burden of Characterization and the Confusion of Meaning in *Sanctuary.*" *College Language Association Journal* 23 (1980): 416–30.

Irwin, John T. *Doubling and Incest/Repetition and Revenge: A Speculative Reading of Faulkner.* Baltimore: Johns Hopkins University Press, 1975.

Jacobson, Richard. "Law, Ritual, Absence: Toward a Semiology of Law." *University of Hartford Studies in Literature* 9, nos. 2–3 (1977): 164–74.

Jameson, Fredric. "Imaginary and Symbolic in Lacan: Marxism, Psychoanalytic Criticism, and the Problem of the Subject." *Literature and Psychoanalysis: The Question of Reading: Otherwise.* Ed. Shoshana Felman. Baltimore: Johns Hopkins University Press, 1982. 338–95.

Kartiganer, Donald. *The Fragile Thread: The Meaning of Form in Faulkner's Novels.* Amherst: University of Massachusetts Press, 1979.

——. "A Marriage of Speaking and Hearing." *Oxford American* 1 (1992): 63–70.

King, Richard H. *A Southern Renaissance: The Cultural Awakening of the American South, 1930–1955.* New York: Oxford University Press, 1980.

Kinney, Arthur. *Faulkner's Narrative Poetics: Style as Vision.* Amherst: University of Massachusetts Press, 1978.

Klinkowitz, Jerome. "Faulkner's Community: Thematic Unity in *Knight's*

Gambit." *The Practice of Fiction in America.* Ames: Iowa State University Press, 1980. 55–70.

Kubie, Lawrence S. "William Faulkner's *Sanctuary*: An Analysis." 1934. *Faulkner: A Collection of Critical Essays.* Ed. Robert Penn Warren. Englewood Cliffs, New Jersey: Prentice-Hall, 1966. 137–46.

Kuyk, Dirk, Jr. *Threads Cable-Strong: William Faulkner's* Go Down Moses. Lewisburg: Bucknell University Press, 1983.

Labov, William. *Language in the Inner City.* Philadelphia: University of Pennsylvania Press, 1972.

Lacan, Jacques. Écrits: *A Selection.* Trans. Alan Sheridan. New York: W. W. Norton and Company, 1977. 30–113.

———. "The Neurotic's Individual Myth." Trans. Martha Noel Evans. *Psychoanalytic Quarterly* (1979): 405–25.

Langford, Gerald. *Faulkner's Revision of* Sanctuary: *A Collation of the Unrevised Galleys and the Published Book.* Austin: University of Texas Press, 1972.

Lévi-Strauss, Claude. *The Savage Mind.* 1962. Chicago: University of Chicago Press, 1966.

Lewis, Clifford. "William Faulkner: The Artist as Historian." *Midcontinent American Studies Journal* 10, no. 2 (1969): 36–48.

Longmore, Paul K. *The Invention of George Washington.* Berkeley: University of California Press, 1988.

Lyotard, Jean-François, and Jean-Loup Thébaud. *Just Gaming.* 1979. Trans. Wlad Godzich. Minneapolis: University of Minnesota Press, 1985.

McDaniel, Linda E. "Horace Benbow: Faulkner's Endymion." *Mississippi Quarterly* 33 (1980): 363–70.

MacKinnon, Catherine A. "Feminism, Marxism, Method, and the State: Toward Feminist Jurisprudence." 1983. *Critical Legal Studies.* Ed. Allan C. Hutchinson. Totowa, New Jersey: Rowman and Littlefield, 1989. 56–76.

Massey, Linton R. "Notes on the Unrevised Galleys of Faulkner's *Sanctuary*." *Studies in Bibliography* 8 (1956): 195–208.

Matthews, John T. "The Elliptical Nature of *Sanctuary*." *Novel* 17, no. 3 (1984): 246–65.

Mellard, James. "Lacan and Faulkner: A Post-Freudian Analysis of Humor in the Fiction." *Faulkner and Humor: Faulkner and Yoknapatawpha, 1984.* Ed. Doreen Fowler and Ann J. Abadie. Jackson: University Press of Mississippi, 1986. 195–215.

Meriwether, James B., and Michael Millgate. *Lion in the Garden: Interviews with William Faulkner, 1926–1962.* 1968. Lincoln: University of Nebraska Press, 1980.

Miller, Perry. *The Life of the Mind in America: From the Revolution to the Civil War.* New York: Harcourt, Brace and World, 1965.

Millgate, Michael. *The Achievement of William Faulkner.* 1966. Lincoln: University of Nebraska Press, 1978.

———. "Faulkner's First Trilogy: *Sartoris, Sanctuary,* and *Requiem for a Nun.*" *Fifty Years of Yoknapatawpha: Faulkner and Yoknapatawpha, 1979.* Ed. Doreen Fowler and Ann J. Abadie. Jackson: University Press of Mississippi, 1980. 90–109.

———. " 'The Firmament of Man's History': Faulkner's Treatment of the Past." *Mississippi Quarterly* 25, supplement (1972): 25–35.

Minter, David. "Notes on Faulkner and Creativity." *Faulkner and the Southern Renaissance: Faulkner and Yoknapatawpha, 1981.* Ed. Doreen Fowler and Ann J. Abadie. Jackson: University Press of Mississippi, 1982. 245–65.

———. *William Faulkner: His Life and Work.* Baltimore: Johns Hopkins University Press, 1980.

Monaghan, David M. "Faulkner's Relationship to Gavin Stevens in *Intruder in the Dust.*" *Dalhousie Review* 52 (1972): 449–57.

Moreland, Richard C. *Faulkner and Modernism: Rereading and Rewriting.* Madison: University of Wisconsin Press, 1990.

Morris, Wesley, with Barbara Alverson Morris. *Reading Faulkner.* Madison: University of Wisconsin Press, 1989.

Mortimer, Gail. *Faulkner's Rhetoric of Loss: A Study in Perception and Meaning.* Austin: University of Texas Press, 1982.

Mueller, Gerhard O. W. "Problems Posed by Publicity to Crime and Criminal Proceedings." *University of Pennsylvania Law Review* 110, no. 1 (1961): 1–26.

Mumbach, Mary K. "Faulkner's Bachelors and Fertility." *The Terrain of Comedy.* Ed. Louise Cowan. Dallas: Dallas Institute of Humanities and Culture, 1984. 221–51.

O'Brien, Frances Blazer. "Faulkner and Wright, Alias S. S. Van Dine." *Mississippi Quarterly* 14 (1961): 101–7.

Ong, Walter J. *Fighting for Life: Contest, Sexuality, and Consciousness.* Ithaca: Cornell University Press, 1981.

———. *Interfaces of the Word: Studies in the Evolution of Consciousness and Culture.* Ithaca: Cornell University Press, 1977.

———. *Orality and Literacy: The Technologizing of the Word.* New York: Metheun, 1982.

Parker, Robert Dale. *Faulkner and the Novelistic Imagination.* Urbana: University of Illinois Press, 1985.

Pikoulis, John. *The Art of William Faulkner.* Totowa, New Jersey: Barnes and Noble, 1982.

Pilkington, John. *The Heart of Yoknapatawpha*. Jackson: University Press of Mississippi, 1981.

Polanyi, Livia. *Telling the American Story: A Structural and Cultural Analysis of Conversational Storytelling*. Cambridge: M.I.T. Press, 1989.

Polk, Noel. "Afterword" to William Faulkner, *Sanctuary: The Original Text*. Ed. Noel Polk. New York: Random House, 1981. 293–306.

———. *Faulkner's* Requiem for a Nun: *A Critical Study*. Bloomington: Indiana University Press, 1981.

———. " 'I Taken an Oath of Office Too': Faulkner and the Law." *Fifty Years of Yoknapatawpha: Faulkner and Yoknapatawpha, 1979*. Ed. Doreen Fowler and Ann J. Abadie. Jackson: University Press of Mississippi, 1980. 159–78.

———. "Law in Faulkner's *Sanctuary*." *Mississippi College Law Review* 4, no. 2 (1984): 227–43.

Posner, Richard. *Law and Literature: A Misunderstood Relation*. Cambridge: Harvard University Press, 1988.

Powers, Lyall. *Faulkner's Yoknapatawpha Comedy*. Ann Arbor: University of Michigan Press, 1980.

Prince, Gerald. "Narrative Pragmatics: Message and Point." *Poetics* 12 (1983): 527–36.

Reed, Joseph W., Jr. *Faulkner's Narrative*. New Haven: Yale University Press, 1973.

Roeber, A. G. "Authority, Law, and Custom: The Rituals of Court Day in Tidewater Virginia, 1720 to 1780." *William and Mary Quarterly* 3rd ser., 37, no. 1 (January 1980): 29–52.

Ross, Stephen M. *Fiction's Inexhaustible Voice: Speech and Writing in Faulkner*. Athens: University of Georgia Press, 1989.

Rossky, William. "Pattern of Nightmare in *Sanctuary*; or Miss Reba's Dogs." *Modern Fiction Studies* 15 (1969–70): 503–15.

Ruppersburg, Hugh M. *Voice and Eye in Faulkner's Fiction*. Athens: University of Georgia Press, 1983.

Samway, Patrick. *Faulkner's* Intruder in the Dust: *A Critical Study of the Typescripts*. Troy, New York: Whitston Publishing Company, 1980.

———. "Gavin Stevens as Uncle-Creator in *Knight's Gambit*." *Faulkner and Idealism: Perspectives from Paris*. Ed. Michel Gresset and Patrick Samway, S.J. Jackson: University Press of Mississippi, 1983. 144–63.

Saussure, Ferdinand De. *Course in General Linguistics*. 1915. Ed. Charles Bally and Albert Sechehaye. Trans. Wade Baskin. New York: McGraw-Hill, 1966.

Schwartz, Barry. *George Washington: The Making of an American Symbol*. New York: Free Press, 1987.

Schwartz, Lawrence H. *Creating Faulkner's Reputation: The Politics of Modern Literary Criticism.* Knoxville: University of Tennessee Press, 1988.

Selzer, John L. " 'Go Down, Moses' and *Go Down, Moses.*" *Studies in American Fiction* 13, no. 1 (1985): 89–96.

Sensibar, Judith. *The Origins of Faulkner's Art.* Austin: University of Texas Press, 1984.

Simonett, John E. "The Trial as One of the Performing Arts." *American Bar Association Journal* 52 (1966): 1145–47.

Singal, Daniel Joseph. *The War Within: From Victorian to Modernist Thought in the South, 1919–1945.* Chapel Hill: University of North Carolina Press, 1982.

Singleton, Carl S. "Gavin Stevens: Faulkner's 'Good Man.'" Ph.D. dissertation, Loyola University, 1982.

Skei, Hans. "Faulkner's *Knight's Gambit*: Detection and Ingenuity." *Notes on Mississippi Writers* 13, no. 2 (1981): 79–93.

Slatoff, Walter. *Quest for Failure: A Study of William Faulkner.* 1960. Westport, Connecticut: Greenwood Press, 1976.

Snead, James A. *Figures of Division: William Faulkner's Major Novels.* New York: Metheun, 1986.

Snell, Susan. "Phil Stone and William Faulkner: The Lawyer and the Poet." *Mississippi College Law Review* 4, no. 2 (1984): 169–92.

——— . *Phil Stone of Oxford: A Vicarious Life.* Athens: University of Georgia Press, 1991.

Soifer, Aviam. "Listening and the Voiceless." *Mississippi College Law Review* 4, no. 2 (1984): 319–26.

Stonum, Gary Lee. *Faulkner's Career: An Internal Literary History.* Ithaca: Cornell University Press, 1979.

Sundquist, Eric J. *Faulkner: The House Divided.* Baltimore: Johns Hopkins University Press, 1983.

Swink, Helen. "William Faulkner: The Novelist as Oral Narrator." *Georgia Review* 26 (1972): 183–209.

Tate, Allen. "A Southern Mode of the Imagination." 1959. *Essays of Four Decades.* Chicago: Swallow Press, 1968. 577–92.

Taylor, Walter. *Faulkner's Search for a South.* Urbana: University of Illinois Press, 1983.

Todorov, Tzvetan. "An Introduction to Verisimilitude." 1967. *The Poetics of Prose.* Trans. Richard Howard. Ithaca: Cornell University Press, 1977. 80–88.

Turner, Victor. "Social Dramas and Stories About Them." *On Narrative.* Ed. W. J. T. Mitchell. Chicago: University of Chicago Press, 1981. 137–64.

Urgo, Joseph R. *Faulkner's Apocrypha*: A Fable, Snopes, *and the Spirit of*

Human Rebellion. Jackson: University Press of Mississippi, 1989.

Vickery, Olga W. "Gavin Stevens: From Rhetoric to Dialectic." *Faulkner Studies* 2 (1953): 1–4.

———. *The Novels of William Faulkner: A Critical Interpretation*. 1964. Baton Rouge: Louisiana State University Press, 1981.

Vining, Joseph. *The Authoritative and the Authoritarian*. Chicago: University of Chicago Press, 1986.

Volpe, Edmond L. "Faulkner's 'Knight's Gambit': Sentimentality and the Creative Imagination." *Modern Fiction Studies* 24 (1978): 232–39.

———. "Faulkner's 'Monk': The Detective Story and the Mystery of the Human Heart." *Faulkner Studies* 1 (1980): 86–90.

Wadlington, Warwick. *Reading Faulknerian Tragedy*. Ithaca: Cornell University Press, 1987.

Warren, Robert Penn. "The Redemption of Temple Drake." *New York Times Book Review* (30 September 1951): 1, 31.

Wasson, Ben. *Count No 'Count: Flashbacks to Faulkner*. Jackson: University Press of Mississippi, 1983.

Watkins, Floyd C. *The Flesh and the Word*. Nashville: Vanderbilt University Press, 1971.

Watson, James G. *William Faulkner: Letters and Fictions*. Austin: University of Texas Press, 1987.

Weaver, Richard M. *The Ethics of Rhetoric*. 1953. Davis: Hermagoras Press, 1985.

Weems, Mason. *The Life of George Washington*. Ed. Marcus Cunliffe. Cambridge: Harvard University Press, 1962.

Weisberg, Richard H. "Quest for Silence: Faulkner's Lawyer in a Comparative Setting." *Mississippi College Law Review* 4, no. 2 (1984): 193–211.

Weisberg, Richard H., and Jean-Pierre Barricelli. "Literature and Law." *Interrelations of Literature*. Ed. Barricelli and Joseph Gibaldi. New York: Modern Language Association, 1982. 150–75.

Welty, Eudora. "In Yoknapatawpha." *Hudson Review* 1 (1949): 596–98.

West, Anthony. "Requiem for a Dramatist." *New Yorker* (22 October 1951): 109, 110, 113, 114.

White, Hayden. *Tropics of Discourse: Essays in Cultural Criticism*. Baltimore: Johns Hopkins University Press, 1978.

———. "The Value of Narrativity in the Representation of Reality." *On Narrative*. Ed. W. J. T. Mitchell. Chicago: University of Chicago Press, 1981. 1–23.

White, James Boyd. *Heracles' Bow: Essays on the Rhetoric and Poetics of the Law*. Madison: University of Wisconsin Press, 1985.

———. *Justice as Translation: An Essay in Cultural and Legal Criticism.* Chicago: University of Chicago Press, 1990.

———. *The Legal Imagination.* Abridged Edition. Chicago: University of Chicago Press, 1985.

———. *When Words Lose Their Meaning: Constitutions and Reconstitutions of Language, Character, and Community.* Chicago: University of Chicago Press, 1984.

Wills, Garry. *Cincinnatus: George Washington and the Enlightenment.* Garden City, New York: Doubleday, 1984.

Wilson, Edmund. "Faulkner and Henley Not at Their Best." *New Yorker* (24 December 1949): 57–59.

———. "Faulkner's Reply to the Civil Rights Program." 1948. *Faulkner: A Collection of Critical Essays.* Ed. Robert Penn Warren. Englewood Cliffs, New Jersey: Prentice-Hall, 1966. 219–26.

Wittenberg, Judith Bryant. *Faulkner: The Transfiguration of Biography.* Lincoln: University of Nebraska Press, 1979.

Wyatt-Brown, Bertram. *Southern Honor: Ethics and Behavior in the Old South.* New York: Oxford University Press, 1982.

Zender, Karl F. *The Crossing of the Ways: William Faulkner, the South, and the Modern World.* New Brunswick: Rutgers University Press, 1989.

———. "Faulkner and the Power of Sound." *PMLA* 99, no. 1 (1984): 89–108.

———. "*Requiem for a Nun* and the Uses of the Imagination." *Faulkner and Race: Faulkner and Yoknapatawpha, 1986.* Ed. Doreen Fowler and Ann J. Abadie. Jackson: University Press of Mississippi, 1987. 272–96.

INDEX

· · · · · · · · · · · · · ·

Stevens, Gavin (*continued*)
  69, 173, 177, 192–207 passim, 220,
  222–24, 247–48 (n. 11); as
  romantic hero, 42, 166–67, 171–73,
  218–19, 224–27; as revision of
  Horace Benbow, 77–78, 84, 90–91,
  92–93, 139, 141, 258 (n. 18); as
  Cincinnatus, 84, 89, 94, 99, 139,
  231; theatrical skill of, 84–87;
  family history of, 94; on race, 96–
  98, 100–101, 105–6, 115; set
  speeches of, 111, 114–17, 118, 120,
  121, 128; as advocate, 155–56, 157,
  161, 163, 230; as poet, 180; tragic
  vision of, 217, 228–30; and bigotry
  against Snopeses, 220–22, 227–28;
  and Labove character, 224–25
Stevens, Gowan, 60, 62, 176, 191–92,
  196–98, 201–2, 207, 241 (n. 2)
Stevens, Judge, 4, 35, 37
Stevens, Temple Drake. *See* Drake,
  Temple
Stevens, Wallace, 253 (n. 12)
Stone, Jack, 7
Stone, James, 7
Stone, Phil, 7, 9, 233–34 (n. 6); as
  mentor, 10–11
Storytelling, 44, 79, 81, 94, 159–60;
  as gift, 45, 47, 80, 121, 154, 160;
  therapeutic dimension of, 45, 176–
  77, 192, 194, 196–97, 200–201,
  202, 204, 205–7; incantatory power
  of, 45–46, 198–99; constitutive of
  community, 47, 82, 120, 154–55,
  206; policing function of, 88–89,
  143–69 passim, 187–89, 209–10,
  221–22; as moral action, 128–32
Sundquist, Eric J., 111
Surveillance, 55, 56, 60–63, 64, 74,
  104, 167, 209–10, 239 (n. 10), 240
  (n. 13)

Sutpen, Henry, 4, 16, 39
Sutpen, Thomas, 38, 216, 256 (n. 4)
Symbolic order, 4, 8, 13, 14, 36, 37,
  148, 161, 181, 190, 234–35 (n. 8),
  256 (n. 4)

"Tall Men, The," 244 (n. 17)
Taylor, Walter, 127
Tennyson, Alfred, 26
Terrel, Bill, 147, 149–50, 152, 154–57
Theater of the absurd. *See* Judicial
  theater
Theatricality of law. *See* Forensic
  practice: theatrical dimension of
"There Was a Queen," 238 (n. 4)
Thompson, John Wesley, 7
Tillyard, E. M. W., 29
Todorov, Tzvetan, 16, 18
"Tomorrow," 4, 78, 142, 147, 148,
  157–61, 165
Town, The, 4, 35, 41, 77, 173,
  208–22, 224–29, 242 (n. 8)
Translation. *See* Stevens, Gavin:
  translation project

Urgo, Joseph, 111, 202, 220

Van Dine, S. S. *See* Wright, Willard
  Hundingdon
Varner, Eula. *See* Snopes, Eula
  Varner
Vickery, Olga W., 127, 135
Vining, Joseph, 22
Volpe, Edmond L., 150, 151, 152
Voyeurism, 40, 56, 63, 73, 239–40
  (n. 13)

Warren, Robert Penn, 183; *All the
  King's Men,* 192
Washington, George, 31, 36, 237
  (n. 24)